The thinking ape

The Thinking Ape

Evolutionary Origins of Intelligence

Richard Byrne

OXFORD

UNIVERSITY PRESS

Great Clarendon Street, Oxford OX2 6DP

Oxford University Press is a department of the University of Oxford.
It furthers the University's objective of excellence in research, scholarship, and education by publishing worldwide in

Oxford New York

Auckland Bangkok Buenos Aires Cape Town Chennai
Dar es Salaam Delhi Hong Kong Istanbul Karachi Kolkata
Kuala Lumpur Madrid Melbourne Mexico City Mumbai Nairobi
São Paulo Shanghai Singapore Taipei Tokyo Toronto

with an associated company in Berlin

Oxford is a registered trade mark of Oxford University Press
in the UK and in certain other countries

Published in the United States
by Oxford University Press Inc., New York

First published 1995
Reprinted 1996, 1997, 1998 (twice), 1999, 2001, 2002

A catalogue record for this book is available from the British Library

Library of Congrand you mustess Cataloging in Publication Data

Byrne, Richard W.
The thinking ape: evolutionary origins of intelligence / Richard Byrne.
Includes bibliographical references and index.
1. Intellect. 2. Animal intelligence. 3. Psychology—
Comparative. 4. Human evolution. 5. Social evolution. I. Title.
BF431.B96 1995 156'.3—dc20 94-20547

ISBN 0 19 852265 7 (Pbk)

Printed in Malta by Interprint, Limited

Preface

In one sense, 'the thinking primate' is ourselves—and me more than you, as philosophers would remind us, since we can never be sure of the private mental states of other individuals! This book, however, is about how human ancestors *reached* the point in cognitive evolution from which the development of modern humans was possible. Instead of speculating about the mental abilities of fossil hominids, on the basis of fragmentary remains combined with modern human psychology, it will explore earlier phases of evolution, with the more solid and testable evidence of human ancestry that is still alive: modern primates and other animals.

Setting out to write on a subject so controversial and topical as the evolutionary origins of human intelligence, I have had to face up to the fact that the result will not be free of error. Likely errors will be of two different types. First, as with any book or paper, there will be errors of fact and misinterpretations of facts. In attempting to minimize these, I have had great help from colleagues who have invested their time in reading and commenting upon drafts. My greatest debt is to Anne Russon, who has painstakingly read the entire document, making numerous invaluable suggestions. Robin Dunbar, Graham Richards, and Rob Barton have also commented upon big chunks, and Michael Booth read the entire manuscript to give an undergraduate point of view. I cannot thank these kind friends enough, for without their efforts the error rate would be higher, and the general comprehensibility lower. The problems of fact and clarity that remain, I must own up to! The second type of error will only become apparent in hindsight. In a fast-advancing field like this, it is inevitable that some of the links, deductions, extrapolations, and glosses that I have imposed on the data will turn out to be wrong-headed. To avoid this sort of error by always playing safe and avoiding risk, is likely to give a result that is dull and lifeless. I have instead tried to pick the interpretation that will turn out to be right in the end, even if the data at present don't quite force its acceptance. Where I have been aware of doing this, I have always pointed out the cracks in the interpretation; but perhaps in some places I haven't even noticed that I was not following the party line. Instead of apologizing for this, I will just hope I've been lucky enough to back winners, so my sins will never be revealed.

In a university position, with teaching and administrative commitments, I would never have completed the essential first draft that I have been revising for the last year at St Andrews: a breathing space was essential. I therefore thank the University of St Andrews for granting me a term's study leave; the Association of Commonwealth Universities for giving me a Fellowship to visit New Zealand; the University of Auckland's Psychology Department for allowing me to spend my sabbatical there; and all the staff of the Department who made me so welcome. I hope one day to be able to repay the splendid hospitality to Jen and myself that made our time in New Zealand so enjoyable and productive: from Mike and Barbara Corballis, Di McCarthy and Frank Metcalf, Mike and Christine Taylor, and especially from Barbara and Clive Evans. And special thanks to Di McCarthy, who even evacuated her own room and computer so that I could use them, as well as helping us to find the best accommodation in Auckland!

One of the most warming aspects of writing this book has been finding how kind my colleagues around the world are when it comes to helping out with photographs or other illustrations. For this, I would like to thank Jim Anderson, Priscilla Barrett (drawings), Robert Barton, Patrick Bateson, Christophe Boesch, David Bygott (drawings), Jen Byrne, Sabine Coussi-Korbel, Robin Dunbar, Jürgen Lethmate, Heather McKiggan, Penny Patterson and Ron Cohn, Daniel Povinelli, Anne Russon, Elisabetta Visalberghi, and Anne Zeller. As will be apparent throughout, their generosity in allowing me to use their illustrative material has contributed greatly to the clarity of the text.

R.B.

St. Andrews
March 1994

Contents

Part 1

Assembling the tools for the job

1
Introduction: the limits of fossil evidence

Palaeonthropology has a problem

Most attempts to say when and how human intellectual abilities arose begin with fossil evidence and end up with modern human achievements. In between comes speculation: careful, plausible speculation. In serious texts the speculation is overt, and justified often by appeals to general rules, such as principles of evolution or how ecological constraints affect animal societies. (These rules have been deduced from the study of mammals and birds in general.) Popular versions, of course, are less up-front about the speculation, and they are rather optimistic about what can in principle be found out.* But, by the inevitable caricature that popularization brings, they have the virtue of making the basic fragility of the whole exercise more apparent.

The genre of semi-popular accounts of human evolution is a well-established one; many texts have come out in recent years, and have been widely read and influential. Nevertheless, the successive stories perform a regular series of U-turns in what is put forward as accepted fact. The same fossil hominids (australopithecines and *Homo habilis*) are portrayed in quick succession as daring hunters of big game, peaceful vegetarians, and nimble scavengers from carnivores. ('Hominids' are the various ancestors or relatives of humans found in the fossil record, and their hallmark is bipedalism.) Others (Neanderthals) are described one year as sensitive and religious people who buried their dead with flowers while speaking human language, the next as animals whose differences from chimpanzees and gorillas would not be immediately obvious to us, beyond their bipedal anatomy. Yet other hominids (*Homo erectus*) have often been envisaged as fire-making dwellers in caves; but according to some new versions the caves were merely where their bones were brought by scavenging animals, and the ash of their hearths just debris of occasional natural bushfires. The examples sound so far-fetched, when put like that, that it might be thought that I have invented them. I have not. What has

* A recent report in the science column of a 'quality ' British newspaper, about the exciting discovery of new fossil hominid skeletons in Spain, concluded that 'more excavation needed to be done before researchers could be sure of their social system'. An extreme example, perhaps, but few editors would allow the tedious repetition of phrases like 'it is uncertain', 'not known yet', and 'we will never be sure' that the reporter would need for an accurate story about a hominid find.

happened in each case is that a careful re-examination of apparently convincing evidence has shown some 'association' to be a product of randomness or some unsuspected artefact. A chance preservation of petals with some Neanderthal bones was seen as 'a burial', a cache of bones in a cave left by a scavenging hyaena became 'a cave-dweller and the remains of his dinner', bushfires that occasionally sweep into the cave were 'the hearth', and so on. These errors were not malicious or even foolish at the time; they are just what must be expected when so much theory has to rest on so little evidence.

Each discovery of new fossil bones is liable to cause dramatic revision in the story offered; one creature after another has been heralded as the key ancestor of modern humans, only to be sidelined by a more recent discovery. The resulting changes of story are embarrassing and are not often pointed out, but they are obvious to anyone whose interest in this fascinating area lasts more than a couple of years. This was vividly apparent to me on a recent visit to the Smithsonian Museum of Natural History, Washington—one of the best in the world. All the recreated fossil landscapes were smart and fresh-looking, but one was strangely covered in little 'Update' notices: the human ancestors diorama. Since 1974, almost all the 'facts' had changed, and a new exhibit was needed unexpectedly soon. But will a new exhibit be any more likely to last?

Also obvious are the major disagreements between writers about the interpretation of the same evidence. *Homo* occurred late, *Homo* occurred early; language is recent, language is ancient; human ancestors went through a seed-eating phase, a scavenging phase, a gestural language phase, even an aquatic phase. The same fossil hominids are, in one version, a series of direct human ancestors forming a chain that leads towards ourselves; in another, they become dead-end branches, with the crucial ancestors few and far between, or missing altogether. (Treatment of *Ramapithecus*, australopithecine species, and the Neanderthals have varied especially, and even *erectus* is now suspected not to be ancestral to *sapiens*.) Reconstructions, especially pictorial versions of life in prehistory, bear an often suspiciously close resemblance to modern apes with suitably increasing nakedness and the skin colour that is politically correct at the time.

Healthy argument is no bad thing, but if the subject is to be a scientific one there must be ways to resolve the disagreements—at least in principle. Much of the subject of palaeoanthropology is simply not science, although it uses many of the tools of science. Theorizing about hominid behaviour is a subject closer to detective work; detective work, however, in which the results are never going to be dramatically confirmed. An *Australopithecus* is just never going to jump out and say 'OK, you got me nailed: I've got my hands up! I admit I had no consonantal phonemes, but I was a really nifty scavenger from sabretooths'. Detective work is great fun, and in the hands of experts in palaeoanthropology it is the best that we can ever hope for in understanding the events of the past 5 million years of our evolutionary history. The signs that the palaeoanthropological detectives have to go on are few and problematic to interpret—just stone artefacts, supplemented only for the past million years by signs of dwellings, cave paintings, and a wider range of bone and other remains. This insufficiency in the fossil record of human ancestors is often admitted, but suggested to be an unlucky and temporary set-back. That view may be optimistic. Hominids were not marine animals, whose bodies would be more likely to fossilize; the fossil record of ancestors of any particular current terrestrial species is probably just as tiny. (According to one interesting theory, in fact, hominids *were* marine, but unfortunately this theory can cite no fossil support.) We can *hope* that the next expedition will put it all right, but we will most likely hope in vain. Because of this, the conclusions will always be speculations, fragile and liable to tumble at the sight of new evidence.

This applies even where sophisticated modern techniques are used. The date of the origin of spoken language has always excited speculation. Computer modelling of the vocal tract of a Neanderthal suggested that their larynx was a very different shape to that of modern humans: Neanderthals could not have produced the range of vowels that we can. However, the same technique applied to chimpanzees 'shows' that they cannot produce sounds that they do in fact produce. Humans can even produce intelligible speech after *removal* of the larynx. Claims about Neanderthal speech are bound to be fragile things. The recent find of a hyoid bone (a small bone closely attached to the larynx) indicates a larynx much like ours in a human of 60 000 years ago, predating most Neanderthals. This date is also 20 000 years before the cave paintings of France and Spain, which are often argued to signal the beginning of symbolic ability in our ancestors—and thus, supposedly, date the origin of language. Finding when language began is clearly fraught with difficulties, and this is just what we must expect. Any bold claims have to be treated with the gravest caution.

The same warning applies to claims about *any* behaviours that do not regularly leave incontrovertible fossil signs. That narrows down the hard evidence of behaviour in early hominids (i.e. 2–6 species of australopithecines and 1–2 of early *Homo*, the exact number varying according to the researcher's taste), to tool-making and diet type—the latter can be studied from the patterns of tooth wear produced by different diets. This evidence is limited in what it can tell us. Only *stone* toolmaking leaves relics, whereas modern peoples who until recent years relied on stone tools also manufactured many wood and bone artefacts. Only the broadest differences in diet type can be recognized from tooth wear under a scanning electron microscope. The marks left by chewing bones can easily resemble the wear from grit on underground tubers, and can never show whether the meat (if it *was* really meat) was hunted or scavenged, and whether it was of a big or a small animal. Processed remains of carcasses (where they can be identified as such) give a little more information, but at the dates of early hominids these are seldom clearly associated with a particular set of hominid bones, let alone the hominids' putative tools. Even with *Homo erectus* the story is little different, and only with some early *H. sapiens* remains do these particular mists clear. Palaeoanthropologists, who study the traces of fossil humans and their relatives, are aware of these limitations, but textbook accounts of the origins of human behaviour tend to neglect them. The reality is that we will never know with confidence the answers to many of the most important questions we would like to ask about what happened in the past 5 million years. Accounts of this period will remain speculative.

What can be done?

Paradoxically, for *earlier* periods, before those past few million years, things get better. A different kind of evidence of behaviour is available about this earlier phase of human prehistory, and is the subject of this book. We will never know for sure the most recent stages in the evolution of our mentality and intelligence, but the earlier stages are there to be studied. Is this some sort of riddle? No, it is perfectly possible to get good evidence of the behavioural repertoire of human ancestors of these earlier times. The evidence is alive and well, the behaviour of other animals. In particular, we must look at the other descendents of those human ancestors we wish to understand. The task of inferring evolutionary changes from living species is sometimes a hard one, but it is not impossible. How do we start?

In order to trace the evolution of any behaviour, we need to use what ethologists call the *comparative method*. This term means much more than simply comparing animals, as will become clear in Chapter 2. With the aid of the comparative method, the evolutionary history of a trait—even a behaviour that leaves no trace to fossilize—can be inferred from its pattern of occurrence in surviving animals. Sometimes the original value of a behaviour in helping now-extinct animals survive and prosper can also be worked out from its usefulness to those animals' descendants today, although we cannot rely on this.

In bare outline, what we have to do is:

(1) find reliable differences between living animal species in their intelligence, and how these differences affect the species' ability to survive under different circumstances;

(2) deduce from this pattern the likely intelligence of the species' extinct ancestors; and then

(3) look for plausible selection pressures that could have favoured the evolutionary changes that we have uncovered—in other words, problems to which they seem to be the solutions.

To take an oversimplified (and fictitious) example, if all carnivores were found to be more intelligent than other mammals one could infer that something in the life of the extinct ancestor of the carnivores promoted intelligence, perhaps the need to hunt; we could test this idea by asking whether more intelligent carnivores *do* hunt more successfully. The emphasis, unfortunately, is on the word 'if'. In practice, of course, life is not so simple. There are two big problems to tackle: discovering all the extinct ancestors of the living species we have available for study, and discovering the living animals' intelligence. The easier problem of the two is to discover extinct ancestors. This is despite the undoubted fact that most extinct animals are highly unlikely to have left any trace in the highly 'imperfect' fossil record, so we cannot expect to discover the extinct ancestors by digging.

Chapter 2 explains the way in which reliable genealogies can be worked out. Then, with the example of the living primates (of which we are one), it goes on to deduce some extinct ancestors that *must* have existed, and works out something of their nature. If this all sounds magical, and exciting, that's good; because otherwise, reading a longish chapter on taxonomic methods and primate geneology may appear a tiresome digression from the topic of cognitive evolution. After that, we will begin the 'meat' of the book, comparing intelligence between animals, at the obvious place: the scientific study of intelligence in humans. Here, the differences are between individuals not species, but there are still insights and cautions to be gained. Animal learning has traditionally been quite a different subject (reviewed briefly in Chapter 4), but recent work on social learning (Chapter 5) and imitation (Chapter 6) has challenged this tidy compartmentalization. The central issue in learning is insight—true understanding, not just success on tasks. The various meanings that this term can take in the realms of inanimate objects, other individuals, and minds, are therefore examined next (Chapters 7, 8, and 9). Having seen a lot of data, we return to the theory of what intelligence might really be, and what aspects of it non-humans lack, in Chapters 10 and 11. The final section of the book returns to evolution, examining the main alternative theories for the origin of primate intelligence and testing them with evidence from brain capacities (Chapters 12 and 13), finally summarizing the 'best bet' scenario for the evolutionary history of the rise of intelligence as modern humans' most specialized attribute (Chapter 14).

Further reading

Most books on palaeoanthropology, understandably, try to give the account that is most consistent with the current evidence, rather than dwelling on the repeated changes of story. Probably the best semi-popular book of this kind at present is R. Lewin (1993) *Human evolution* (3rd edn, Blackwell Scientific Publications, Oxford). J. Reader (1981) *Missing links* (Collins, London) is unusual in giving a chronological account of the discoveries, which shows how dramatically views have changed in the past 100 years. Contemporary revisions are mostly in journals or more technical books, such as Binford (1981), Eldredge and Tattersall (1982), Dibble (1989), and Gargett (1989).

2
How to reconstruct evolutionary history

Can the evolutionary history of a living species be worked out if its fossil ancestors cannot be found with certainty? Surprisingly, the answer is 'yes'; the method relies on a subject called evolutionary taxonomy.

Linnean taxonomy

'Taxonomy' means classification of individuals into groups, and classification of these groups into bigger groups, on the basis of some sort of similarity. Each group is technically called a 'taxon' (Greek; plural: taxa). In animal or plant taxonomy, the groups are always hierarchical. 'Hierarchical' means nested: the only way an individual can be a member of two groups is when one includes the other. For instance, people are classed as primates, and primates are classed as mammals, so people can be classed as both primates and mammals. The system of classification that is used routinely today was originally devised by the Swedish botanist Carl von Linné (Carolus Linnaeus) for classifying all living things. The smallest taxon is usually the species (a group of potentially interbreeding individuals). Closely similar species are first grouped into a 'genus' (plural: genera). Latin was the language of science at that time, so the Latin names for an organism's genus and species form its scientific name, such as *Homo sapiens* or *Iris reticulata*. Genera are next grouped into larger units, such as a 'family', and families themselves are grouped into an 'order', and so on.

Evolution

When Linné was working (his system was published in 1758), creationism was unquestioned. The similarities between species that were obvious to all naturalists were interpreted as reflecting the original intentions of a Creator: in doing taxonomy Linné was unravelling the thought processes of God. By the nineteenth century, many thinkers questioned whether species always stayed the same. The alternative possibility, that they might change over time, was given the name 'evolution'. Many people thought evolution a more reasonable explanation for the similarities between living species, and one that could also explain the fossils found in the earth—as remains of former species that had evolved into modern forms. What was more difficult to think of was a mechanism for evolution, short of a God who continued idly to tinker with his creation for the fun of it. (In fact, almost as odd an idea as that *was* indeed believed by many: Cuvier's 'doctrine of repeated creation, the seventh being the last and current one; fossils are the remains of the other six. The first 'evolutionists' were evidently very keen to retain their belief in original creation.)

A workable mechanism was finally discovered—twice. In both cases the discovery was made by men influenced by Malthus's ideas on the effect of exponential growth of populations on resources which could themselves only increase linearly. This combination inevitably means that many individuals must fail to leave descendents—the key to the explanation. As is now familiar, the basic idea is that variations in survival abilities of different individual members of a species would automatically serve to 'select' the fittest, in a way analogous to the artificial selection practised by plant and animal breeders. Less fit individuals would die or fail to breed as successfully, so they would leave fewer offspring behind them. 'Fitness', in this sense, has little to do with aerobics and jogging. It means only 'having whatever it takes to reproduce' and is measured by the number of offspring that survive to reproduce in future generations (even the death of the individual only matters when this reduces the potential number of its offspring). The variations in these survival skills between individuals are random, not organized or planned. Looking at the system 'from the outside', we might judge some variations better or worse according to which turn out, retrospectively, to promote successful reproduction; but unlike artifical selection, the system works without our judgements, quite automatically. Selection is a 'blind' process: the need for a Creator, to explain the marvellous variety of species and their apparent clever design, has been completely removed. (Evolution by natural selection does not explain the *origin* of life in the first place, and evolutionists may still attribute this to a Creator.)

Provided variation between individuals continues to provide raw material, then this 'natural selection' will allow populations to change gradually in response to the environment. If a species is found in several areas in which different skills or bodily traits are valuable for survival, the separate populations will grow apart and eventually be unable to reunite and interbreed; they will then be separate species. Anything that puts barriers in the way of populations mixing, such as large rivers, inhospitable deserts, or the seas between islands, will increase the chances of new species forming. In this way new species will be formed continually in response to new environments; species that fail to adapt sufficiently may die out altogether, and these extinct species are what are sometimes found as fossils. 'Adaptation' has become a technical term for the process of natural selection of advantageous traits.

Charles Darwin was one of the originators of this discovery of the process of species change. From a crushingly respectable background, he hid his work in a safe with instructions to publish after his death, presumably to gain the eternal honour of discovery without the fight and shame of publicizing an idea that he knew many would see as irreligious. But then he received a letter from a younger man, written between bouts of malaria while in the jungles of the Celebes Islands (now Sulawesi, Indonesia), describing the exact same insight. This was Alfred Russel Wallace, not a pillar of society but a travelling collector of insects and other animals, with rather left-wing views. He was all for publishing, regardless of what the Church thought. So they did, and ever since then we have regarded ourselves as part of a still-going evolutionary process, and believed that we are related to animals by a shared descent in the distant past, most closely to the lemurs, monkeys, and apes that make up the order Primata, the primates. We seem very different from all the non-human primates, and not surprisingly we put ourselves in a unique family—the Hominidae. The Hominidae, together with the great apes, Pongidae, and lesser apes, Hylobatidae, make up the superfamily Hominoidea.

Evolutionary taxonomy: cladistics

'Cladistics', or evolutionary taxonomy, is the classification of species in such a way as to reflect correctly their evolutionary history, not merely their present appearance. Usually, appearance is a good guide to relatedness, but not always. When one line of descent suddenly starts to evolve very quickly, it can leave some of its close relatives so far behind that they look as if they are really no relation at all. As a result, there are some dramatic cases where superficial appearance is no guide to the real evolutionary relationship. Birds are now known to be descendants of one type of dinosaur, which resembled them in many ways. The closest living relative to the dinosaurs is a small lizard-like animal, the tuatara, which shares sea-bird burrows on a few islands off New Zealand; also, crocodiles are more closely related to dinosaurs than they are to modern lizards and snakes. These facts are not in dispute, but put together they give some surprising family trees. Birds and tuataras, form a valid group in cladistic taxonomy (a valid group is called a 'clade'), since they have a common ancestor that is not ancestral to any other species. Birds, tuataras and crocodiles also form a valid clade. But lizards, tuataras, snakes, and crocodiles are not a valid clade—despite the fact that they are similar in so many ways and even have an name, reptiles. 'Reptiles' is, of course, a useful term for most everyday purposes, but it doesn't reflect the path of evolution. The first common ancestor shared by these modern reptiles is also an ancestor of birds (and, for that matter, mammals). Since modern reptiles do not share a common ancestor that is unique to them, they are not a clade, a coherent evolutionary group. The most ancient fossil reptiles *were* a clade, but some of their descendents—mammals and birds—have since changed radically from the more conservative modern reptiles. So much so, that for all purposes except tracing evolution it makes more sense to put them in different groups, defined by the new adaptations they possess (warm blood, hair, and milk glands; warm blood, hard beaks, and feathers). Modern reptiles, then, are what is 'left over' among all the descendents of ancient reptiles when the mammals and birds are taken out. Their shared characters are *primitive* ones. In cladistics, this term means a character retained from earlier ancestors (or a species that retains many of these primitive characters). It is crucial that only *derived* characters—new ones—are used to identify clades, otherwise misleading groupings will result; however, working out which characters are derived ones is not always easy. Taxonomists call a group based on shared primitive characters a paraphyletic group. Confusingly, 'evolutionary taxonomy' is occasionally also used for a hybrid system that reflects relationships up to a point, but *not* in these dramatic cases where it still uses paraphyletic groups. The term 'cladistics' removes this ambiguity and aims to reflect only relatedness (Fig. 2.1).

Apart from avoiding this particular sort of grouping, modern evolutionary taxonomy proceeds much as Linné did. Now that we realize that similarities among species can be the result of their sharing a common evolutionary history, it is clear that we should beware of features that

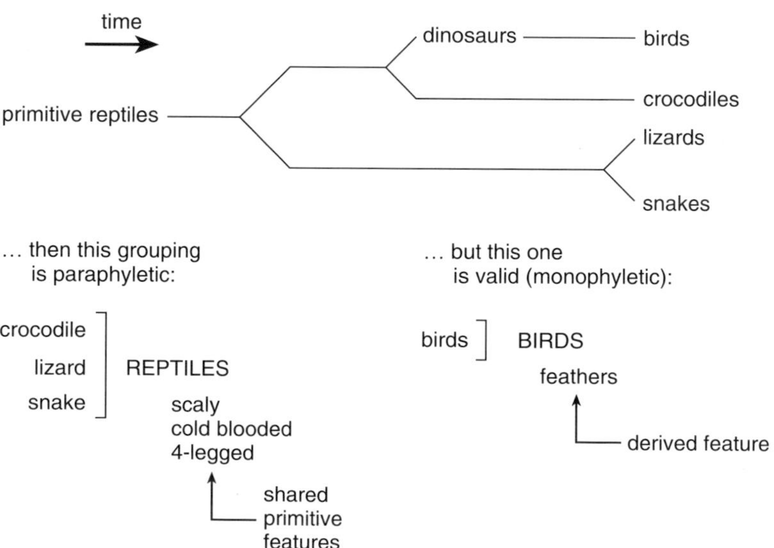

Figure 2.1 Diagrammatic illustration of the relationship between cladistic terminology and evolutionary history.

might be the same for some other reason, and use only certain, 'good' taxonomic characters for classification. What is a good taxonomic feature? Answer: one that is very *unlikely* to have evolved, and is therefore very, very unlikely to have evolved twice. Repeated evolution of the same feature in different species certainly does occur, and this makes sense. If some device is a good one (for leaving more descendents), and not too unlikely to turn up in the random variations of individuals, then several unrelated species can all end up with features in common. This is called 'convergent evolution', and has resulted in some fascinating parallel tracks being followed by quite unrelated species. One of the most obvious is the way in which bees, birds, and bats have all evolved flight; the rather different parts of their anatomy that make up the wings is one clue that this is a case of convergent evolution. Telling convergence from common descent is not always that easy. In Australia there live small animals that burrow underground all their lives and throw up little hills of earth, animals that glide from tree to tree on membranes of skin between their legs, and animals that eat only termites with a long tongue that emerges from their long, narrow head. These animals are not closely related to moles, flying squirrels, or anteaters; all share more recent common ancestry with a kangaroo, but that's hard to remember when watching them. Sometimes even professional taxonomists can be fooled. Kipling called the Elephant's child a 'promiscuous pachyderm' in the *Just so stories*. The term 'pachyderm' (it means 'thick skin' in Latin) commemorates the days when it was believed that elephants, hippos, and rhinos inherited their thick skins from a common ancestor, whereas now taxonomists are sure that hippos are more closely related to pigs, and elephants and rhinos to horses.

What is rather odd, when we remember that the theoretical basis is so different, is that Linné, as a creationist, arrived at such a similar classification to a modern, evolutionary one. Both schemes agree that features like colour and size are 'bad' taxonomic characters and avoid them, and tend to agree about what is a 'good' taxonomic feature. One explanation may lie in the patterns of co-occurrence of features that common ancestry leaves in related species. Suppose Linné began entirely neutrally, classifying species by *all* the characters they showed, then most of the time he would have found an unambiguous result because strong groupings would emerge, with just a few 'oddities'. For instance, if colour, size, feathers or hair, beak or none, suckling or egg-laying, fins or feet, means of locomotion, and many other features were all used, the similarity of crows to sperm whales (they are both black) would be swamped by all their other similarities to other birds and mammals, respectively. Characters that usually got swamped (like colour and size) are troublemakers; so groupings that depend mainly on those characters can be avoided as being unreliable ones, even without a theory of why this should be. Probably Linné did not actually carry out the purely neutral stage of this process. (Although the method, called numerical taxonomy or phenetics, is used quite often today for sorting items where there is no clear principle to show the best features, such as classifying neolithic burials by the types of grave goods found in them.) The human brain is well adapted to picking out patterns of covariance among features, and Linné and his successors no doubt just found it 'obvious' that some features were not useful.

Complicated characteristics, especially ones that are very specific and yet could, in principle, have been quite different, are the best ones to use for evolutionary taxonomy. The chance of an inherently unlikely piece of design evolving *twice* is minimal. The vertebrate backbone is a classic example: multiple cylindrical bones separated by hard flexible pads, held together and moved by muscle all round, is neither the only nor the most obvious way of structuring a semi-rigid skeleton. Cars, helicopters, submarines, all get around without using this design, although they sometimes suffer from their greater rigidity. Wings, however, are almost essential for flight, and we shouldn't be surprised that they have evolved repeatedly. Taxonomy has always been held back by the scarcity of such ideal characters as the vertebrate backbone for use in classification—until the advent of molecular biology. Molecules give a new, and often better, level of detail at which to compare species' characteristics to deduce their relatedness.

Molecular taxonomy

Most biological molecules are proteins, and most of our genetic material encodes instructions for making proteins. Proteins are very large molecules, but function at small 'active sites'; the job of the rest of the protein is structural, affecting how the protein folds and where it fits, so that the active site can catalyse a reaction in a specific way. Random variation in the active site would stop the protein working, probably be lethal to the organism, and the last we'd see of that variation. But random variation at other points in the immense molecule would not matter unless it seriously affected the overall molecular shape. Copying errors in genetic transcription (mutations) cause variations to creep into molecular structures; the errors survive—unless, of course, they are detrimental or lethal ones—and are copied themselves. Very occasionally a mutation might even make a protein work better or do a new, useful job, and so be actively selected by evolution. But most errors seem to be neutral, and these neutral mutations gradually accumulate over time. When two populations have diverged sufficiently for their interbreeding to cease (that is, when biologists would recognize them as separate species), all further neutral copying errors will cause their biological molecules to grow slightly dissimilar in their structure at the most detailed level, yet still function in the same way. If we can compare the 'same' protein (that is, the one that does the same very specific job, in a very specific way) in the two species, then the longer the species have been separate, the more different will be the two molecular structures at neutral sites. Alternatively we could compare the instructions for making proteins, encoded on another large biological molecule (deoxyribonucleic acid, DNA), in ways described below.

In comparing molecules, we might even get a sort of clock—the more differences, the longer time separated. To be most useful, a clock must run at a steady rate. It would therefore be awfully convenient for taxonomists if the rate at which mutations accumulate did not vary: if the probability of a neutral copying error was the same at each generation, and in all species. This idea of a regular rate of mutation began life as a rather wild hope of molecular taxonomists, but oddly enough seems to be correct. Since apes breed slower than flies and fewer generations give fewer opportunities for copying errors (which only occur at genetic transmission), the clock must be corrected for generation time. Then, to find out what speed the clock is running at, it must be calibrated against the known fossil record. Once we have a calibrated clock to measure species' divergence points, charting evolution becomes enormously easier. And certainly there is no risk of convergent evolution of whole proteins from different origins, since the molecules are each so huge and highly complex (and so inherently improbable as structures) that their common descent is virtually certain. Several methods are employed, and different molecules (which change at different rates) are used. The results have been compared and a very robust story is emerging; the broad facts keep coming up the same, however they are obtained. Calibrating the clock is a more controversial matter, but even on that there is now quite good agreement.

The first technique to be discovered involves the specific antibodies that the body manufactures to destroy any foreign protein found in the blood. The antibodies are highly specific: antibodies to smallpox are no help in fighting plague. In experiments, antibodies specific to any particular protein can be made; for instance, a rabbit might be injected with a little human blood serum protein, and later its blood will automatically include antibodies to this protein. Even in a test-tube, the antibodies will react with human serum protein and give a distinctive precipitate. It was noticed that if, instead of human serum protein, that from a chimpanzee is used, the antibodies still work but less efficiently and with less precipitate. With a rat, the reaction is weaker still. In general it seemed that the antibodies' effectiveness depends on the degree of relationship of the species to the one for whose protein the antibodies were generated. In other words, the longer ago that two species last shared a common ancestor, the weaker the immune reaction. As long as the molecular changes creep in at a constant rate, or a rate whose variations are known, the 'immunological distance' measures the time since the species had identical serum protein, the age of the last common ancestor. The classic paper of Sarich and Wilson (1967) used this measure to shatter preconceived views about the human/ape relationship.

A much more direct method would be to compare two species' DNA, since it is on this molecule that genetic information for building all proteins is held during an individual's lifetime. DNA is a long, chain-like molecule, which folds into a complex pattern and eventually crystallizes into a rigid structure. If we imagine the molecule laid out straight, its structure is ladder-like, but the ladder is twisted into a helix. The famous discovery of Crick, Watson, and Franklin was that the two sides of the ladder were exactly complementary to each other, so one side alone could be used to generate the other. Each 'rung' of the ladder consists of two nucleic acid bases joined together, but only if the correct match for each base is attached to it will the rung be the right length, and so allow the twisting and folding of the final helix. In fact, there are four bases involved; for illustration, call them A, T, C, and G (people do). A and T form a pair, as do C and G. If one strand of the helix is CCATGCGTATT then the other strand must be GGTAGCATAA, or they will not form a stable molecule. This, the researchers realized, could produce the accurate replication necessary for copying genetic information from one molecule to another, and they rightly guessed that DNA was the basis of inheritance. In normal cell division, the double helix is unwound and split apart and the complementary bases then attach to each side, producing two identical copies of the original molecule.

What can now be done routinely in the laboratory, is to take the DNA from two species, unwind the helices and allow them to combine to produce a 'hybrid' molecule. Of course, this resulting chemical will not be as stable as either of the two normal DNAs would be. In fact, its instability can be measured very simply, since the more base pairs that fail to join up, the lower the melting point of the DNA crystal: every 1 per cent of base pairs that do not match reduces the melting point of the DNA by 1°C. This gives a direct measure of the similarity of the species' genomes, a wonderful taxonomic aid. Just as with immunological distance, if the changes are at a rate that is constant or varying in a known way, they can be used as a clock to date the splitting points of different taxa.

Since protein structures are coded in DNA, it might seem an equally good taxonomic technique to compare proteins (as immunological distance measures do) or to compare DNA, but it has recently been found that much of the coded text on DNA molecules is never read. So-called 'junk DNA' is simply copied from cell division to cell division, generation to generation, without producing any effect on phenotypes (a 'phenotype' is the developmental result of the 'genotype' in the particular environment in which it affects growth, and is usually synonymous with 'adult individual'). This means that junk, unexpressed DNA is not subject to any selection pressure from its effects on the resulting organism, so that the assumption that mutations are 'neutral' will hold much better for DNA than proteins. True, most of a protein molecule is not close to any active site, but there may still be structural effects causing selection of some mutations over others.

Perhaps the very best taxonomic character that could ever be imagined would be to read off the coded information from genomes of individuals in two species, and compare the 'text'. Even this can now be done, by a complex series of methods known simply as 'DNA sequencing'. The major limitation on these techniques is simply expense, and big chunks of the detailed genetic code on DNA have now been read for several species.* Since it is too costly to decode all the DNA of a species, in practice only relatively small parts of the genome are compared, a few thousand or tens of thousands of bases long. Particularly useful to taxonomy are sequences of certain parts of the genome which are believed to be unexpressed in the phenotype and therefore not under active selection—the so-called pseudogenes. Conveniently, there is a second sort of DNA in all animals, which mutates at a faster rate than that of the nuclear genome. This is mitochondrial DNA, and since the molecule mutates much quicker, it can act as a sort of 'second hand' on the molecular clock. Mitochondria are the organelles in most cells which produce the metabolic energy for the cell, and they are believed to have originated in distant geological time as independent organisms, and to retain their DNA from this earlier existence. Mitochondrial DNA is only passed down the female line, so the results need to be interpreted somewhat differently.

Just as in conventional taxonomy, there are potential problems of convergent evolution. Only a limited set of possible changes can occur to a DNA base pair, so the range of ways in which one amino acid can become another is also limited. However, the sheer size of the molecules involved, and careful choice of molecules least likely to be under active selection, minimizes this worry. In addition, even molecular taxonomists still have to be careful to avoid paraphyletic groupings, in which the members of the group are only similar in their conservative retention of primitive features—just as crocodiles and snakes are similar because neither has diverged as much as birds from the primitive reptiles of the Permian and Triassic. These known problems have been taken into account in recent work, and we can now be confident in the overall pattern of relationships that the molecular evidence shows. In general, all the techniques give a consistent overall pattern, and the primates (Fig. 2.2) have been particularly well studied.

Primate and human evolutionary relationships

It is just as well that the data on primate relationships are reliable, since there are surprises in store, quite different results from the traditional

*In protein synthesis, triplets of adjacent bases along the DNA molecule are decoded to link a particular amino acid in sequence along the protein molecule. These sequences can also be read ('amino acid sequencing'), and the sequential similarities between species compared for each protein.

(a)
(b)
(c)
(d)
(e)
(f)
(g)

Figure 2.2 Typical species of some of the less well-known groups of primates. Strepsirhines (a)–(d): (a) golden bamboo lemur (*Hapalemur aureus*), (b) ring-tailed lemur (*Lemur catta*), (c) white sifaka (*Propithecus verreauxii*), (d) aye-aye (*Daubentonia madagascariensis*). The first three are more-or-less diurnal, whereas the aye-aye is strictly nocturnal, probing for insects below tree bark with its single thin and elongated finger; all are lemuroids. Note the wet nose-tip (rhinarium) and the tendency to large, powerful back legs (especially in the sifaka) allowing leaps between vertical treet-runks. Platyrrhines: (e) woolly spider monkey (*Brachyteles arachnoides*), (g) golden lion tamarin (*Leontopithecus rosalia*). The woolly spider monkey, the largest South American monkey, is an ateline with the prehensile tail typical of this group; the lion tamarin, a typically small callitrichine, comes from the other main branch of Platyrrhines (note the human hand: the animal is being fitted with a radio collar during a field study). Catarrhines: (f) Hanuman langur (*Presbytis entellus*). The langur is a colobine, a fore-gut fermenter able to eat mature leaves; other catarrhine primates are well illustrated in the rest of the book.

story, and rather a jolt to common sense. From an evolutionary point of view, we will now look at the correct classification of the primates, and at what approximate dates the various branches split off.

The major division among the primates is between the monkeys and apes and their allies, on the one hand, and the lemurs and their allies on the other (Fig. 2.3). This distinction used to be between simian primates (just the monkeys and apes) and prosimians (all other primates), but more recent work (including the incontrovertible molecular evidence) shows that a group of Asian prosimians called tarsiers are actually more closely related to the simians, so now the split is between what are called strepsirhines (the lemurs of Madagascar, the African bushbabies, and the slow-moving lorises of Asia and Africa, but not the tarsiers) and haplorhines (monkeys, apes, and tarsiers). Strepsirhines have wet rhinaria on the tips of their noses, like dogs and cats, a device to enhance their sense of smell, whereas haplorhines have lost this primitive* character and must rely more on their other senses. Since wet noses leave no fossil trace, it is not easy to distinguish strepsirhine fossils from tarsier fossils, so palaeontologists still find the term prosimian useful. Tarsiers are little known, so the useful categories for our purposes will be *strepsirhines* and *simians*. All the

*Remember that the word 'primitive' does not mean inefficient or unsuccessful. For characters to be retained in surviving species they must work well: primitive characters in modern animals cannot be inefficient. Where apes, monkeys, and strepsirhines (several species of bushbaby) live alongside each other in Africa, the strepsirhines have complete domination of the forest at night and occur at high densities: primitive species are often very successful. The strepsirhines' wet nose is primitive because it is shared with most other mammals and is obviously an ancient and still excellent device; dry noses are a derived character which developed in the common ancestor of tarsiers, monkeys, and apes, so was bequeathed to its modern descendants.

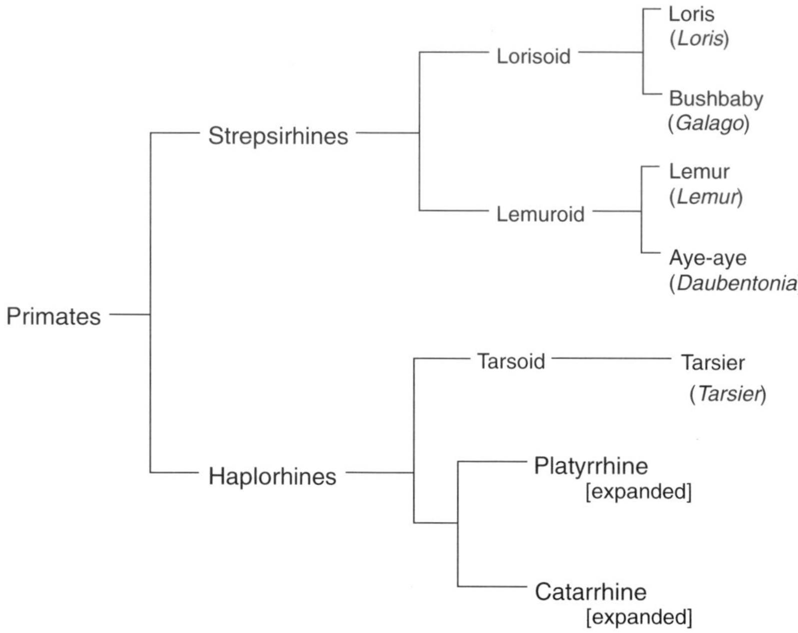

Figure 2.3 Evolutionary relationships among the modern primates: an overview, with no detail of platyrrhines or catarrhines. Representative genera are given for each major branch of the strepsirhines and tarsioids.

early primate fossils resemble modern strepsirhines. It is therefore presumed that the many shared features of all modern strepsirhines would have been possessed by these early primates. Modern tarsiers are often thought to be similar to the earliest ancestors of monkeys and apes, but there is no strong evidence for this belief because they are not closely related to any modern simian. Fossils date the earliest primates to at least 65 million years (My) ago. The first simian fossils are found at 30 My ago and do not closely resemble either modern monkeys or apes, but dental characteristics suggest they are ancestral to modern monkeys and apes which live in the Old World. These dates are used to calibrate the 'molecular clock' for dating the many modern primate taxa which have left fewer fossils or none.

Among the simians, there is a major division between the New World and Old World species. The New World ones are called platyrrhines because of the clear separation of their nostrils—dogs, cats, and mice also have separate nostrils, therefore it is a primitive character. These animals include a wide range of different types and the full detail of their evolutionary relationships is only just emerging (see Fig. 2.4), but molecular evidence suggests they diverged from Old World species as long ago as 40 My. Superficially the most striking division among them is between the

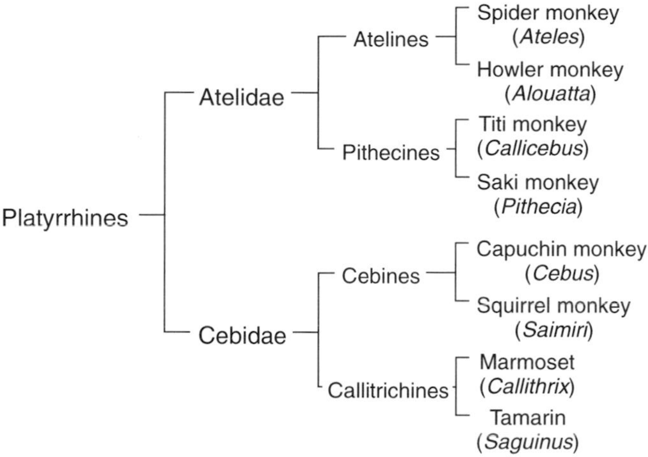

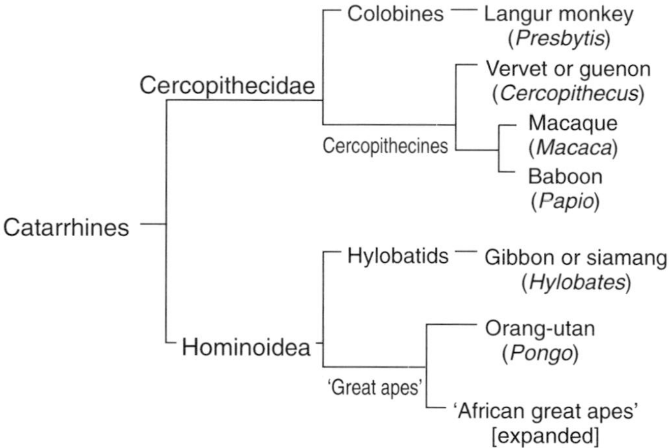

Figure 2.4 Evolutionary relationships among modern monkeys: (a) Platyrrhine primates. (b) catarrhine primates; Representative genera are given for each major branch, but no detail of the African great apes is given.

marmosets and tamarins, and larger species. However, modern evidence suggests that the small and rather squirrel-like marmosets and tamarins, now called callitrichines, that have lost the primate 'hallmark' of finger-nails on many of their digits, are related to the more monkey-like squirrel and capuchin monkeys, now called cebines. (Capuchins are the ones that formerly helped organ grinders and are now sometimes trained to help paraplegics as 'auxiliary hands'.) The atelines, including the howler and spider monkeys, which can hang from their prehensile tails alone, and the strange pithecines, like the bare-faced uakari, and the nocturnal night monkey, form the other grouping. Few of the species are well known so these groups are not yet important for comparative cognition.

Old World monkeys and apes are classified as catarrhines, because their nostrils are separated by a thin septum, as in humans; no other animals share this feature, which must therefore be a 'derived' character of the ancestral catarrhines. Old World monkeys (technically called cercopithecoids) separated from the apes around 30 My ago, and they have further diverged into several types, as shown in Fig. 2.4. Species that are important in arguments about cognitive evolution belong to the Colobinae, which have specialized stomachs for eating mature forest leaves, and the cercopithecine monkeys, the very well-studied macaques and baboons, the mangabeys and the guenons.

Apes differ radically from monkeys in appearance, and this largely comes from their adaptation to a quite different manner of locomotion. All Old and New World monkeys and some strepsirhines are essentially quadrupedal. Even if they can hang, swing, and jump well, they can also walk easily on all fours on a level surface. Tarsiers and most strepsirhines are cling-and-leap animals, able to jump powerfully with massive hind legs from one vertical tree trunk to another; they find walking awkward as their front legs are much smaller. Various other mammals are adapted to cling-and-leap travel, some of them aided by membranes between hind and front legs allowing long glides at each leap. Ape locomotion is unique among mammals, and depends on their much more mobile arms. The ape shoulder-blade is not tightly bound to the ribcage as in monkeys, but can slide over it; this allows the arm to be swung overhead, as in overarm bowling in British cricket. More to the point, it allows apes to hang beneath branches with ease, but not to walk quadrupedally like a monkey. Humans, adapted to bipedal walking, have legs too long and heavy to make brachiation easy or efficient.

For monkeys and strepsirhines, molecular taxonomy has only had minor effects on how their evolution is interpreted, apart from allowing assignment of approximate dates to the divergence of those groups that are not represented as fossils. Ape classification, however, has been revolutionized. Until the 1960s, the group was divided into pongids and hominids, groups thought to have separated about 25 or 30 My ago. Sometimes the pongids were divided again into lesser apes (gibbons) and great apes (two species of chimpanzees, gorilla, and orang-utan); hominids included only humans, along with our extinct relatives or ancestors such as Neanderthals, *Homo erectus*, *Homo habilis*, and australopithecines. The most obvious distinction is that hominids walk bipedally (two-legged) on the ground whereas pongids brachiate (arm-swing) in trees.

None of this picture is quite the same now. Most dramatically, a cladistic interpretation of molecular taxonomy (whichever biochemical method is used) shows that humans are not a separate lineage from the modern apes: we *are* apes, and specifically we are close relatives of the gorilla and especially the chimpanzee. (This doesn't mean common usage will change. English is uncomfortable with nested categories—we talk about 'birds and animals' yet birds *are* animals to a zoologist. So 'ape' is likely to remain commonly used to mean 'apes but not humans' (paraphyletic though that group is), instead of 'apes including humans' (Hominoidea)—which more properly acknowledges that we humans are a kind of ape. The everyday sense of the word 'ape', which excludes humans, and the term 'pongid', must be abandoned when we are talking about evolution. Non-human apes are just what the words imply, a paraphyletic grouping formed by subtracting humans from the valid clade of apes-including-humans. Put at its most sensational, if we were chimpanzees, our closest relatives would not be those big black animals in nearby forests that look rather like ourselves, let alone those reddish Asian animals that hang from the trees, but the naked and bipedal humans. Certainly, humans do show signs of having undergone very rapid evolution, leaving the more conservative chimpanzees resembling gorillas in physical appearance (just as tuataras and crocodiles resemble lizards not birds). But chimpanzees and humans share a common ancestor unique to themselves, more recently than either shares ancestry with any other living animal. The implications of this may be upsetting for those who prefer a discreet distance to be kept between themselves and brute beasts, but it is exciting news for the study of the evolution of cognition. Had humans no living relatives from the last 30 My of their evolution, the chances of understanding how our unique human intelligence evolved would have been small. Many psychologists still believe that the chances *are* small, but now their pessimism (when it does not simply reflect ignorance of molecular taxonomy) is based on flimsier grounds—the belief that all the important intellectual changes happened in the past 5 My, since the human and chimpanzee lines diverged. This might of course be so, but it would be rather surprising. There is certainly every reason for taking a close look at the evidence before concluding that the job of reconstructing the evolution of intelligence is hopeless.

With the best modern evidence, how does the family tree of our closest relatives look? The apes (including humans) diverged from monkeys at most 30 My ago, from fossil evidence. But there is then a long period before the ancestors of modern gibbons (Hylobatidae) branch off at 19–17 My (if we take 30 My, as the monkey divergence date—and this is conservative, it could be even more recent). By this time we know the ape line had already evolved the ability to arm-swing, since every descendant shows the distinctive shoulder-blades. Gibbons took arm-swinging to a pinnacle of skill; on the ground, however, gibbons are clumsy and vulnerable bipedal walkers. Gibbons' small body size and very long arms allow a kind of brachiation (and sometimes the term is reserved for gibbons' specialized form of movement) in which upward pulling actions of the arms provide forward propulsion, just as on a child's swing arm-pulling is used to make the whole body swing back and forth.

The collection of animals on the other branch of the lineage at this point, including humans, have no agreed Latin term as yet, since the revision is too recent (Fig. 2.5). However, the English 'great ape' is adequate, provided we remember that it *includes* humans. Great ape molecular taxonomy has been much studied; the currently most reliable studies are probably those of Bailey *et al.* (1992), sequencing 30 000 base pairs of a pseudogene, calibrated with a 30 My date for the ape/Old World monkey divergence, and Horai *et al.* (1992), sequencing 5000 base pairs of mitochondrial DNA, calibrated with a 16 My date for the orang-utan/African ape split by Waddell and Penny (1994); I will give both here. The first divergence in the great ape line was that of the modern orang-utan's ancestor, dated at 14.0 ± 0.5 My by Bailey *et al.* (1992). Unusually there is good fossil evidence of what and when this animal was: a well-preserved skull of *Sivapithecus* is so like

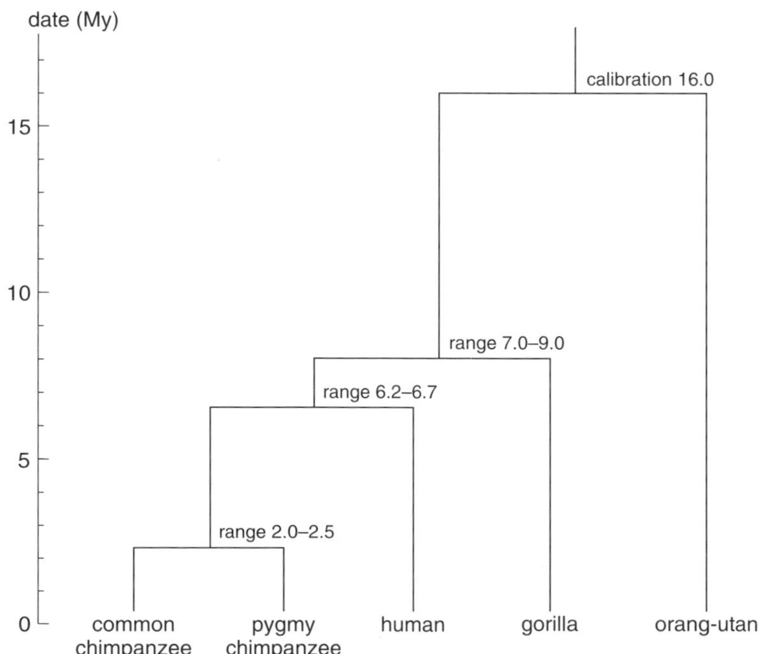

Figure 2.5 Approximately dated cladogram of the great apes; see text for sources and explanation.

a modern orang-utan that there is little doubt of their close relationship (Pilbeam and Smith 1981). The earliest *Sivapithecus* are dated to 12 My, but they are thought to have taken 2–6 My to acquire their unique features, giving the calibration date used by Waddell and Penny (1994). This also shows that orang-utans have changed little in the past 12 My and can probably be considered primitive. If so, a modern orang-utan gives us a good idea of what the common ancestor of all great apes was like, making their study of great interest (although skeletal remains of *Sivapithecus* suggest more monkey-like movement than a modern orang-utan). Orang-utans are effectively four-handed, able to clamber and swing among tree branches in any orientation, but are not efficient brachiators like gibbons. On the ground they walk on all fours with most weight taken on the short, back legs, the hands held as fists, flat on the ground as a support, or resting on various 'knuckles' depending on the joint most flexed. Often one hand is supporting one way, the other quite another. Locomotion of orang-utans is less well understood than that of other great apes, and is an important topic because the hand and foot anatomy of australopithecines is rather similar to that of an orang-utan, suggesting that they too retained primitive characters from the ancestral great ape despite their ability to walk bipedally. Two subspecies of orang-utan (Sumatran and Bornean) split apart around 1–2 My ago, but seem to have diverged little in behaviour.

Once again, there is as yet no agreed scientific name for the remaining group of apes including humans (hominid has been suggested, but this conflicts with the established usage of hominids for bipedal, walking primates), but the English label 'African great apes' is fine for the present, if modern humans originated in Africa. (This clever guess of Darwin's is now supported by most of the available evidence.) The next ape lineage to diverge from the human line was the gorilla, at 7.5 ± 1.0 My ago (or 8.0 ± 1.0 My). The gorilla's close anatomical similarity to the two chimpanzee species suggests that their (and therefore our) common ancestor was not too different from a modern gorilla or chimpanzee. If so, it was a specialized knuckle-walker, with hand modifications to allow much more efficient travel on the ground than modern orang-utans, modifications now lost in human hands. In knuckle-walking, most weight is taken on the short, back legs as in the orang-utan, but the back of the hand is held roughly in line with the lower arm and the supporting weight is taken on the folded knuckles, with the wrist flexing as shock-absorber. Gorillas, as well as the two chimpanzee species, travel like this on the ground (Fig. 2.6). They use terrestrial travel extensively and actually prefer it for long-distance movements; in trees they arm-swing but lack the speed and finesse of the smaller gibbons.

Finally, the chimpanzee lineage separated from that of humans at only 6 ± 1 My (or 6.5 ± 1.0 My). Remarkably, this is much the same date as that suggested in the original work of Sarich and Wilson (1967), but it is now

Figure 2.6 The ape that stood up. In fact this particular common chimpanzee can knuckle-walk very well; he is the animal at the rear in the lower photograph. Raised partly by humans, he habitually walks upright some of the time, showing how small an evolutionary change in anatomy would be needed to reach bipedalism from the African ape body form.

based on a far more solid basis of evidence. The two chimpanzees separated from each other at around 2.0–2.5 My ago; however, unlike the *subspecies* of orang-utan, they have become markedly different since, hence their *species* status. Many zoologists have pointed out that a relationship as close as that of human to chimpanzee (as it is now known to be) would normally apply to species in the same genus ('differences at only 1 per cent of DNA base pairs' is one way of dramatizing the similarity).

'*Pan sapiens*' grates somewhat, and, in any case, *Homo* was used prior to *Pan* so rules of biological naming would require *Homo troglodytes* and *Homo paniscus*. As members of *Homo sapiens*, we are somewhat biased in the matter, but there are some real reasons against this solution. A minor point is that it obscures the obviously much closer relationship of *troglodytes* to *paniscus*, but more importantly it obscures massive differences in anatomy between *sapiens* and the others, especially the many adaptations that allow bipedal walking.

Bipedalism is common in birds and was the normal mode of locomotion of many dinosaurs, but is rare in mammals (hopping by kangaroos and gerbils is quite different from walking and running on two legs, which is what 'bipedalism' normally implies). Therefore it is a good derived character among primates for defining a clade, and this group is usually called the hominids; it comprises modern humans, Neanderthals, *H. erectus* and *H. habilis*, and a number of forms of australopithecine. Keeping the traditional division between hominids (*Homo* and *Australopithecus*) and *Pan* is simple, does not violate evolutionary taxonomy, and is almost bound to happen anyway. The real losers in this are the chimpanzees, because designation as *Homo* just might have changed the often appalling ways in which they are treated by humans, by raising serious ethical questions about their status. (In fact, since I wrote these words, 'The Great Ape Project' has been launched, a campaign to give all great apes the ethical status of those humans who lack full adult cognition, such as children or the mentally retarded.) The ethical questions, of course, are not settled by the Latin name, but are better decided by knowledge of the actual behaviour and cognition of chimpanzees than by their family history.

Inventing ancestors

With a reliable set of family *relationships* of the living primates in hand, we can go on to 'reconstruct' the extinct ancestors of these animals. To do this, the taxonomic method of cladistics is turned on its head. This sounds so much like a free lunch that the logic is worth emphasizing.

So far, what we have been doing is to use a shared character of several species within a related group as evidence *that those species are closely related*—provided that the character is not commonly found outside the related group of animals. (If it is, possession of that character is instead taken to be the primitive state, and not evidence of closer than average relatedness.) As long as the shared character is not found more generally, then it is good evidence that those species had a common ancestor not shared by other primates. For instance, some primates have mobile shoulder-blades; this is not found in dogs, rats, lizards, or fish. The primate species with mobile shoulder-blades (apes, including ourselves, lumped under the name hominoids) are then taken to be of closer than average relatedness—reflecting their descent from a single ancestor. Similarly, very few species apart from humans and the extinct Neanderthals and *Homo erectus* have such a massive brain for their body size. This again suggests that they shared a common ancestor, one that is not also ancestral to modern chimpanzees or gibbons, and it helps to define the group *Homo*. However, some hominoids have small brains, and this was once wrongly used to define an evolutionary group, the pongids. Remember that dogs, rats, lizards, and fish all have small brains too: so a small brain does not tell us that those apes derived it from a single, small-brained ape ancestor. A small brain is a retained primitive character, and the real derived character is actually possession of a *large* brain.

Now, if a character is derived in several species by common descent from their unique common ancestor, the character *must* have been present in this ancestor. So, in the examples just given, the ancestral hominoid must have had mobile shoulder-blades (and therefore been able to swing in trees if it wanted), and the ancestral *Homo* must have had a large brain relative to other apes (and therefore been good at activities needing a large brain). In other words, reversing the logic enables us to deduce ancestral traits. What is more, this does not just apply to *good* taxonomic characters.

As I have argued above, the best way of settling the details of relationships is by cladistic molecular taxonomy, not by looking at phenotypic features; but once the relationships are worked out, we can use the distribution of phenotypic characteristics in modern species to deduce those of the extinct ancestors. For a bunch of modern species that form a clade at any level (e.g. African great apes, apes, catarrhine primates, primates, mammals), *any* derived characters they share will be characters of the common ancestor at the appropriate level (Fig. 2.7). The ancestral catarrhine must have had a sinus membrane in its nose, the ancestral primate must have had fingernails, the ancestral mammal must have been warm blooded, and so on. This approach is not limited to anatomical features; it can be used just as easily to trace the evolution of large molecules, and to trace the evolution of behavioural traits that leave no fossilizable record. If all simians, but no other mammals, had colour vision, then we could conclude that colour vision originated with the first simian, and that this animal—alone among its mammalian contemporaries—could discriminate colours. (This is NOT true, although it is widely imagined to be; in fact some strepsirhine primates and many other diurnal mammals have some colour vision.) If all apes, but no other primate, could count (this is not true either, as far as I know), then we could conclude that counting originated with the first ape, which could count. When reconstructing extinct ancestors by this method, unlike the case of inferring relationships, primitive characters are also useful. In the first fictitious example I gave, it would be reasonable to attribute 'lack of colour vision' (the primitive state) to extinct ancestors of all mammals other than simians, and to the common ancestors shared by simians and other mammals. The only problem

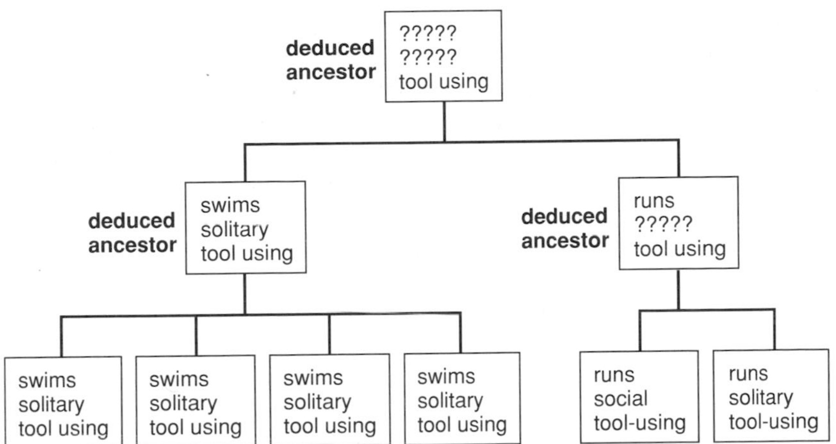

Figure 2.7 Hypothetical taxonomy—deducing the characteristics of extinct species by the comparative method. Each 'box' represents a species, living forms at the bottom of the pyramid.

emerges if some, but not all, of a clade have a character; then it gets tricky, and no firm deduction can be made.

This is evidently a very powerful method—to 'invent' and then describe extinct animals, their form, both molecular and large-scale, and their behavioural aptitudes. Is it really this simple and reliable? Consider how it could be fooled. If some ability had evolved several times, but *only* in the species of a single clade, in most of them but in no other. Then, we would falsely attribute the ability to their shared ancestor, and wrongly date the trait's antiquity. This is possible, but it is rather far-fetched and it is exactly the same problem always faced by evolutionary taxonomists. The same logic applies: confidence is built up if the character is unlikely in the first place, found in as few other places in the animal kingdom as possible, found in every one of a sizeable group of species that form a clade. With characteristics like 'mammalian bipedal walking', or 'spoken language', found in only one species, all we can be sure of is that it evolved *since* the last shared ancestor with other species: during the past 5 My, in both cases. To narrow that down, the best bet is the fossil record, despite its imperfections. A skeleton that would have allowed efficient bipedalism has been found in Ethiopia and dated at 3.6 My (and called *Australopithecus afarensis* by some palaeontologists), and bipedal footprints have been found in Tanzania and dated at 3.75 My, narrowing the time gap to 1.25 My. (In fact, rather wider than that since *each* of these dates has an associated error, whether it comes from molecular taxonomy or potassium–argon dating of volcanic glass; when dates are added or subtracted their associated errors must always be *added*.) But language leaves little trace, and we may never know its date of origin for sure. This has not stopped people trying, as we saw in Chapter 1.

Evolutionary reconstruction through the study of modern species is quite different from that sort of speculation. It has little to say about those years in our history since humans last shared an ancestor with another living primate. Instead, it can make a solid and reliable attempt to answer questions about our earlier evolutionary history. What capabilities would the ancestral hominid have inherited from its earlier ancestors that enabled it to evolve the cognitive, social, and physical characters of modern humans? In what order and at what times did these characteristics evolve?

Only when we can be sure of the answers to these questions will it be safe to tackle the most interesting questions about our intellectual origins, the 'why' questions. Why did we evolve large brains, the ability to lie and to recognize lying, the means to speak our minds, the minds themselves, the use of teaching and apprenticeship, our family relations and our larger social units? There are many theories and speculations in answer to these questions, but scientific testing of them is in its infancy. Proper evaluation of theories again needs evidence from modern species, and will not emerge from the fossil record. For instance, if some special feature (like meat-eating or monogamy) is claimed to have led to brain enlargement in evolutionary history, then, at the very least, brain enlargement should correlate with the feature nowadays. For these reasons the rest of the book is divided roughly into two parts, concerned with *what* we can know about the behavioural aptitudes of our common ancestors with other animals (Chapters 3–11), and *why* might these aptitudes have evolved (Chapters 12–14). The questions are, of course, not really separate, but the levels of confidence we can have in the answers are quite different.

Further reading

To really understand the theory of natural selection, R. Dawkins (1988) *The blind watchmaker* (Penguin, London) cannot be too highly recommended; but if you want every detail, M. Ridley (1993) *Evolution* (Blackwell Scientific, Oxford) is comprehensive and reliable, and his *Evolution and classification: the reformation of cladism* (Longman, Harlow, England, 1986) is the best full account of modern taxonomy. The *Cambridge encyclopedia of human evolution*, by S. Jones, R. Martin, and D. Pilbeam (Cambridge University Press, 1993) is authoritative and careful, especially useful for finding more about the primate fossil record and how molecular methods are used in practice.

3
What is intelligence and what is it for?

If we are going to use the comparative method to reconstruct cognitive evolution in humans, we need first to describe and measure the intelligence of various animals. Especially, we will need information on the relative intelligence of strepsirhines, New and Old World monkeys, gibbons, orangutans, gorillas, and the two species of chimpanzees, in order to cover the succession of early ancestors of humans that must have existed. It sounds straightforward, put like that, but it is not.

Politics of intelligence

The very idea of applying the concept of intelligence to animals is fraught with perils, because of what the measurement of intelligence in humans has been used for in recent history (see Gould 1981). Calm, unbiased science cannot be performed in a climate of doubt as to whether findings may be used to justify refusal to allow residence in a country, let alone mass murder. Intelligence testing is now a minefield of potential social and political abuses, impassioned polemic, and misuses of science in general. The polarized opinions associated with testing human intelligence will spill over into any work that seems to compare human intelligence to that of animals, for obvious reasons.

Understandable as this is, we needn't panic: fears of debasing humans by attributing intelligence to animals are *not* justified. The subject of human intelligence testing (psychometrics) seeks to grade and label potential within one species, the human. These individual differences will inevitably be small compared with the common potential for intelligence shared by each individual human, by virtue of being this species. When we talk of 'differences in intelligence between species', this is always a shorthand: strictly, intelligence is necessarily an individual-level phenomenon, allowing individuals to devise flexible solutions to problems they meet. Even though there are individual differences among individuals of a species in such flexibility, they all share a 'common denominator' of ability. Differences in this common denominator intelligence of different species are what we mean by species-level intelligence; this is bound to be genetically based.

The possibility that variations in human intelligence have a strong genetic component is one of the greatest fears of those who forsee misuse of human testing data. If the species-level human intelligence is genetically based, doesn't that mean that individual variations will also be strongly influenced by gene differences? Not necessarily. Any trait with a strong genetic basis, subjected to strong selection for the trait—and presumably high intelligence is strongly advantageous for people—will tend to reduce over many generations in its genetic variability, within the species. Genetic variants that are expressed as lower intelligence will be weeded out quickly in periods of strong selection pressure for high intelligence; since gene mutations occur at a steady rate which is not influenced by selection pressures, the range of variation in the genes of the species will be reduced. The variation gets narrowed down—used up, in a sense. Therefore, current variation between humans in intelligence is unlikely to be related to the much greater, species-level difference between human intelligence and that of our relatives—which is what interests *us*. Whether differences in intelligence among humans are much influenced by gene variation or not is a major controversy, but not one that matters here.

There is no need now for anyone to fear proper scientific comparisons among intelligence of different animal species. The idea that some human races might be closer to apes in intelligence would indeed be laughable, had it not been such a prevalent one in the past 100 years and been used to justify so much abuse and suffering.

IQ tests for animals?

Putting aside political and social objections to comparing species' intelligence, we are still left with major problems of how to go about doing the job. An obvious starting point is to see how the small variations in intelligence among humans are measured; surely these sensitive measurement tools can be adapted for other species? In practice, this isn't easy. One reason is a lack of consensus about what the term 'intelligence' means, when applied to humans—let alone animals. Although most people treat intelligence as something that can be deduced from everyday behaviour, psychologists have often preferred to define intelligence *operationally*, as what IQ tests measure. As a result, we can draw upon sadly little expertise in psychometrics on how to infer human intelligence from behaviour.

Many IQ tests are, however, readily available. Although some can be adapted to test animals, attempts to do so have been disappointing; this seems to be because IQ tests are so bound up with successful performance in a world of language and culture. Modern tests have often been 'calibrated' against existing IQ tests, but ultimately these were devised by selecting test items that correctly predicted educational success, and throwing out those that did not. This embodies a strong theory of what intelligence is—the ability to profit from the current educational system. This seems to be circular and enshrine the educational status quo, and certainly has little relevance to non-humans. At best, it is only one aspect of what the term 'intelligence' means to non-psychologists: there remains much controversy as to whether IQ tests measure anything like people's everyday notion of intelligence (see Sternberg 1985).

In any case, most IQ tests depend on language for their administration, so cannot directly be applied to animals. To some extent, this last difficulty can be overcome. The procedures developed by behavioural psychologists for studying learning in rats allow a sufficiently ingenious experimenter to pose any questions that can be reduced to picking the next in a series, the odd one out, the best match, and so forth. Even this may still leave the results hard to interpret. Human intelligence testing has shown the very great problem in taking a test, standardized on people of one culture, and using it on people from another; the difficulty is obviously far greater across species. However, much work of this kind has been done with primates and other animals, and the results will be summarized briefly in Chapter 4.

Intelligence as adaptation

If IQ tests give a narrow view of human intelligence, what do people fully mean by the term? When researchers come to formalize the vague, everyday understanding of the meaning, they often arrive at a definition that makes sense for variations within one species but does not help in comparing species. Focused on how to measure individual differences, their definitions have no relevance to the commonality between individuals of a species, which is what we need to compare across species. For instance, Wechsler (1944) suggested 'the aggregate or global capacity of the individual to act purposefully, think rationally, and to deal effectively with his environment'. If 'purposefully' means the same as 'in a goal-directed way', and 'rationally' means the same as 'optimally', this definition is suspiciously close to that of biological *adaptedness*. This resemblance almost seems explicit in some definitions, like 'the faculty of adapting oneself to circumstances' (Binet and Simon 1915), though they were presumably using the word 'adapt' only in its everyday sense.

To ethologists (scientists who study animal behaviour and its ecology and evolution), the word conveys a technical meaning. When they observe an animal acting in an apparently purposeful way, with a result that seems to be the best available given the animal's natural environment, they usually assume that the behaviour has arisen by natural selection—as an 'adaptation'. This assumption does not mean that they think the behaviour is entirely encoded on DNA and emerges fully formed when needed. The developmental origin ('ontogeny') of many animal behaviours is well understood and often involves a subtle interplay between genes and environment. But if almost all members of a species usually acquire a behaviour under any remotely normal circumstances, then the tendency to do so is seen as genetically controlled. All living animals are evidently, by their very survival, adapted to their particular environments. But if 'intelligent' for an animal species means the same as 'well adapted to the environment', then presumably all species are intelligent in their own ways! Small wonder then, that some biologists have doubted whether intelligence is an appropriate measure by which to compare animals at all. Animal adaptations are fascinating, but calling them 'intelligence' adds nothing to our understanding. The use of the term intelligence should be restricted to that quality of flexibility that allows individuals to find their own solutions to problems; genetical adaptations, by contrast, are fixed and inflexible, however well-tuned to special environments they are.

This very understandable mistake is in unholy alliance with that legacy of pre-Darwinian arrogance, the assumption that animals merely learn, and only humans are intelligent. According to this view, very widespread among social scientists, human intelligence is unique. This does not mean 'unique as each species' intelligence is unique', nor does it mean 'uniquely large'; both these are very reasonable beliefs to hold. It means 'incomparable', and anyone seeking to compare animal and human intelligence must be silly. If anything can be said about the origin of human intelligence (and many researchers with these sort of views would say that it cannot), real intelligence is seen as a consequence of language and speech, since these traits are also unique to humans. Any use of the term intelligent for animal performance is dismissed as simply metaphorical or (worse) anthropomorphism.

Now, in the end it may turn out that the gulf between human intelligence and that of any other animal is a very large one; but to assume that there is no comparison is an approach that makes good sense only when coming from a creationist. Strangely, adherence to the view is much more widespread than that. In fact, the determination to believe in many 'unique' traits of humans is rather pervasive, and definitions of the traits get changed to rule new facts out of court. Language, for instance, used to be defined as a communication system with *arbitrary* relation between concept and signal pattern; until the deciphering of the dances of bees forced a re-think. Bees encode the distance and compass direction of a source of honey in their waggle dances, performed in the dark inside the hive. The bearing of the flowers to the sun is encoded in the bearing of the angle at which the bee dances to the vertical, and the distance away is measured by the waggle rate, both awkwardly arbitrary relations. So, language became the ability to learn and bestow *new* relationships, which bees can't do. But this has been challenged by experiments with captive chimpanzees (challenged, that is, if the idea that language is uniquely human must be sacrosanct). Now, 'real' language has become equated with *syntax*, with which chimpanzees have trouble. No doubt this will persist until some animal turns out to use syntax to structure its communication.

It looks very much as if preserving human uniqueness has become a goal of its own.

Intelligence is a much more slippery concept than language, so anyone determined to keep animals out will have no trouble. Since this sort of definitional argument is a 'dead end' for those interested in how human intelligence evolved, we must look for a better definition of intelligence to help us out. But in doing so we must not underestimate the seriousness of the problem that many performances of animals *look* intelligent, yet there is every reason to suppose that their development is under tight genetic guidance. Although the shorthand of talking about species-level intelligence is convenient, we must not forget that the importance of the species' potential is in *individual* flexibility in learning and problem-solving. The marvellously complex societies and built structures of ants, wasps, bees, and termites *resemble* the products of intelligence, but they are not. Individual social insects have no roles except as cogs in a genetical machine, and have been described as 'silicon chips with legs'. Those structures and societies that we marvel at are produced by a genetic recipe, not by intelligence. Actions that are specified in advance by genes are a different matter from superficially similar ones we call intelligent in people (such as the civilized society of ancient Athens, or the road-building of Rome), and it does not help to overextend the term.

Dangers of everyday observations

Of course, few are fooled by social insects' behaviour into imagining that their actions are at all like our intelligence. But many cases are much less obvious and do fool people, including me—as I noticed recently. I will digress briefly, to recount my error, as a cautionary tale of how careful we must be in inferring species-level intelligence.

I underestimated sheep. Most people do, I suspect, particularly in comparison with sheep-dogs. Black and white dogs sometimes called border collies (although exactly which border is unclear) are famous for outwitting sheep. The classic image is the sheep-dog, responding to mere whistles of a shepherd with flawless outmanoeuvring and controlling of 100 sheep. Who could doubt that clear differences of animal intelligence exist? Of course, any ethologist would point out that this wonderful performance depends on the innate anti-predator reactions of sheep. Bunching and running in tight-packed flocks when attacked makes it difficult for a wolf to single out a potential kill, but easy for a sheep-dog to manoeuvre a group. The black and white wolf-descendent is also equipped with innate hunting tactics, which can be seen in any untrained sheep-dog let out to chase some sheep. In training, the shepherd does just that and then painstakingly 'labels' each tactic with whistles, giving the appropriate command whistle after the dog has run in a certain direction, sat down, crouched, and so on.

Eventually one day the dog notices the whistle–tactic association, and from then on will obey each by making the appropriate action. This is all the training needed because the dog's reward is simply to please the shepherd, who has usurped the wolf role of pack leader. After it has made the connection between whistle and action, the sheep-dog follows the human's intentions.

But still, the dog is able to deploy its tactics to order; the sheep are unable to overcome their innate restrictions—so surely they are dumb, in comparison? Well, not necessarily. Recently I was able to spend some time with Gujarati shepherds on the Little Rann of Kutch in India (Fig. 3.1). They whistle their commands just like British shepherds; it seemed a familiar scene of sheep being pushed around because they are not overly bright. Eventually, I noticed the sheep-dogs—asleep. In fact the sheep in Gujarat learn to understand the shepherds' commands and follow them, treating the shepherd as herd leader. The dogs' role is not one of herder, but a source for the flock of protection from wolves. I suspect that pet dogs seem especially intelligent to people largely because they happen to use facial musculature for visual communication, giving rise to expressions that resemble our own and happen to have similar meanings. Because of this we can 'see' what they are thinking. Sheep are very foreign and cryptic because they are not primates like us, and so we easily underestimate their capacities.

Figure 3.1 Shepherds with their flocks in Gujurat, India.

Innate tendencies and learned behaviour

When we search for really *diagnostic* actions with which to deduce variation in intelligence between species, we must therefore beware of anthropomorphism, and watch out for powerful genetic influences. We have to understand an animal's own world view as far as we can, before jumping to conclusions about its abilities.

It is tempting to believe that the search can be simplified by first separating all animal behaviour into discrete categories, 'innate' and 'learned', and then only using the latter. Unfortunately, life is not that simple. Most animal behaviour is influenced in important ways by both genes and learning. For instance, passerine birds such as European chaffinches (*Fringilla coelebs*) are predisposed by their genes to copy songs that match a particular, but loosely specified, pattern. Youngsters remember very exactly the song that they hear; months later, when they are adult and it is spring, they successively improve their attempts at singing by comparing their own song with this memory. Is chaffinch song, then, innate or learned?

Learning and genetic predispositions are intricately meshed in an animal's development, and the same is even apparently true for skilled human behaviour. For instance, it would seem that all adults, male and female, are predisposed to talk to babies (and pet animals, and even occasionally house-plants) in a particular way: 'What's that you've got there? A nice, red ball, is it? Isn't that pretty? Wouldn't it be fun to drop it?', and so on. This speech is singularly low in novel information, which is largely obvious from context anyway. Yet it is flamboyantly rich and complex in syntax—the largely unconscious, everyday grammar that allows people to structure a limited set of words into phrases and sentences with an unlimited range of meanings. This kind of talk also has an exaggerated intonation pattern, making both the syntactic structure and those individual sounds (phonemes) of speech that distinguish meanings more obvious than in normal adult speech. Syntactic forms are often repeated in successive utterances, and the tendency of adults to interrupt themselves or tail off into incomplete sentences is missing. It is, in short, an ideal vehicle for helping the child (if not the house-plant) to learn phonology and grammar. Mothers and other caretakers who talk this way are unaware that their speech has this special function in language development. If the same principles apply to such disparate organisms as babies and chaffinches, perhaps there is no need to go beyond this sort of explanation to understand all intelligent-looking behaviour. Could all differences between animals result from species' differences in the channelling of simple, individual learning processes by genetic* predispositions?

---

*Here and elsewhere, I use the word 'genetic' loosely, to include cytoplasmic factors. Also, the idea of 'channelling' of learning is not meant to imply direct action on the neural processes of learning, at the time of the learning; only, that guidance is imparted to learning, most likely through effects actually operating during neural development.

Why bring in 'intelligence' at all? There are two answers to that question. The first is that psychologists have less confidence than in the past that learning is simple and well understood. Traditional learning theory held two convenient beliefs: that learning processes are identical in all situations and organisms (and therefore best studied in a laboratory animal, where experimental control is greatest), and that by just these processes and no others animals can learn anything. Learning now seems to differ from species to species, and not all information is equally learnable; this is particularly true in social learning contexts. It is not simply that different species are channelled into acquiring different knowledge according to their needs; species turn out to differ in overall flexibility of learning. To most people, intelligence includes the ability to learn, so variation in flexibility is part of animal 'intelligence'. This way of looking at intelligence is matched by another type of definition of human intelligence, one that stresses *understanding*, for instance 'grasping the essentials in a situation and responding appropriately to them' (Heim 1970).

The second reason is that intelligence is surely not just learning ability, even if social learning is included. We need to 'flesh out' the scope of the term, to examine its various facets.

Facets of intelligence

In humans, intelligence certainly means more than flexible learning: terms like 'thinking clearly', 'solving difficult problems', and 'reasoning well' recur in attempts to define the ability. The scope of intelligence is quite wide, including learning an unrestricted range of information; applying this knowledge in other and perhaps novel situations; profiting from the skills of others; and thinking, reasoning, or planning novel tactics. (Which should remind us not to expect that intelligence is a single 'thing', but a bag of devices and processes, endowments and aptitudes, that together produce behaviour we see as 'intelligent'.)

What all these (possible) components of intelligence have in common is that they contribute to general purpose skills, not highly specialized ones. This may help understanding of what intelligence is *for*. All the abilities listed above are what one should expect in generalist animals: intelligence should most benefit extreme generalists, species adapted to exploit continually changing environments, since they must daily cope with novelty in order to survive. Creatures adapted to unvarying environments, however intricate, would be much better off with reliable, if inflexible, methods: genetically coded strategies, or genetically channelled learning of a narrow range of information. In a given species, then, one might expect a trade-off between special-purpose, hard-wired abilities serving particular biological needs, and general-purpose 'intelligence' which can be applied widely.

Those inborn tendencies that allow reliable learning of songs by passerine birds and grammar by children, however remarkable and well-adapted, imply *restrictions* on generalized learning capability.

According to this view, the flexibility given by having superior intelligence is an adaptation to a life of change and unpredictability, just as being able to run fast or breathe infrequently are adaptations to quite different selection pressures. This shows that there is nothing unscientific about calling one animal intelligent and another less so. (Although it would be nice to be able to go further than that, and specify exactly what mental mechanisms result in the intellectual difference.) The difficulty is only a practical one: does any evidence exist that enables us to say one species is more intelligent in some way than another?

Behaviour and representation

In trying to compare animals' intelligence, I will often speak as if animals mentally represented information (about the world, or about their behaviour). This way of talking is natural to people; we talk about knowledge, belief, memory, and ignorance as if they depended on stored information in our minds. Behaviourists have long pointed out that this way of talking is not necessary. One can always replace these statements with ones that describe only behaviour. For instance, 'remembering the way to water' becomes 'having the behaviour of moving to the site of water, in circumstances of water-deprivation or salt administration'. This clumsy-sounding version has the advantage that the things it mentions are all observables, which can be studied directly, unlike memory representations of information, which have to be inferred. It is true that representational terms can always be replaced with behavioural histories, but it is not necessarily virtuous; behavioural accounts rapidly become very clumsy and hard to follow. Presumably one can just as easily run the maxim in reverse, and replace all behavioural histories with ones that hypothesize mental representations. The resulting *cognitive* versions have the advantage that they are much easier for people to understand; and, provided that our hypotheses are always supported properly by observable facts, should give no cause for alarm. Using these representational terms also enables comparisons in equivalent terms to be made between animal ethology and cognitive psychology—where mental representations are routinely inferred on the basis of observed behaviour.

In this cognitive way of talking, then, intelligence must involve an individual animal's ability to:

(1) gain knowledge from interactions with the environment and other individuals (and specify whether there are constraints on the type of knowledge it can represent, and the circumstances from which it can extract knowledge);

(2) use its knowledge to organize effective behaviour, in familiar and novel contexts; and

(3) deal with problems, using (if it is able) 'thinking', 'reasoning', or 'planning'—in fact, any ability to put together separate pieces of knowledge to create novel action.

To judge what an animal knows, and who or what it learnt it from, we have to see how it uses this knowledge to deal with problems: evidence for the three aspects is tangled together. The list above therefore does not make a useful organization to follow in this book. Instead, we will first look at knowledge that is acquired individually, and to what extent it is restricted (looking at it negatively) or channelled (looking at it positively) by genetic constraints in different species. Then, in Chapter 5, we turn to whether other individuals function as sources of knowledge, and whether animals actively understand this or are simply passively influenced. This will prepare the ground for the bigger questions, of what do animals really understand and whether they can be said to think.

Postscript: developmental and cognitive ideas on intelligence

In ransacking mainstream psychology for ideas on how to compare species' intelligence, I have concentrated on psychometrics, which is concerned explicitly with measuring intelligence differences. There are two other branches with useful things to say about intelligence: developmental psychology and cognitive psychology. Both have contributed substantially to the theory and data reviewed in later chapters.

As we have seen, one problem with using ideas from psychometrics is that they often seem inappropriate for describing species differences, which rely on comparing the shared 'common denominators' of intelligence in each species. Developmental psychology has always been more concerned with understanding the commonality of human intellect than the minor individual differences. This focus means that developmental ideas often relate easily to the understanding of intelligent behaviours in other species. Most dramatically, the developmental psychology of Jean Piaget has given rise to a possible 'scale' of intelligence. Studying the developmental changes in abilities and verbal explanations of young children, Piaget saw intelligence as built up in stages; at stage transitions, skill in all spheres of ability would change together, since all performance depends on underlying mathematical structures. He believed that these stages inevitably occurred in the same order, because each stage built on and was logically dependent upon the last. If this applies to intelligence in general, as Piaget hypothesized, species evolution must also have moved along the same ordered series of stages. (This sounds a bit like a 'progression towards human perfection', but Piaget's argument is not anthropocentric; he believed that the underlying mathematical nature of intelligence defined the ordering, so any intelligent species must be on the same trajectory.) This immediately raises the possibility that other animals could be compared with each other and ourselves by the Piagetian stage they have reached.

In practice, difficulties are encountered. Whether there really are discrete 'stages' even in children's development is now much less clear—the alternative being a hotchpotch of different rates of achievement, out of step with each other. And close comparison of abilities in different species does not find a single ordering of stages: a species often exhibits higher stages in some spheres than others, and development in some species misses out some stages altogether. Nevertheless, 'comparative developmental psychology', as it is called, has certainly inspired some of the most interesting work in the field, whether or not its premises are strictly true. It has focused attention on many of the skills now seen as important—such as imitation, empathy, and symbolism—and there certainly are cases in which direct comparison between the performance of primates and young children makes sense (as we shall see in later chapters).

The other area of psychology that relates to intelligence is cognitive psychology. This was only brought into existence by advances of the 1940s and 1950s in computing and artificial intelligence; psychology texts before the mid 1960s did not mention the subject. In those days, it was not believed that intelligence (other than differences in IQ) could be analysed scientifically, and more peripheral information processing (such as object or face recognition) was seen as too obvious to be worthy of study. Cognitive psychology is concerned with the mental storage systems, encodings, and processes by which information is manipulated—central to what we have been been calling 'intelligence'. Most work in the subject has concerned language and speech, or at least relied on language for experimentation, so cannot be directly related to animals. Nor is cognitive psychology at all concerned with comparing different types or levels of intelligence. But my own background is in this subject, and its influence will be very apparent throughout the book: in the way of thinking about what animals must be doing mentally to produce the observed behaviours.

Further reading

Menzel's typically thoughtful article 'How can you tell if an animal is intelligent?' in Schusterman *et al.* (1986) gives further insight on the problem raised in this chapter. Good introductions to measuring human intelligence are A. Heim (1970) *Intelligence and personality* (Penguin, London) or K. Richardson (1990) *Understanding intelligence* (Open University Press, Milton Keynes, England). For an ethological approach to animal behaviour, giving proper treatment of genetic and environmental influences on development, there are several excellent texts, such as A. Manning and M. S. Dawkins (1992) *An introduction to animal behaviour* (4th edn) (Cambridge University Press, Cambridge), or D. McFarland (1993) *Animal behaviour* (2nd edn) (Longman, Harlow, England). Developmental comparative approaches to intelligence are well illustrated by the chapters in Parker and Gibson (1990); there is no introductory text to this approach.

Part 2

Changing views of learning and imitation

4
How animals learn

The traditional story of animal learning

The explanation of how animals gain knowledge and solve problems used to be a simple one; here is a brief résumé. (For the moment, I shall talk as if all this were still accepted fact.) There are three strands: learning, imitation, and insight. Learning happens by an associative process. This takes two different forms, but in each of them an initially neutral event becomes associated with a valuable reward or an unpleasant punishment, a 'reinforcer' of positive or negative valence. In *classical conditioning*, the neutral event is presented by an experimenter, or simply occurs naturally in the world, shortly before a reinforcer; after a number of such coincidences, the neutral event alone brings on the reaction appropriate to the reinforcer—such as salivating to food. In *instrumental conditioning*, the neutral event is a behavioural act by the animal itself. Since the animal has to discover for itself that a certain behaviour will be followed by a reinforcer, this is often called *trial-and-error learning*. The same rules (or 'laws') apply in all situations, so the tight control of laboratory experiments can be used to unmask laws that will apply equally well to the complexity of real life. With the mechanisms of conditioning, an animal will associate any pair of events that occur next to each other, as long as it is able to detect the events at all. By building up a mass of associations, therefore, the animal will gradually come to behave appropriately.

Social influences have little place in this picture, but *imitation* by animals has long been seen as important—usually as a problem getting in the way of testing whether animals have any *insight,* a more powerful intellectual ability than 'mere' learning. Since birds such as parrots and hill mynas (*Gracula religiosa*) can imitate so perfectly, even when they clearly have no understanding of the human words they copy, copying new behaviour by imitation must be a 'cheap' way of appearing clever, a sham of intelligence. Many species of animals can imitate, because there are many well-documented cases of the spread of behaviour as traditions among animals. A well-known example concerns the spread among species of small birds (mostly tits, *Parus* spp.) of the habit of tearing off the cardboard tops of milk bottles to obtain cream (first reported by Fisher and Hinde 1949). More recently, tits in Britain learnt to peck holes in metal foil tops, before being finally defeated by cartons! Imitation of clever behaviours, in its full flowering among the monkeys *Macaca fuscata* of Koshima

Figure 4.1 Food washing performed by a Japanese macaque monkey. (Photo by E. Visalberghi.)

Island in Japan, has led to a whole range of cultural differences from other Japanese monkeys. These monkeys clean their sweet potatoes by washing, carrying them to sea-water for preference, presumably because of the taste (Fig. 4.1). They separate wheat from the beach sand (on which the wheat is spread by people) by throwing the messy mixture into the sea, whereupon the lighter wheat floats and can be skimmed off, a technique also invented by humans who called it placer-mining. And they have a vocalization, not used by unprovisioned Japanese monkeys, that indicates the discovery of plenty of food.

What most animals lack, on this traditional account, is *insight*. Insight learning has been treated as diagnostic of intelligence. The classic demonstration that at least one species of animal can show insight was by Köhler (1925). He gave the puzzle of raking in a reward with sticks to several chimpanzees; in one version, no stick was long enough. After many attempts, the chimpanzee gave up, and Köhler stopped observing. A few minutes later the keeper excitedly reported that the chimpanzee had succeeded. The animal had been playing with the sticks, and had happened to join two sticks together. It then suddenly jumped up and used the joined pair to solve the puzzle—apparently after a sudden realization that now the tool was long enough (Fig. 4.2).

Figure 4.2 Other great apes than chimpanzees readily learn to solve the sort of task used by Köhler to study insight. His most famous task involved reaching an object with a stick, when no single stick was long enough. Here an orang-utan (a) joins two sticks by means of a hollow tube, (b) carries the resulting extended tool, and (c) successfully hooks in the food reward. (Photos by J. Lethmate.)

These three pillars of animal abilities—associative learning, imitation, and insight—have all had to be modified in recent years in how they are understood. The current picture is a much more exciting one for anyone interested in reconstructing the evolutionary origins of human intelligence.

Individual learning channelled by genetic constraints

It is now known that animals do *not* find all events equally easy to associate. Garcia and Koelling (1966) gave rats water that was novel to them, either in its taste (sweet or salt) or in that a flashing light and clicking noise always accompanied drinking. They paired these with aversive reinforcement (i.e. punishment), either by illness which was in fact brought on by X-rays, or by painful electric shocks. If rats feel ill after they have drunk novel-tasting water, they then avoid water with this taste in future; but if they feel only a shock, they apparently do not associate this with their novel drink. The opposite happens after drinking 'bright-noisy' water. The pain of an electric shock causes the rats to avoid bright-noisy drinks in future, but nausea has no effect. Furthermore, Garcia *et al.* (1966) showed that learned aversion to a novel drink or food can be caused by illness up to 12 hours after consumption. It seems that rats are specially prone to associate feeling ill with the last novel food they ate or liquid they drank: a wonderful mechanism for an explorative animal, used to foraging opportunistically on a wide range of dietary possibilities, to learn which items are poisonous. Humans, too, seem prone to this kind of food-aversion learning; most people have experienced 'going off' some unusual food that preceded nausea, even when they know very well that the nausea was really caused by some infective illness. Garcia's results have led to a plethora of research on the specificity of reinforcers in classical conditioning, and just the same kind of 'favoured pairings' of some events over others has been found in instrumental conditioning. To give just one example, hamsters (*Mesocricetus auratus*) readily learn to rear up or scrabble when they are hungry, if an experimenter gives them food rewards every time they do so. Yet they fail completely to increase the rate of washing their faces when this behaviour instead is rewarded (Shettleworth 1975). Animals cannot learn just any pairing of events or event and reward; they show what has been called 'constraints on learning'.

It is clear from this work that animals are equipped to learn some things better than others. Genetic predispositions to learn certain sorts of things but not others have even been blamed for our own absurd tendency to learn fear of (harmless) spiders and snakes, yet our slowness in learning appropriate fear of motor cars and electric sockets. Of course, early ancestors of man in Africa encountered dangerous snakes and spiders, but no cars or power points. This sort of reasoning works more generally: most apparent 'constraints' on learning make perfectly good sense on an evolutionary time-scale. For instance, it is very plausible that at no point in their own evolutionary histories would a rat have been at risk of poisoning by bright-noisy water, or a hamster have been able to affect its evolutionary fitness by scratching more. The usual term, constraints on learning, is a rather misleading one since it suggests the evolution of incompetences. In reality, what have evolved are tendencies to learn efficiently just those specific kinds of information that have favoured survival. These cases are all better viewed as *channelling of animals' selective attention by genetic predispositions*, towards certain aspects of the environment and not others.

Putting it this way highlights common ground with the way in which songbirds learn their songs. The chick of a bird like a chaffinch has a predisposition to listen to sounds that approximately resemble the song of its own species (that is, it finds these songs reinforcing—given the chance, it will even work to hear more). The chicks seem to have an approximate 'template', defining a proper song for a chaffinch, in a rough-and-ready way (Fig. 4.3). The closest match to this template that the chick hears in the nest will be its father's song, or perhaps the song of a neighbouring male of the same species. The chick remembers whatever it hears until next spring, when lengthened days trigger hormonal changes that cause it to begin singing itself. At first, its own song is only an approximation to a chaffinch song, not an accurate copy of what was heard last year. In fact, this first song is no better than the efforts of youngsters that have been artificially prevented from ever hearing a real chaffinch song. But after

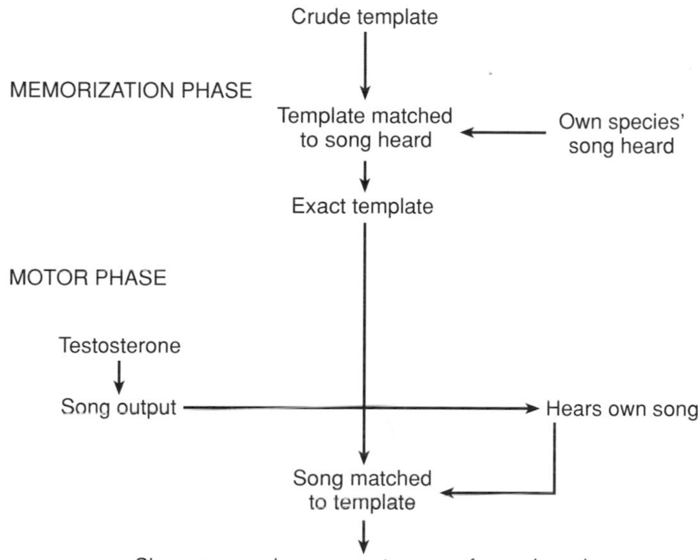

Figure 4.3 The 'template theory' of song learning in birds (based on Marler 1976).

hearing itself sing, a normally reared chaffinch is able to compare this with its memory of what it preferred listening to, months earlier. It then changes its singing, always in the direction of a closer resemblance to its memory version, until quite soon it is singing an almost exact match. The specificity of the innate template is known from experiments: if the chicks are reared by hand and played only blackbird (*Turdus merula*) song, they are not influenced by it. If they are played both blackbird song and reversed chaffinch song (by playing a tape backwards), they later give an accurate copy of the reversed chaffinch song.

A similar parallel can be made with imprinting, a very rapid form of learning found in the young of precocial birds—that is, in birds that are ready to leave the nest almost as soon as they are hatched, like chickens, gamebirds, or ducklings. The chicks attend to and follow conspicuous objects as soon as they are steady enough on their feet. In the natural condition this 'conspicuous object' is usually the mother bird. But Konrad Lorenz, who discovered the phenomenon, showed that it could also be a person, or something equally inappropriate in the ethologist's laboratory. Patrick Bateson (1973; Fig. 4.4), using various artificial objects, found out that chicks will not 'imprint' on just anything, they too have innate preferences: the innate specification is very approximate, obviously. By focusing

Figure 4.4 The apparatus used by Bateson to measure the strength of imprinted chicks' following tendency; the revolutions of the wheel are counted automatically (photo by P. P. G. Bateson).

their attention on whatever best fits their innate idea of what should be followed, they learn its characteristics in greater detail. After that, they will not follow other conspicuous objects, ones that would have been equally attractive to a naïve chick. In this way, they successively narrow down their preferences to (eventually) one particular conspicuous object—in the natural state, selecting their own mother rather than any other hen.

In all these cases—food aversion, song learning, and imprinting—the organism is equipped with predispositions and preferences that increase the chance that useful, adaptive information will be acquired by learning. It is worth thinking about what alternatives could in principle exist, that evolution *might* have equipped animals with. What range of options are theoretically available? At one pole, 'pure genes', each baby chaffinch could have been genetically programmed to sing the chaffinch song; this does indeed happen in some songbirds. Each baby chicken could have been equipped with a recognizing device that could tell its mother from not only trees and foxes, but every other female chicken. That would take a lot of specification, and have to be different for every mother chicken; it is really not remotely feasible. If every baby rat were equipped with an innate avoidance of natural poisons, then rats would never learn avoidance to new poisons; a great deal of money has been spent proving this is not true! Moving to the opposite pole, 'pure learning', it is not obvious how any birds would ever acquire species-specific songs, nor how precocial chicks would survive their formative learning experiences with foxes, stoats, and motor cars! Genetically channelled learning is evidently a powerful and efficient tool for giving animals what they need to survive.

The mechanisms of learning themselves, classical and instrumental conditioning, are best regarded as devices for ensuring that animals learn useful—that is, adaptive—information. This interpretation is suggested by the finding that two events that reliably occur together in time do *not* always become associated by classical conditioning. If one element is a *redundant* predictor of another, the two remain unassociated in the animal's mind. For instance, suppose a red light has been paired with food repeatedly, so that just seeing the light evokes salivation in a dog. Later, both red and green lights together are repeatedly paired with food, but the (redundant) green light will not come to evoke salivation on its own (this phenomenon is called 'blocking'). With an adequate predictor of the food already learnt, there is nothing further to learn, and the redundant cue is ignored, whereas on the traditional view it should be classically conditioned.

A better interpretation of classical conditioning is that it is a correlation-learning device (Dickinson 1980). This makes good evolutionary sense: with a mechanism for learning correlations, an animal will automatically come to learn the pattern of event probabilities in its environment. The animal would indeed seldom be misled if it treated these correlations as *causal*, although this would not be strictly correct. Certainly, we humans tend to see causes in mere correlations. Occasionally this leads us into error, forcing us to notice our false logic. Mistaking correlation for cause suggests that classical conditioning still functions powerfully in humans—evidence of its evolutionary effectiveness as a learning system.

Instrumental conditioning, too, has been reinterpreted recently; it has been likened to evolution by natural selection (Skinner 1981). Like natural selection, it is an automatic process by which behaviour patterns with beneficial consequences are selectively increased in frequency, among the many types of behaviour produced by the animal. The mechanism is quite different in the two cases, however. In instrumental conditioning, reinforcement increases the probability of advantageous responses to what the animal perceives in the world; unhelpful *responses* become 'extinct', the animal lives on. Natural selection is more drastic and slower to produce change, since whole individual animals survive or die, and the selection effect on genes is therefore much less efficient. Rapid changes of behaviour in response to changing environmental circumstances *only* come about by learning. Instrumental conditioning functions automatically to record the significant results of exploration and experiment, ensuring that an animal profits from its experience and need not repeat its errors.

While precisely *what* an animal focuses on to learn can be heavily channelled by its genetic predispositions, the rules of associative learning seem to apply rather generally (Roper 1983). At first sight, the many examples of apparently remarkable learning feats in otherwise unremarkable animals would seem to require 'special' kinds of learning for each one. For instance, fledglings of some species of bird learn the axis of rotation and star configuration of the night sky for later use in navigation (Emlen 1970); and elephants (*Elephas maximus*) can remember 600 other elephants as individuals (Moss and Poole 1983). But these prodigies may also be explained as a result of narrow channelling of attention rather than as special kinds of learning. This has the advantage of making it quite clear that it would be inappropriate to describe the impressive adaptive feats as 'intelligent', or to compare (on a unitary scale of 'intelligence') differences in what animals are predisposed to learn.

With the two kinds of learning mechanism, to record corrrelations among what it perceives in the world and the results of its own exploration, a solitary animal is well equipped to learn. What it learns is also nicely adjusted by genetic constraints on its focal attention, in ways that vary from species to species and accord well with the species' survival needs. But some animals are not solitary, and they consequently have further advantages in how they can discover about the world—to which we turn next. Social animals can learn from the trials and errors of other individuals, in some cases even individuals in past generations. Darwin, in his later writing, argued for a more efficient genetic mechanism than natural selection, one that could pass the benefits of practice and experience to future generations. This is the idea of selection of *acquired* characteristics, called Lamarckism—after the original proposer of the idea long before

Darwin and Wallace had their insight into how natural selection could work. Sadly, it is now abundantly clear that the nice idea of inheriting acquired characteristics simply does not happen. But social learning can deliver some of the same rewards.

Further reading

T. R. Halliday and P. J. B. Slater (1983) *Animal behaviour,* Vol 3: *Genes, development and learning* (Blackwell Scientific, Oxford) has several very useful articles on animal learning; P. Bateson describes imprinting, P. J. B. Slater song learning, and T. J. Roper and N. J. Mackintosh put the modern view of learning in a biological context. At a more detailed level, Dickinson (1980) is probably the best modern text on animal learning.

5
Why animals learn better in social groups

The demise of imitation as an explanation of all social learning in animals

We tend to dismiss someone's apparently creative insight if we discover it was 'merely imitation'. In the same way, as we have seen, animal imitation used to be dismissed: a cheap trick that animals often use, which produces a spurious mimicry of real intelligence. From this lowly status, imitation has recently been promoted to a sign of remarkable intellectual ability, one which involves a symbolic process—except when it is vocal imitation by birds, perhaps an anti-bird bias. And ironically it is *now* suggested that imitation can only be done by humans. How has this come about?

When humans want to acquire a new and complex skill without excessive effort, they watch and imitate a skilled performer. It used to be axiomatic that many species of animals also used this strategy, but a few doubts about the strength of evidence for animal imitation have recently snowballed; and questioning the role of imitation sometimes has far-reaching implications for popular belief.

Consider the famous cultural behaviour of Japanese macaque monkeys ('cultural' is used here in the lay sense of local tradition, rather than the symbolic sense meant by anthropologists). This is commonly believed to be transmitted by imitation. The original innovation and subsequent spread of some cultural variants was even witnessed. Imo, a monkey in the Koshima troop, in September 1953 began to wash sand off a dirty sweet potato (this food had been provided by researchers since 1952 to provision the monkeys), and over the next 9 years this habit spread to many others in the troop. Most of this spread was to young animals, especially to Imo's own relatives; other cultural behaviours such as the placer-mining of wheat showed similar patterns. However, Green (1975) pointed out that all the special cultural differences involved food processing or—in the case of the vocalizations that he was studying—food calling; and that provisioning gives the opportunity for quite unintentional conditioning by the human provisioners. Suppose monkeys that called dramatically, or fed in ways considered cute by people, were consequently fed just a little more than average; this is not an unreasonable supposition, since monkeys do not usually do anything so striking. This would, from the animals' perspective, conditionally reward certain acts and not others—automatically tending to increase the frequency of those acts by instrumental conditioning. If this has happened, the cultural spread observed might have been a human artefact, based on reinforcement of chance variations in behaviour. The potato washing and placer-mining were, according to this interpretation, not spreading through the monkey troop because their mechanical efficiency prompted imitation by other monkeys, but because people thought they were interesting. Except that Imo, a monkey, must have innovated the actions in the first place without selective reward, they might better be regarded as part of *human* behavioural repertoire—just as we might treat the tricks of circus animals as human actions transferred into the animal repertoires by training.

For this 'human reinforcement' explanation to work, the behaviours have to be part of the natural repertoire of each monkey (though only with low frequency, and in an approximate form only), or reinforcement has nothing to work with: no acts to selectively increase in frequency. Surely such an unusual behaviour as food washing is highly unlikely to occur by chance exploration? Maybe not. Visalberghi and Fragaszy (1990) gave dirty pieces of fruit to a social group of capuchin monkeys (*Cebus apella*) under close observation in an enclosure. Each monkey learnt food washing within 2 hours. But these monkeys showed no sign of watching what others did, and instead assembled the whole pattern in a piecemeal way. Some threw the fruit around, and bits sometimes landed in the water. Others, or the same monkeys at different times, found these (now clean) bits of fruit and ate them. Gradually each monkey started to do both these actions, sometimes in the 'right' order. Apparently, separate components were assembled by a coincidental history of chance events—such as finding clean food under water.

The whole value of imitation, when done by people, is that it is a *quick* way of acquiring a complex skill, avoiding time-consuming and potentially dangerous errors. Imitation is useful for learning to tie shoelaces or operate a corkscrew or tin opener; but a waste of time with simpler skills like jumping a fence, when trial and error is amply good enough for all but the professional athlete, and involves less mental effort. Foodwashing is intermediate in complexity between these. This suggests an additional clue as to whether the Japanese macaques of Koshima learnt their skills by imitation: the speed with which the skill spread. Reinforcement has to wait for variation to occur naturally before anything can happen. This is a slow job, even when a scientist or animal-trainer is constantly trying to reward a particular set of actions selectively; with unintentional reinforcement by people who only sometimes favour monkeys with clever tricks a little more than others, it could take years. In fact, the washing of sweet potatoes took 4 years to spread to those eight of Imo's contemporaries who learnt to do it at all: an average of 2 years since Imo began demonstrating the trick. Now, perhaps the macaques just didn't immediately try to learn; dirty food was still edible, after all. But the suspiciously slow appearance of the new habits, added to Green's suggestion of human influence, provoked Galef (1988) to doubt the whole story.

Once doubt began to be voiced, many claims of imitation in animals were reviewed and found wanting. When the claims were tested with tight experiments, time after time animals showed no evidence of imitation! In the case of birds learning to remove milk-bottle tops to obtain cream, for instance, naïve birds shown a bottle with the top already pecked open learnt just as quickly as those that saw a bird actually pecking a top and gaining cream (Sherry and Galef 1984). This even applied to monkeys, so famed as imitators. Most cases, like the Japanese macaque skills, could easily have resulted from associative learning, mimicking imitation—even without human intervention.

Perhaps imitation is restricted among animals to the special case of birdsong acquisition (and the tricks of domestic parrots and myna birds that depend on the same ability), with only humans able to imitate actions? This would be a very dramatic turn-about, so we should look carefully at the alternative interpretations before accepting that one. What other mechanisms are used to 'explain away' the frequent social learning that used to be called imitation? Explanations have taken several forms, but they share the fact that the action must *already* be a part of the animal's repertoire before it can be affected. (The term 'action' is not meant to imply a single movement, but might be an already learnt sequence of movements.) And in each case probability of performing the action is ultimately affected by reinforcement. What happens can look surprisingly like imitation. But, since the mechanisms depend on modifying existing behaviour, they cannot account for the acquisition of really novel actions without a history of trial-and-error learning, whereas imitation can. True novelty without a history of reinforcement will therefore be an important element in discovering if any animals can really imitate. One 'action' can be a sequence of component movements: the *novelty* will very often be in the new ordering, rather than in the component movements themselves. Indeed, it might be argued that all novel behaviour of individuals consists of novel organizations of species-typical basic motor actions 'program-level imitation' (Byrne and Byrne 1993). We will return to this idea in Chapter 6.

The next three sections look at the various explanations that rely on existing brain records to explain apparent imitation; they are grouped according to whether the record is a stimulus, a response, or a goal (Fig. 5.2).

Stimulus enhancement

The commonest explanation of what initially might look like imitation is called *stimulus enhancement* (Spence 1937). The idea is that the probability of an animal approaching or contacting something in the environment is increased by seeing an individual of its species interacting with it. Once an animal's responses are limited to a small part of the environment or a particular object in an experiment, the chances of it discovering by trial and error the correct technique to gain reward are then much increased. The similarity in the animals' behaviour, which attracts attention and leads to claims of imitation, results from them both engaging with the same stimulus conditions, which then shape similar response patterns. Stimulus enhancement would enable much more efficient learning, so it is just the sort of simple rule that we might have expected natural selection to have equipped social animals with. It would also make good sense (and still not require much in the way of genetic pre-specification) for animals to approach more readily if their conspecific is obviously getting a good meal than otherwise. Similarly, avoidance ('negative enhancement') of places where other animals were seen to be hurt would also be functional. This consequence-sensitivity would greatly increase the power of enhancement to produce social learning that looks like imitation. At its most general, then, stimulus enhancement could in principle cause an increase or decrease in the probability of approaching or contacting parts of the environment, contingent on seeing a conspecific interacting with these parts and what happens to it. This would allow rapid learning which might easily be mistaken for imitation of the conspecific's behaviour.

Stimulus enhancement is clearly helpful for social species, and is probably the major factor in many cases of culturally transmitted behaviour of ecological importance. A few of the many studies will serve to make this point; sources are found in Byrne (1994). Juvenile baboons (*Papio ursinus*) learn the palatability of a new food rapidly once one animal has tried it. But propagation of the same knowledge is slow in vervet monkeys (*Cercopithecus aethiops*) in the same habitat. This difference matches the spatial organization of the troops, young baboons tending to be found close to each other, and young vervets not. Greater potential for learning by stimulus enhancement may be one reason why baboons show such flexibility in the environments that they inhabit, from subalpine grassland and semi-desert to quite dense forest, whereas vervets are more specialized, living almost exclusively on forest edges. As noted in Chapter 4, we should expect intelligence to evolve in generalist species like baboons; one component of baboons' intelligence is their ability to learn socially.

Some species are not merely found in a wide range of environments; they are opportunists, able to colonize new habitats rapidly. A striking example is the red-winged blackbird (*Agelaius phoeniceus*), a major pest of crops in the USA. Red-winged blackbirds have been shown experimentally to acquire food preferences by watching conspecifics feeding. They also learn to avoid foods which they have seen a conspecific eat shortly before it was sick; this shows that stimulus enhancement can really produce opposite effects on an observer, depending on what happens to the observed animal: negative enhancement *does* occur. The benefits of stimulus enhancement to such an opportunist species are obvious and unfortunate for farmers. In domestic cats, observation by a kitten has been found to enable rapid learning of tasks which were learnt slowly or not at all by individual trial-

and-error learning. Squirrels (*Tamiasciurus hudsonicus*), allowed to watch an experienced squirrel feeding on hickory nuts (for them a novel food), after 6 weeks' experience were using only half the time and energy to gain the same food as a group which had no model to watch. All these behavioural changes are likely to be due to stimulus enhancement rather than imitation, but their biological significance is considerable.

Avoidance of anything seen to be aversive to others can be useful in other ways. Young rhesus monkeys (*Macaca mulatta*) have no inborn fear of snakes. Mineka *et al.* (1984) allowed some young monkeys, reared in captivity with no prior experience of snakes, to watch their wild-born parents while they met a snake and displayed their intense fear. From that moment onwards, all the young monkeys were also frightened of snakes, and this lasted a long time (probably throughout their lives). The common observation of children acquiring their parents' fears (such as an irrational fear of spiders) no doubt taps the same phenomenon. In both cases, the object for which fear is easily learnt is of a specific class—neither we nor rhesus monkeys readily learn fear of certain things. Monkeys are much less likely to acquire fear of flowers than of snakes, and children are notoriously slow to learn fear of mechanical perils like cars. Socially acquired response to danger involves a bit more than just stimulus enhancement, since the young monkeys show signs of *fear* and not merely avoidance of the snake (and it is sometimes given another name, 'observational conditioning'; Galef 1988). Monkeys' own responses, their specific emotions and actions, seem to have been affected by seeing those of others. The possibility that responses as well as stimuli may be 'enhanced' by seeing them in others brings us to the other main way in which social learning may happen.

Response facilitation*

Large flocks of shore birds when alarmed perform remarkable synchronized movements in flight, which are thought to decrease the vulnerability of any individual to predators. When part of a flock takes to the wing or turns in flight, the rest follow suit immediately: the responses seem to be *contagious* (Thorpe 1963). A less obviously functional example of contagion is the way adult humans respond to the sight of a person yawning, by yawning themselves. These contagious behaviours might sometimes be mistaken for imitation, but only concern a few, rather fixed behaviour patterns. Human babies soon after birth respond to an adult's smile or tongue protrusion

*Social effects that act directly to encourage or initiate actions have usually been called *social facilitation,* but unfortunately several quite different phenomena have been given this same label (for instance, an indiscriminate increase in general activity, proposed by Zajonc (1965)—see Fig. 5.2). For this reason, I use the term 'response facilitation' for what I describe here.

with smiles or tongue protrusions of their own. If the babies' behaviour is interpreted as imitation (and it usually is), this raises the interesting question of how the child works out what act in its repertoire is 'the same' as the adult's, with no obvious way of comparison or matching. The puzzle is solved if facial expression mimicry in babies is a special case of contagion in neonate humans. Babies at birth are no doubt equipped with a number of functional responses to special stimuli; only when the responses and the stimuli that trigger them just happen to be 'the same' would this mimic imitation; for instance, a rule like *if (mother's face shows smile)* → *(make smile)*. Genetic endowment with simple rules like this is quite plausible: it would have a clear function in controlling the behaviour of adults to the baby's advantage. If this view is correct, there will only be a limited range of actions that a neonate human could mimic, but this is hard to test when a baby's range of behaviours is small anyway. This ambiguity in interpreting babies' matching responses to certain facial expressions shows that what looks like imitation need not be cognitively complex.

The intellectual problem, of how an individual can recognize that a behaviour is 'the same' when performed by itself and by another, is much less acute when the behaviour does not involve the individual's face. Single neurones in monkey brains have been found which respond to a specific action, for instance picking up or rotating an object, whether the action is done by another or by themselves (Perrett *et al.* 1989) . Presumably, then, monkeys could be taught to execute simple actions which look to them the same as what they are shown. Although monkeys have not succeeded so far when researchers have attempted to do so, pigeons certainly can. Naïve pigeons watched a trained bird which used a specific technique to obtain food; the demonstrator either rotated or lifted up a small handle (Palameta 1989). When the subjects were tested with the apparatus arranged so that only one method would work, those birds that had seen the 'helpful' demonstration learnt much more quickly and efficiently. This does not imply imitation, since it is quite possible that the simple actions were already part of the birds' repertoires, but it is powerful evidence of the importance of social learning for a generalist forager like a pigeon. These experiments suggest the existence of *response facilitation* (Byrne 1994), a kind of social effect that selectively enhances responses: watching a conspecific performing an act (often one resulting in reward) increases the probability of an animal doing the same. Unlike imitation, only actions already in the repertoire can be facilitated. The sparse current evidence for response facilitation suggests that it may not be common in animals.

Emulation

Finally, an animal's *goals* might be influenced by watching another animal's actions: duplicating the results of other individuals' behaviour but

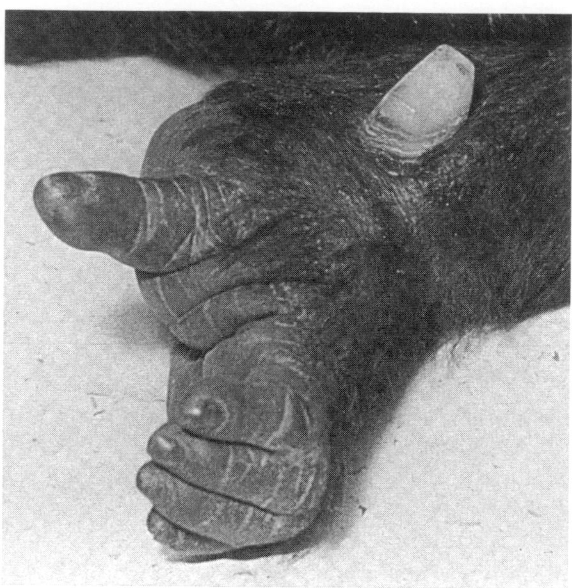

Figure 5.1 The gorilla, Koko, has put a lump of ice on her foot, after seeing a human do this in order to ease pain: this may be a case of *emulation*, copying a result rather than the action used to obtain it (photo by F. G. Patterson and R. H. Cohn.)

not their methods has been termed *emulation* (Wood 1989). When a child sees a ball hit into a net and wants to do the same, but uses its own idiosyncratic way of hitting to do so, this is emulation. At present there is no clear experimental demonstration of emulation in animals, but the possibility that some species copy in this way must be borne in mind when evaluating evidence for imitation (Fig. 5.1). Michael Tomasello (1990) has argued that many of the elaborate tool-using behaviours of wild chimpanzees (*Macrotermes* termite-fishing, *Campanotus* ant-dipping, *Dorylus* ant-fishing, use of hammer and anvil stones to crack *Panda* nuts, etc. See Chapter 7) could be learnt by emulation of the results of expert adults, rather than imitation of their methods as generally believed. Cultural traditions of chimpanzee tool use are very specific—for instance, in some populations both ends of probe tools are used, in others only one—so chimpanzee social learning would seem to go beyond emulation of observed results and include copying of *methods*. However, the possibility of emulation shows that we must not make the assumption that, just because *we* would certainly imitate a chimpanzee's skilful actions if we wanted an efficient way of catching termites or ants, that another chimpanzee would do so too. Chimpanzee tool use may depend on imitation, but this is not always easy to prove.

Modelling social influences that affect existing brain records

The great attraction of associative learning as a mechanism is its extreme computational simplicity. Yet I have now had to introduce both 'stimulus enhancement' and 'response facilitation', and perhaps even 'emulation', in order to understand data from social learning: three separate kinds of rule to modify learning. Has all hope of simplicity been lost? Not necessarily. Computationally, all types of learning that show these effects can be modelled mechanistically by adding the single notion of *priming* to animals' associative mechanisms, since all the 'new' types affect existing records in the brain.

Imagine an animal whose foraging is handled by a brain system that chooses a location or object to go to (or stay at), a current goal to seek, and an act to perform, on the basis of the highest salience or *activity level* of units that represent the possible choices. These activity levels vary independently of each other according to the motivations and past experiences of the animal, but the activity levels of corresponding location, goal, and act units are incremented ('primed') each time the animal sees a conspecific perform an act in some location with a desirable result. This system automatically generates the categories of behaviour I have described as stimulus enhancement, response facilitation, and emulation (Fig. 5.2). The animal would give an impression of highly 'intelligent' social learning in some circumstances.

Even if only response facilitation and stimulus enhancement were to influence an animal on the same occasion, their combination would be a powerful one, quite apart from the possibility of emulation. Imagine that the animal observes a conspecific performing a particular act (one also in its own repertoire*) to a certain object, in a certain place, and gaining food in the process. The likelihood would then be increased that the observing animal would go to the location, contact the object, and perform the same act—a sequence so intelligent-looking that it is understandably likely to be called imitation. Yet the underlying mechanism of learning would still be trial and error, without any real understanding of the situation being necessary. What must be emphasized is that none of these priming mechanisms can give rise to novel and complex sequences of behaviour without trial and error learning: they can only affect existing brain records, whether of stimuli perceived, of goals desired, or of responses executed. To build up new behaviours (or new sequences of old behaviours) by

*The 'act in the repertoire' need not be a simple action, nor an innate pattern, for the priming theory to apply. Adults of long-lived species may have learnt to combine several acts in sequence, like a 'macro' in computing: the resulting behaviour was of course novel, when first done. However, once practised—as a fixed sequence—this becomes just another act in the repertoire, and can be primed as a whole.

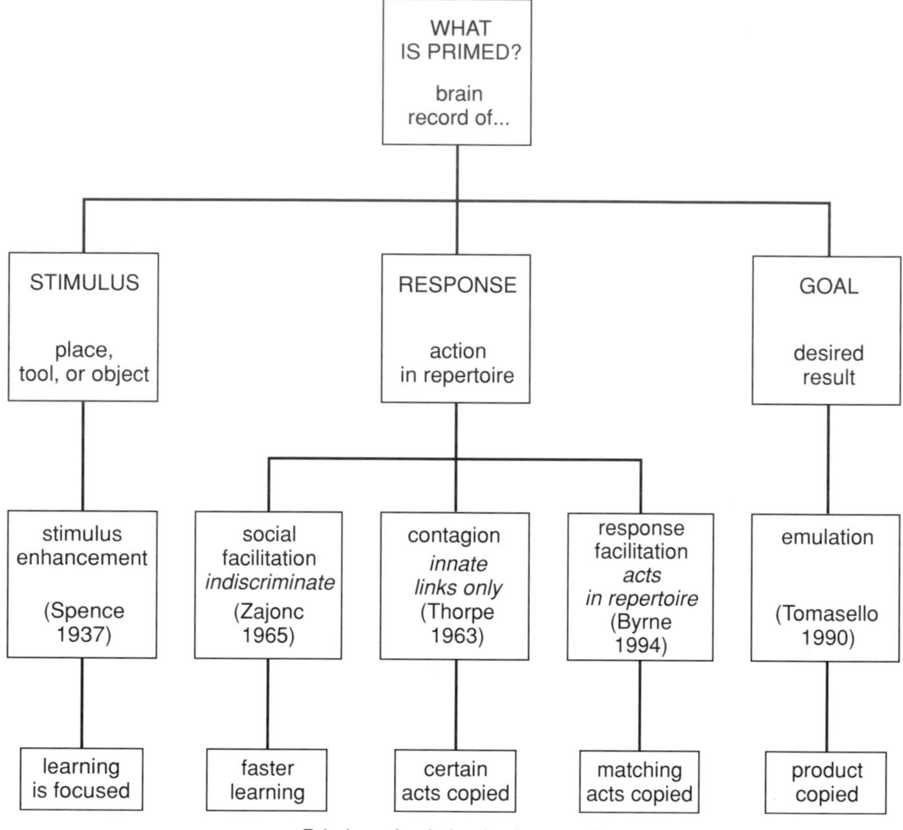

Figure 5.2 Priming of existing brain records. A classification of the various explanations of social learning that can be subsumed by the idea that existing brain records are *primed* by observation.

observation alone, imitation is required. These priming effects are no doubt important to humans as well, but we can also imitate. Just as trial-and-error learning may become more powerful when it is channelled by social effects, imitation may occur to greater effect when influenced by these simpler mechanisms that themselves rely on no more than priming.

We next move on to see if *any* evidence still holds up that animals can imitate—and if so, which animals, and what can they imitate? What has become clear in this chapter is that only the *acquisition of novel behaviour* can be safely used in diagnosis of imitation in animals. Of course, in humans we often refer to 'imitation' when there is no way of ruling out stimulus enhancement and response facilitation as explanations. Partly, no doubt, this is our species bias towards assuming that we clever humans do things the smart way; partly, though, it only makes sense to require better evidence for unlikely or disputed phenomena than for routine ones, and humans imitate routinely.

Further reading

Galef's (1988) article set the scene for much of the re-analysis discussed in this chapter. A good, critical review of the evidence on monkeys' social learning is by Visalberghi and Fragaszy (1990). In the same edited volume, Tomasello (1990) makes the case that even chimpanzee cultural behaviour may not depend on imitation (he uses 'cultural' in the sense of 'taught or imitated', as opposed to the wider 'transmitted over generations by social learning', used by most biologists).

6
Imitative behaviour of animals

Behaviour that appears intelligent can be underwritten by a notion as simple as priming (Chapter 5). Now that this is apparent, the difficulties of studying *imitation* in animals must be obvious. It is not surprising that attempts to define imitation have, implicitly or explicitly, concentrated on the rather negative approach of excluding the 'lower-order' explanations for given data. Defining by exclusion has the risk of producing a heterogeneous category of hard-to-explain behaviour, as Hinde (1970) pointed out. This is perhaps why 'imitation' in animals now includes two very different things: copying of sounds by various birds, which is easily demonstrated, strikingly accurate, yet not obviously related to any intelligence the birds show in other spheres; and copying of novel motor skills, shown by very few animals at all.

Imitating sounds

Hill mynas readily copy human speech to such a close tolerance that the formants are reproduced faithfully (Thorpe 1967). This is a very remarkable feat, because of the way in which the formants of speech—the bands of major energy that are seen clearly on a speech spectrogram or voiceprint—are produced. Speech relies on cavity resonance in the supralaryngeal vocal tract. Sound with a broad range of frequencies is produced low down the vocal tract, either by the vocal cords ('voiced' sounds) or simply by the rushing of air through a constricted space ('unvoiced' sounds, or whispering). This is then filtered by cavity resonance. The air inside a cavity will vibrate at a characteristic frequency when air rushes through or over it, and the frequency of vibration only depends on the cavity size and shape; anyone blowing across the top of a bottle with varied amounts of water in it will soon find that smaller cavities resonate at higher pitch—that is how church organs work. The supralaryngeal cavity—throat, mouth, and nose passages—is not fixed like an organ pipe, but can be varied in shape and size in many complex ways by movements of the tongue. This produces the many subtle and rapid components of human speech, which have proved their complexity by the slow progress of machine imitations of speech since the first attempts of the 1950s. Hill mynas have no similar resonant cavities, and must copy the formant structure in a quite different way to normal formant production by humans, yet they manage to do it.

Not only are some birds' imitations very accurate, their repertoire is sometimes very large. Francoise Dowsett-Lemaire (1979) has shown that an average European marsh warbler (*Acrocephalus palustris*) mimics 78 species of other birds, many learnt in sub-Saharan Africa during the warbler's very first winter migration. She has noted 212 species' songs and calls copied in all, and even this may be an underestimate—there are considerable problems identifying the marsh warblers' wide and eclectic selection. The function of vocal imitation by birds of this kind is presumably that a larger repertoire of songs pays off either in deterring rival males or attracting females. There are many plausible rival theories of why this should be. On the Beau Geste principle, more song types might seem like more birds and send late-arriving males away from the 'crowded' area; or the effort invested in complex singing might demonstrate underlying fitness, on the grounds that the male must have plenty of strength to be able to afford such waste; or females might just prefer good singers, so good singers will have many mates and thus many young—of which those that are male will have good songs and thus more mates because females prefer this—an escalating feedback loop.

Whatever the correct explanation, in vocal mimicry by birds imitation seems only to function in augmenting the repertoire, and no more intelligence is suggested by this than by the chaffinch's tendency to copy songs heard as a juvenile. Copying is not selective, and birds show no understanding of what is copied. (Some British song thrushes (*Turdus philomelos*) even learn the electronically produced ringing of Trim-phones, with sometimes chaotic consequences for phone owners.) Slater *et al.* (1980) showed that chaffinches' acquisition of song types by imitation is, in fact, well simulated by random copying with a fixed error rate. This means that the propagation of bird-song types is a nice example of cultural transmission where precisely *what* is copied has no adaptive consequence. In contrast, intelligent copying is necessarily directed at problem-solving, where the precise behaviour copied is crucial. We must set aside vocal copying, for all its interest to biology, in the search for evidence of intelligence in animals.

Imitating actions

Imitation, in the sense of copying novel motor acts from the repertoire of another individual, is surely a very different phenomenon from these 'tape recording' skills of birds. Does this sort of imitation indeed exist in animals? Ruling out the cases where apparent copying can be explained by some form of priming such as response facilitation or stimulus enhancement, then clear cases are few and far between, even in simian primates. In fact, the ability of monkeys and apes to imitate has been repeatedly doubted in recent publications. Why *should* it be difficult to copy a novel motor task? There are two main conceptual difficulties: first, that of seeing the world from another's perspective; and, secondly, that of putting together complex behaviour without constant guidance from direct experience to build up the whole from several parts. Let's look at each in turn.

Mental perspective-taking and impersonation

How does an animal recognize that its behaviour is 'the same as' the actions of another? In vocal imitation, a simple test would suffice: matching its own sounds against a memorized trace of those heard from another. This has long been suggested as an explanation of how birds produce accurate song learning and vocal copying, although, strictly speaking, the birds would also have to compensate for differences in sound transmission. A bird's own song is heard partly by transmission through bone as well as through the air, whereas others' are heard directly through air; compensating for this would not be simple—remember the difficulty of recognizing your own voice on a tape recorder for the first time? But at least that is a matter of matching, logically a straightforward task. This is not always so.

An action caried out by the muscles of limbs or face can look radically different from different viewpoints (most extreme when the act is a facial expression), so its imitation may need to involve more than simple comparison. The distinction is a matter of degree: raking in a peanut does not look all that different when performed by one's right hand than by the hand of a conspecific sitting to one's right. But certainly some kinds of imitation require 'putting oneself into the shoes of another', in order to understand the physical viewpoint of another individual. This would be much more straightforward for an animal if it could understand, as well as the other's geometric perspective, what the other was trying to do. To take the other's 'viewpoint'* in this special sense requires the ability to represent mental states—for instance, to understood what the other individual intended, what it knew, and what it failed to understand. The logical difficulty of understanding an action's form viewed from another perspective has sparked off much research on imitation.

Most of the researchers have been very concerned to ensure that the animal acquiring the action really did copy what it watched, and did not just invent its own version by trial and error. They have therefore restricted their attention to behaviour that duplicated the fine detail of acts, and imitation of the detailed form of actions is sometimes called 'impersonation'. (Readers who have lunged for a dictionary to help with these confusing terms will have found that imitation, impersonation, emulation,

*Because for ourselves, 'seeing is believing', we tend to assume that being able to understand the physical viewpoint of another individual—which is all we need to learn to tie shoelaces or a bow tie—is the same as understand the knowledge gained from that viewpoint. This is not necessarily true for animals or even all people, as we shall see in Chapter 8.

and even mimicry all mean much the same. In the psychology of learning, like Humpty Dumpty in *Alice in Wonderland*, we just have to take a firm line and make words mean what we want them to.) If the fine details are indeed copied from the model's behaviour, this is strong evidence of the ability to understand another individual's physical (and perhaps mental) viewpoint. But remember that gaining behaviours that the mimic can *already* perform can be achieved by response facilitation just as well as by imitation. As I argued in Chapter 5, novelty is crucial: only cases of copying the fine detail of actions not previously in the repertoire are conclusive evidence of imitation. Although the term is sometimes used more widely, I shall consider here only impersonation that results in acquisition of novel behaviour.

Organization in serial actions and program-level imitation

In learning a complex skill largely by trial and error, as we do with many motor skills, we begin with a few fragments of the whole skill (bits and pieces that we actually *can* do), and gradually, through practice, we build them together into a structured whole. Our progress is made much easier if we occasionally get the chance to watch the fluent performance of a skilled practitioner, because we can then copy the sequence and co-ordination of the fragments—the logical structure of the task. This is true even if we do not need to impersonate any of the fine detail since we already have adequate ways of doing each little action. When we imitate a structured skill as a whole in this way, we need cognitive sophistication of a quite different type from that involved in seeing another individual's point of view. (Of course, we often do both at once when we imitate a novel and complex action, but the problems involved in impersonating detailed actions and copying logical structure are very different.)

Karl Lashley (1951) was the first to draw attention to what he called 'the problem of serial order in behaviour'. What this means is that behaviour of an animal or human that superficially appears as a string of separate acts, often turns out to be better understood as having a hierarchical organization. For instance, when the behaviour breaks down under stress or brain damage, whole chunks remain together and are reassembled in a different structure; each little bit does not move independently. This raises a big problem for 'linear' theories, such as the chains of associations in behaviourist explanations. The problem becomes extreme for human speech, which has a multi-layer hierarchical structure. Distinctive features like voicing, nasal quality, or sibilance are structured into phonemes, the 'letters' of speech; phonemes are structured into morphemes, the basic units with any meaning; morphemes are structured into words, so 'sing' plus a past tense morpheme becomes 'sung'; words are structured into sentences, and so on. At each level, the units are affected by becoming part of the higher level of organization. A phoneme is pronounced slightly differently in different morphemes, morphemes change when combined into words, words are affected by the sentence intonation pattern, and so on. These kinds of integrative modifications are characteristic of a hierarchical organization. Stringing long chains of language bits together by reinforcement is simply laughable as an explanation of language learning, and it was duly ridiculed by Noam Chomsky (1959) in his famous review of B. F. Skinner's attempt.

Skilled behaviour is hierarchically organized, and imitation can, in principle, occur at any level of the hierarchy: from slavish copying of each act in sequence to copying only the outline logical structure (Fig. 6.1). The sort of imitation called impersonation refers only to copying at the lowest, motor-act level. We need a new term, for copying at the structural and organizational level, and I have called this *'program-level imitation'* (Byrne and Byrne 1991, 1993). Unfortunately, with the tendency to focus on impersonation, most laboratory studies of imitation in animals have used single-step tasks—where there is no task structure to be learnt. The question of level becomes interesting, however, when behaviour involves some real logical complexity, such as requiring several subgoals to be achieved in the process of achieving the main goal. The mountain gorillas (*Gorilla g. beringei*) that my wife, Jen, and I have studied give good illustrations of this (Byrne and Byrne 1991). Consider the way one deals with a large stalk of wild celery (*Peucedanum linderi*) in order to eat the pith (Fig. 6.2). First the stem must be bitten or snapped into manageable segments; then a segment partly peeled by biting the outer case and stripping it off with a pull against the teeth; then some exposed pith can be carefully picked out with delicate finger work; then more stripping is needed, and so on—maybe for 15 min with a big 10 m stalk. All mountain gorillas do this in much the same way, and it seems most likely that they copy some aspects of the skill from mothers in the first 3 years of life. With a task that can be divided into several stages, it is a real issue whether:

(1) the logical structure is copied (program-level imitation), but the motor-act sequences used in achieving each stage are not;

(2) some motor-act sequences are copied in detail (impersonation), but an idiosyncratic logical organization is used, or

(3) the entire sequence is copied, which could involve either or both mechanisms.

Figure 6.1 Hierarchical levels of imitation. (a) An infant mountain gorilla examines a strand of the herb *Galium* while on her mother's head; the mother is processing *Galium* herself, and the technique is complex. (b) Imitation would help the infant, but could occur at several levels: the text uses words to give an idea of the level of detail that might be copied. The top (most fine-detailed) level would be called *impersonation*, the bottom one *stimulus enhancement*, but other kinds of

(a)

(b) **Levels at which galium technique can be copied:**

'pick out a strand of green galium from the mass with any precision grip of the left hand and transfer the hold to a power grip by the other fingers of this hand, then repeat this cycle while still holding the picked strands in a power grip of the other fingers of the left hand, until the bundle is sufficiently large; then fold in any loose strands by using the right hand to bend in any loose strands while loosening and re-grasping the mass of stems in the left hand; or, if this is easier at the time, by letting-go with finger and thumb of the left hand so that bundle is held only by other fingers, then rocking the hand to allow grasping of both loose and gripped strands by finger and thumb again, then repeating this process so that the other fingers grasp the bundle firmly, and repeating the whole cycle until all strands are held; then grip the bundle of galium loosely with half-open left hand, pick out any debris with pad-to-pad precision grip of the first finger and thumb of right hand, then grip the bundle tightly with left hand and eat by feeding into the mouth until full, then shearing off the rest by a molar bite, repeating when mouth empty again'

'pick out a strand of green galium from the mass, then repeat this while still holding already picked strands until the bundle is sufficiently large, then fold in any loose strands with the other hand (or rocking motion of the hand holding the bundle with repeated letting-go and re-grasping of strands if this is easier at the time), then grip bundle of galium loosely with half-open hand, pick out debris with first finger and thumb of other hand, then grip tightly and eat with shearing bites'

'repeatedly pick green strands of galium with one hand, then use other hand to fold in loose strands, then hold the bundle loosely with one hand and remove debris with other hand, then eat'

'pick a bundle of galium, tidy it up, remove debris from it, then eat'

'eat galium'

Figure 6.1 (*cont.*)

imitation could occur between these extremes. Copying the process structure and organization, approximately the third level here, is called *program-level imitation*.

(a)

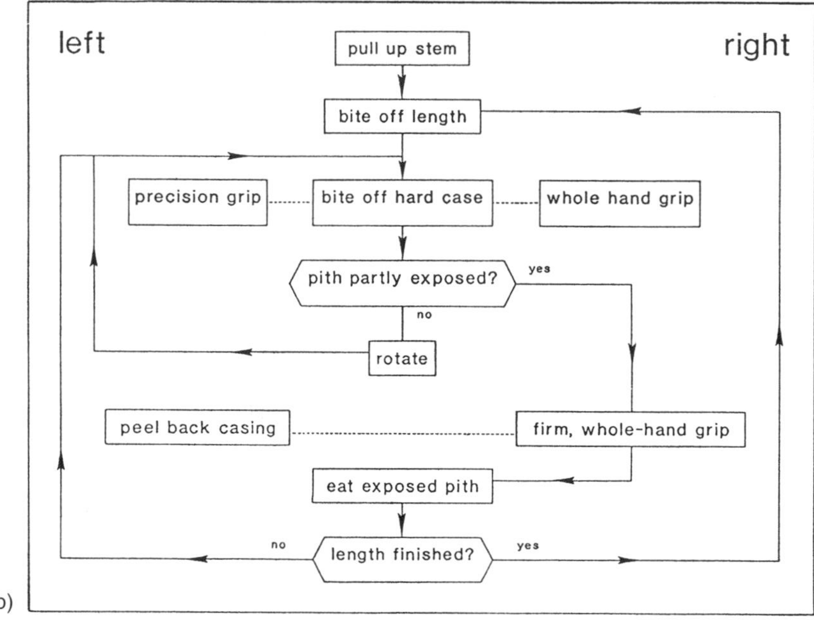

(b)

Figure 6.2 Eating celery (*Peucedanum linderi*). (a) An adult female mountain gorilla showers her 2-day-old baby with debris in the process: infant gorillas do not have far to go to learn which foods are edible. (b) The approximate flow chart shows hierarchical complexity. The process begins at the top, and actions performed systematically right- or left-handed are on the right or left of the figure. The dotted lines show co-ordination between the two hands used in different roles, or between both hands and the mouth. Otherwise the notation is that usually used for flow charts: diamonds for choice points, rectangles for actions. (Photo by J. Byrne.)

Young gorillas might copy the exact hand actions of their mothers, the overall way of tackling the task, or a bit of both.

To copy the logical, hierarchical structure of behaviour, the minimum required is to copy the sequence of *subgoals* reached along the way to successful performance; how to achieve each may then be learnt by trial and error. The subgoal structure of behaviour is often 'visible' in its consequences, so the ability to understand mental states is not strictly necessary to imitate at the program-level. A young gorilla—by seeing that mum first arrives at a manageable short length of celery, then gets part of the length stripped of the hard casing on one side, then removes the pith—could learn task structure without copying any detail of actions. All that is required is an ability to identify as subgoals the key results to achieve along the way (perhaps by emulation), and to structure a sequence of goals. Children as young as 16 months display program-level imitation. Bauer and Mandler (1989) found that children's imitations of adults' sequences of action require less observation and are more accurate if the sequences are of actions that are causally related, such as the steps in bathing a teddy bear. Any actions unrelated to the job in hand tend to be missed out in the childrens' imitations. (Children of this age can also impersonate actions, even where they probably do not understand the logical relations among them, often apparently in order to 'be like mum'.)

From the perspective of an animal or human learning new and complex behaviour, the ability to perform program-level imitation—copy organizational structure—will be useful, whether or not the individual is also able to impersonate—copy detail of motor actions. The two aspects of imitation are logically separate, and a species may well have evolved the ability to do one without the other.

Evidence of imitation by animals

The flexible 'ideal learner' would use program-level imitation to copy complex action structures, and acquire the fine details by using trial and error learning, emulation, or impersonation—whichever was easier. To be most useful in problem-solving, imitation requires both this ability to understand and copy the logical organization of programmes of action, *and* to copy detailed action patterns from others—where these cannot be achieved by methods already known or easily derived by trial and error. Program-level imitation and impersonation are thus complementary skills. With these conceptual distinctions in mind, what aspects of imitation have been recorded?

Little evidence of impersonation has been found in experiments, despite many attempts. Heyes *et al.* (1992) allowed rats to see a demonstrator rat gaining food by either a left or right press of a joystick. The observers were in front of the demonstrator, so their 'left' was the demonstrator's 'right': the rat had to take the different perspective into account. Before they were themselves tested, the joystick was rotated through 90° so that the place where it had previously finished after a left push was now the place where it would finish after a right push—with this arrangement, stimulus enhancement would impede learning. Nevertheless, the rats copied the direction of pushing. Response facilitation could be argued to explain this result, since the rat's response was not a novel behaviour. However, even this would need the rat to view responses as 'left' or 'right' from the point of view of the demonstrator: rats can certainly take the visual perspective of others into account. Convincing evidence of impersonation has recently been found in the African grey parrot (*Psittacus erithacus*). Moore (1993) used the parrot's well-known ability at vocal mimicry to remove ambiguity as to what action his parrot intended to imitate, and recorded its behaviour on closed-circuit television to remove any possibility of unintentional cueing by the experimenter. Over 5 years, the parrot was shown a few stereotyped actions each day, accompanied by words or phrases as labels. The parrot did not make immediate imitations, but over the years it came to imitate many actions in impressive detail. One such routine, labelled by 'Ciao!', consisted of opening the door with left hand while waving with the right, then closing it with the right while waving with the left. The parrot copied all of this, waving first with right foot and then with left, meanwhile vocalizing both 'Ciao!' and finally the door click! Other actions imitated include head-nodding (saying 'nod'), tongue protrusion ('look at my tongue') and holding an imaginary peanut ('peanut') and dropping it ('whoops, dropped the peanut'). The richness of these imitated actions, many quite foreign to normal parrot behaviour, shows that at least one species of parrot can impersonate actions at will.

Among mammals, monkeys have yet to give any good evidence of impersonation, but the great apes show more promise. Hayes and Hayes (1952) report the ability of the common chimpanzee, Viki, reared in their home, to learn and respond appropriately to the spoken command 'do this'. The experimenter spoke the command and then, for instance, whirled on one foot, or stretched the mouth with two forefingers; Viki soon learnt to impersonate the act immediately. However, Hayes and Hayes report 'many of our 70 items were difficult for her ... [the difficulty] often seemed to involve the execution of the act. For example, she apparently saw clearly enough that we put a card in an envelope, but her attempted imitation was too clumsy to succeed'. Impersonation is evidently not the simple matter for chimpanzees that it is for ourselves. Nevertheless, it is widely reported that chimpanzees which have spent long periods with humans will put on lipstick, tie shoelaces, brush their teeth, and so on. None of these acts has been rewarded, some are heavily discouraged; it therefore seems most likely that chimpanzees can impersonate many actions when they want to. If this evidence is accepted, the fact that captive orang-utans, pygmy chimpanzees, and gorillas have often shown similar behaviour would mean that they, too, can impersonate (Fig. 6.3). There is similarly good observational evidence in bottlenose dolphins (*Tursiops* sp.), which mimicked the behaviour of humans and a sealion using their aquarium pool (Taylor and Saayman 1973). An adult dolphin impersonated the swimming mode, grooming actions, and sleeping posture of the sealion, all movements entirely foreign to a dolphin. When a human blew a cloud of cigarette smoke

(a)

(b)

(c)

Figure 6.3 Great apes living with people readily copy human actions. (a) An orang-utan attempts to saw wood; (b) she combs her long arm hair—neither activity was encouraged or rewarded by humans. (c) The gorilla, Koko, helps with washing-up. (Photos (a) and (b) by A. E. Russon, (c) by F. G. Patterson and R. H. Cohn.

at the pool's glass just as an infant dolphin looked in, 'she immediately swam off to her mother, returned and released a mouthful of milk which engulfed her head, giving much the same effect as had the cigarette smoke' (Fig. 6.4). Another dolphin mimicked the scraping of the pool's observation window by a diver, even copying the sound of the air-demand valve on the SCUBA apparatus while releasing a stream of bubbles from his blowhole. These and other carefully described impersonations are convincing, and of a different order of complexity to the rat's copying of a left rather than right joystick movement. (This is despite the rat's inherently greater similarity of sensory and motor apparatus to the human, variables often felt to underlie apparent phylogenetic differences in intelligent behaviour.) Interestingly, dolphins can also imitate sounds (Richards 1986).

It is no coincidence that the strongest observational evidence of impersonation comes from apes, parrots, and dolphins copying behaviour of *other* species. In these cases, all that must be ruled out is individual acquisition by trial-and-error learning. If instead an animal were apparently to mimic

Figure 6.4 An infant dolphin blows milk to mimic a human's puff of cigarette smoke (drawing by P. Barrett from description in Taylor and Saayman 1973).

the behaviour of a conspecific, much stronger evidence would be needed that the behaviour change was not just a result of normal maturation: a species-typical pattern emerging without any specific influence of the animal's experience on the form of the behaviour.

The best evidence for program-level imitation in wild animals comes from the plant gathering of wild mountain gorillas, mentioned above. Celery is not an isolated problem; the techniques gorillas use to eat their major foods are all complex, multi-stage skills. For instance, to eat stinging nettle leaves requires the following sequence: accumulation of a bundle of leaves, detaching the particularly virulent petioles from the more innocuous leaf blades, and then folding the blades so that the least stinging surface is presented to the lips (Fig. 12.7). Only the mother and the leading adult male of a group tolerate infants near while feeding, and adults use their left and right hands in unvarying roles during complex processing; yet we found that offspring hand preferences match neither their mother's nor the leader male's. The result suggested that impersonation cannot have been the main means of acquisition, and this was confirmed by finding that fine details of processing are in general idiosyncratic, each animal has its own preferred methods (Byrne and Byrne 1993). (However, impersonation may be important for some details, such as folding the leaf blades. One mother and her son do not do this, and must suffer greater pain as a result; they do not seem to care much for nettles. Female gorillas immigrate at adolescence, and this particular mother was brought up in a lower zone of the mountains, where nettles do not occur commonly. Her failure to discover the trick by trial and error, and her son's similar failing, suggest that perhaps this detail is usually copied by impersonation.) Trial-and-error acquisition of whole techniques seems highly implausible, given their complexity and structural uniformity across animals. Genetically encoded action sequences similarly make no sense, as skills are specific to plants of very limited altitudinal and geographical range. Since none of the other alternatives seem possible, program-level imitation is the likely explanation—perhaps by emulation of each intermediate result in the sequence of processing stages, perhaps also using impersonation for a few difficult actions.

To obtain clear evidence of program-level imitation a complex, multi-stage task is necessary, but unfortunately the natural lives of most animals (and the experiments usually devised to test imitation) are lacking in this complexity. The richer environment of humans gives more scope, and it is from human-reared apes that good evidence comes. Anne Russon and Biruté Galdikas (1993) have recorded orang-utans, during rehabilitation into the wild after illegal capture, copying rather elaborate human actions. A camp assistant to the rehabilitation programme obviously valued tidiness, since he was often seen chopping off weeds from the edges of forest paths and sweeping them up into a row of neat piles. One day, an adult female orang-utan was seen following him, using a stick to chop off weeds he had missed and making extra piles, similarly in a neat line in the centre of the path. Other orang-utans have been seen copying a range of other human activities: anointing the body with (pilfered) insect repellent, attempting to siphon liquid with a hose, and tying a hammock between two trees by winding the rope round each tree several times, then threading it through a metal ring on the hammock, finally winding it round the hammock sling itself (Fig. 6.5)—although no rehabilitant orang-utan has yet copied a knot properly. More frightening, Russon watched an adult female, Supinah, trying to start a fire, imagining that the liquid the orang-utan was using was water (Fig. 6.6). Supinah picked up a stick from the dying fire and blew on the hot end several times until it glowed, then removed the lid from a can and scooped up some of the liquid with a small cup, finally dipping the stick in the cup and fanned the stick repeatedly with the lid. This was unsuccessful, but she persevered and by the fifth stick she had produced billowing smoke from her little pile of damp sticks. By this point Russon was beginning to suspect (rightly) that the liquid was in fact paraffin, and luckily Supinah gave up her project soon after.

Figure 6.5 This orang-utan has, unaided and without human encouragement, managed almost to tie up a hammock between two trees (she still holds the end of the cord in her left hand, since her second knot failed to hold). (Photo by A. E. Russon.)

(a) (b) (c) (d) (e) (f)

Figure 6.6 Some of the orang-utan Supinah's fire-raising activities. (a) Removing the round lid from the paraffin container; (b) pouring fuel from the cup back into the container; (c) tipping the container to pour fresh fuel into the cup; (d) plunging the burnt ember into the cup of fuel; (e) fanning the burnt ember in the fuel with the round lid, holding it upright as do the local cooks; and (f) blowing on the extinguished ember. Copyright 1993 by the American Psychological Association; reprinted by permission. (Photos by A. E. Russon.)

Throughout, she had followed the techniques used by the camp cooks and used the very same tools: blowing on and fanning embers, decanting paraffin with a cup, putting smouldering sticks together; obviously, any behaviour of this sort is not encouraged or rewarded in these orang-utans, since it could be highly dangerous. These cases of imitation show program-level copying of task organization, and may rely on emulation of the results of task stages (e.g. (1) weeds that are cut; (2) neat piles). The copying of actions like side-to-side fanning with a lid and siphoning by sucking at a tube strongly suggest that orang-utans can also impersonate human actions. Interestingly, in some cases orang-utans will repeatedly practise their imitations—specifically when they are unsuccessful the first time (Russon and Galdikas 1995). Supinah, the heroine of the fire-making, once imitated hammering nails into wood, after watching construction work. She copied closely, but used insufficient power, and her nails fell out. However, she returned repeatedly over subsequent days, reassembled the necessary nails, hammer, and wood, and tried again. This 'internally driven' repetition should be sharply distinguished from the repetition of stimulus-controlled behaviour, which follows conventional laws of learning. Imitation requires a mental, symbolic representation of the desired result in advance of its achievement.

From the patchy current evidence, it seems most unlikely that any species apart from great apes and dolphins possess anything approaching the flexibility I described as 'ideal' for a social learner. Rats can take account of the different physical appearance of a task in a simple way (left for right). Parrots, dolphins, orang-utans, and chimpanzees (and perhaps gorillas) can impersonate the form of actions, although only the great apes among this collection have the manual dexterity to show close approximations of the human behaviours they copy. None of the evidence is completely watertight, but the sheer mass of strongly suggestive examples tends to convince; that dolphins give the strongest evidence is perhaps because their actions are so different from those of other mammals that when they copy another species it is more obvious. Great apes are the only taxon to give evidence of program-level imitation, but this is a little unfair to most species who have seldom been set tasks requiring several stages to complete. No animal, except the human, can be said definitely to show both aspects of imitative ability that have been distinguished: program-level imitation of task organization and goal structure, and impersonation of the detail of actions. In principle, then, humans should be able to gain novel skills efficiently from others, normally using program-level imitation, but buttressed by impersonation of any aspects resistant to trial and error acquisition. In practice, humans are less godlike. Those who work on animal imitation sometimes tend to overrate human capability, whereas those of us who recall trying to tie a bow tie or a reef knot by imitation (without verbal instruction) sometimes wonder if humans can impersonate at all.

It will be clear that, for an animal to imitate by putting itself mentally in the place of another or by understanding the logical structure of another's behaviour, some sort of insight is implied. We have thus already begun consideration of what 'insight' might really mean. There seem to be at least three senses or components to insight: understanding the mechanics of cause and effect; understanding what others know, think, or feel; and being able to plan or simulate actions without carrying them out, in order to solve problems by thinking. We will look at these in turn in the subsequent chapters.

Further reading

The data used in this chapter are largely recent, reported in academic journals. However, A. E. Russon, K. A. Bard, and S. T. Parker *Reaching into thought: the minds of the great apes* (1995) has chapters that describe orang-utan imitations of humans (Russon and Galdikas), gorilla plant-feeding skills (Byrne), and imitation in signing orang-utans (Miles), and related issues. Assessing dolphin capabilities is made harder than it need be by scientific researchers' understandable reluctance to associate with the 'New Age' enthusiasts' views; the net result is that little has been published on imitation since Taylor and Saayman's article. Much the best source is Schusterman *et al.* (1986).

Part 3

Insight

7
Understanding how things work

An understanding of mechanical function, of cause and effect between physical events, is what in everyday language we call 'understanding how things work'. This can include knowledge of object properties (Is it heavy/solid/soft/large? Does it always stay the same? Can it be deformed?), knowledge of relationships between objects (inside/outside, touching, above/below, interlocking), knowledge of how to achieve modifications (apply force by hitting/pushing, tear by twisting/levering, move by rolling/dragging), and knowledge of how things are constructed (subtraction of unwanted parts, combination of several appropriate objects, joining things together). Several lines of evidence imply insight of this general sort in some animals.

Object permanence

One of the most basic attributes of objects is that they usually continue to exist in time and space. Without a represention of objects as enduring entities, an organism would be hindered in building up knowledge of the properties of objects and the relationships among them. Having an idea of 'object premanence' might seem trivial, but there is evidence that young children do not have it. While adult monkeys and apes evidently *do* have representations of objects as still existing when not in view (for instance, they give evidence of having 'cognitive maps' of their home ranges, as we shall see in Chapter 13), the age at which object representation develops could affect the richness of what a primate learns about the physical world.

Whether a child has a mental representation of an object is usually assessed by tests involving invisible displacements of an object, first done by Jean Piaget. An object is hidden in a container, then this is passed behind several screens, behind one of which the object is surreptitiously dropped off and the empty container shown to the child; searching the route of the container indicates that the child has a representation of the object—as something with permanence. However, Piaget emphasized that this task can also be solved in practical, non-representational ways, and until recently attempts to assess monkey and ape object concepts have failed to exclude these alternatives (Natale *et al.* 1986). Francesco Natale and colleagues introduced 'catch' trials in which the container hiding the object was not moved, and tested a young Japanese macaque and a young gorilla at a similar developmental level of achievement. The monkey did not act any differently in these catch trials, showing that when she got the task right (as she often did) it was on the basis of a simple rule like 'search where the experimenter's hand moved'. But when the catch trials were repeated many times, the monkey gradually began to discriminate them, and her search strategy also changed. As the gorilla had always done, the monkey now began to search systematically back along the path of the object, abandoning her earlier (and initially successful) strategy of going straight to where the object was usually dropped off. Did she have a concept of object permanence after all? A further refinement of the test showed that the answer was no. Normally, there is only one possible place for the object to be hidden; when a second possible hiding place was introduced, the monkey always searched the one nearest to the container first, even when the container had only travelled to the other hiding place. The gorilla never made this error. It is too early to generalize from one individual of each species, but it may be that early in their development great apes, but not monkeys, have a representational concept of objects' permanent existence. If so, this would tend to delay young monkeys' understanding of the characteristics of objects, hindering development of mechanical skills depending on this knowledge.

Solving problems with the insightful use of objects

We have already met in Chapter 4 the most famous and historically one of the earliest hints of mechanical understanding by an animal: the discovery by one of Wolfgang Köhler's chimpanzees, Sultan, that two short sticks when fitted carefully together can make a tool long enough for the problem in hand—raking in food that is out of reach. Sultan's behaviour has long been hailed as evidence of 'insight', but the conclusions that can be drawn from Köhler's original work should be qualified. Schiller (1952) showed that chimpanzees with no experience of the raking-stick problem will sometimes join sticks together in play even where there is no reward to be gained. The crucial behaviour of stick-joining could therefore have happened as part of Sultan's play, even if he had not been set the problem. Stick-joining may have occurred in Sultan's play before the day of the test, and so been already part of his repertoire. This is not to denigrate the achievement of the chimpanzee: he still had to recognize that a relationship he had created (putting two sticks together) as a part of play or in the past was now relevant to the current problem. It only shows that Sultan's solution was not necessarily mentally computed entirely *de novo* from the mechanics of sticks, but may instead have been appropriately deployed out of a repertoire of past experience. The *appropriateness* of the deployment shows that he understood the cause and effect relationship between stick-joining and extra length.

The same is likely to be true in much human problem-solving, and more often than we perhaps realize. I once studied problem-solving in complicated everyday tasks, by asking people to 'think aloud' while they planned (Byrne 1975, 1977). Often my subjects would give up on some perplexing aspect for a while and work on some other part of the task instead, only to suddenly interrupt themselves with an 'Aha! I've got it!' when the answer to the abandoned problem became apparent at last. Everyone experiences these sudden insights, apropos of nothing; sometimes the phenomenon is called 'incubation' by psychologists. It certainly feels as if an unconscious part of one's mind has been working away on the abandoned problem all along and finally this process gets a result and interrupts the conscious flow. But my 'think aloud' protocols told a different story. Just before the dramatic realization, in each case there had been a train of thought that was in fact closely related to the insight that—in retrospect—seemed to have come from nowhere. The little burst of excitement at solving the irritating problem had been enough to make the subject forget the end of the previous train of thought, and so they could not see any connection. What had happened would be better described by saying that the subject 'noticed' the answer to the unsolved puzzle in their current mental activity, rather than unconsciously set in motion a parallel train of problem-solving that only burst into consciousness when it made a discovery.

The analogy with the chimpanzee's behaviour is close: recall that Sultan had been playing with two sticks *after* he had given up trying to reach the food; then he jumped up and produced the 'clever' solution. In the chimpanzee case too, the intelligence seems to be a matter of *noticing* a solution when it comes by, not calculating it by some logical process. In order to notice a useful solution, the problem must be mentally represented in a certain way: a clear outline of an adequate solution must be set up, in Sultan's case a rigid rod of sufficient length. Early researchers on human problem-solving called such an outline a 'schematic anticipation' of the solution.

In the phenomenon of incubation, or in Sultan's famous success, the breakthrough is to *notice* a possible solution in current experience. More normally, skilful problem-solving doesn't require incubation: instead, resemblances are noticed between novel problems and remembered *past* experiences, and these enable the novel problem to be solved. 'Intelligence' in problem-solving, on this view, amounts simply to having plenty of similar past experiences to draw upon, and an efficient memory. Not only does this make sense for chimpanzees with sticks, but it has been proposed and tested as an explanation of skill in chess-playing humans. Master players should have a more extensive repertoire of board configurations in their memory, to compare with any current state of play. If so, researchers argued, then masters should find a complex board configuration—an array of pieces and their exact positions—much easier to remember than does a novice, after a brief look. And they certainly do (de Groot 1966). Just better memories, all round? No, because where the array did not come from a real game but was simply a random placement on the board, masters and novices were equally poor at remembering it. Only arrays that come from real, serious games are easy for the expert to remember—real games are rich in memorable patterns of relationships among the pieces, and the patterns are largely 'known' already from the vast experience that goes to make up a master player's skill.

Explorative play with objects

Returning to the more concrete problems that confront animals, perhaps here, too, differences in ability derive from differences in memory: in individuals' different repertoires of the cause-and-effect rules that enable effective use of objects. How might animals best build up repertoires of useful rules; on what experiences can they draw?

To be useful, the past experiences only have to be similar in mechanical cause-and-effect terms to the current problem; they do not have to come from past problems that were serious at the time. Playful experience would serve very well to build the repertoires of useful rules, and has the advantage of avoiding any unpleasant consequences that failure at 'real' problems might have. A tendency to *play* with objects in childhood might then have the biological function of building an augmented repertoire of possible solutions. ('Play' in animals and pre-verbal children is notoriously difficult to define; some researchers have given up, and use the word 'exploration' instead. Here, I mean all object manipulation out of the context of a real problem.) If this is right, then we should predict that chimpanzees whose childhood lacked the normal opportunities for object play, should be poor at problem-solving later in life with tasks that involve objects. Play has indeed been shown to benefit some chimpanzees in solving problems. Birch (1945) showed that captive chimpanzees that fail to solve the stick-raking problem benefit greatly from a period of unstructured play with sticks, in that they are then likely to succeed in the task. A lack of object play could have affected many captive-reared chimpanzees in zoos in the past, before zoos became more conscious of a need for environmental enrichment, and many chimpanzees in laboratories even now.

The idea that play with objects functions to augment object problem-solving skills has implications for species other than chimpanzees. Most animals, in fact, *lack* a strong tendency in their childhood to play with objects (as opposed to social play, or locomotor play in branches, for instance). Only common chimpanzees and humans, among the great apes, regularly invest much time in play with detached objects. But under the artificial conditions of captivity, young gorillas also play with objects. This may be the causal explanation of a paradox: that gorillas regularly show skills in tool use and even tool-making in captivity, yet tools seem to have no part in their natural lives (McGrew 1989). In the wild, the gorilla problem-solving repertoire may be deficient in cause-and-effect rules most relevant to tool use, as a result of almost no play with detached, inanimate objects in childhood. Gorillas live in cohesive groups, and youngsters play with each other, not with objects. Solutions based on using objects (i.e. tool solutions) are then simply not available later when they might be needed. The immediate, causal explanation of the differences between chimpanzees and gorillas in tool use may well be that object play in childhood is necessary for efficient adult tool use, and young gorillas prefer social play; only in captivity are play partners rare, and the 'second best' object play becomes frequent. A functional explanation is nevertheless also required: gorillas evidently have the latent potential to play with objects in childhood, and to use tools to solve problems in adulthood, yet they do neither in the wild—why? The functional explanation lies in their ecology, as McGrew points out. Gorillas have less need of tool use than common chimpanzees because of differences in how they exploit their environment—either they can obtain the same foods by other means, or their dietary needs are accommodated in other ways. For instance, both gorillas and chimpanzees eat ants and termites, but only chimpanzees use sticks to do so. Lowland gorillas use their greater strength to overturn termite mounds, whereas chimpanzees in the same forests have to probe with thin tools to obtain termites; mountain gorillas eat safari ants (*Dorylus*) by hand instead of using a stick as chimpanzees do, presumably because the stings are less painful to their tougher skins. (It is tempting to apply this account to the 'lack of tool use' in wild orang-utans and pygmy chimpanzees. However, these species are more arboreal, so harder to observe, and much less studied: the facts are less certain. Recently a wild orang-utan was recorded (on film) using a large leaf as a 'glove', and pygmy chimpanzees have been found regularly to signal with tools (see Chapter 13). Until both species are much better known in the wild, any claims are premature.)

In monkeys and strepsirhines, object play is largely lacking even under captive conditions.* This is not to say that the young of these primates do not show curiosity towards novel objects—far from it. But when the curiosity has once been satisfied, the object will not be a focus of attention again. Nor does it mean that other primates do not play in ways that sometimes include objects. For instance, young monkeys often jump off branches repeatedly in play; when the monkey troop lives near water, their play may included repeatedly jumping into the water from a branch. Young monkeys, especially females, are sometimes seen to carry soft or hairy objects against their chest or to sit with them, just as if they were 'cuddling a baby'. In all these cases, an object is involved because it meets one or two simple requirements for an activity to be carried out: a firm, high platform above the desired area for jumping; a yielding, warm object of the approximate size of a baby. The

*An exception to this generalization is the capuchins monkey; capuchins in captivity are highly oriented to explore and play with objects, and regularly acquire tool use—conveniently for the hypothesis of the previous section. Their understanding is examined later in the chapter.

activity itself is the goal, the object is just 'filling a slot' in the programme of behaviour, reasonably adequately. This sort of play is not likely to result in learning more about the object itself—what can be done with it, what effects it is good for, and so on. The most that might be learnt is that the chosen object is not, after all, any use for that single purpose, when it will be discarded. In this sense, none of these cases are 'object play'. The manipulations of a stick by an infant chimpanzee—which include tickling, probing nooks and crannies, masturbation, flailing, clubbing and throwing, and prodding others to initiate social play, as well as infantile attempts at termiting—provide a generalized exploration of stick properties and uses.

The play of species other than primates also sometimes involves objects, but again not in ways that would suffice to learn object properties and potential functions. The play of a kitten with a ball of wool or cotton-reel is the most familiar example, and this clearly belongs in the category of slot-filling (in this case, the slot is labelled 'prey'), rather than potentially serving to build up a repertoire of information about object properties and uses. If a kitten's play with inanimate objects *is* functional, it is because it encourages practice of specific action patterns or builds up physical fitness in general; Caro (1980) found little evidence for any beneficial effects at all, however.

Tool-using and tool-making

Of all animal aptitudes, using tools seems most likely to offer a window into their understanding of cause-and-effect relationships in the mechanical world. The great interest over many years in animal tool use reflects this hope, although the key role that tool use is often given in depictions of human origins has also spotlighted animal tools. A 'tool' is, somewhat arbitrarily, defined as a detached object applied to another object to achieve a result. On this definition, neither an orang-utan's use of a living sapling to pole vault between two solid trees, nor a human's levering the top off a beer bottle with teeth, 'count', although these acts are conceptually close to tool use.

Many animals, from insects to apes, use detached objects as aids in their actions—as hammers, probes, anvils, weapons, sponges, lures, and many more. For tool-using species that are known, three things are usually true:

(1) the habit is not shared by closely related species;

(2) individuals of the species use one type of tool, and for a particular purpose only;

(3) all individuals use the tool in the same way, given the same opportunities.

These facts bring into question whether animal tool use necessarily reflects intelligence. For instance, Galapagos woodpecker finches (*Camarhynchus pallidus*) carefully select cactus spines and use them as probes for insects under bark. This enables them to fill the niche that woodpeckers (Picidae) occupy in Eurasia, the Americas, and Africa (by virtue of their long tongues), and a strepsirhine primate called the aye-aye (*Daubentonia madagascariensis*) occupies in Madagascar and the striped possum (*Dactylopsila trivirgata*) occupies in Australasia (by means of their one extra-long and thin finger on each hand). No other Galapagos finch uses a tool; woodpecker finches use objects for nothing else but probing. If you watch a woodpecker finch long enough, it will eventually do the trick. These facts do not encourage any idea that the tool use is indicative of intelligence or special insight into cause-and-effect relations. Rather, it is best seen as an adaptation to a particular set of ecological circumstances, just like the aye-aye's long finger. In some cases, such as the Egyptian vultures (*Neophron percnopterus*) which break ostrich eggs by throwing rocks at them, only certain populations show the habit, so it must be learnt socially—probably by stimulus enhancement acting to focus individual exploration on to the rocks. Even cetaceans, despite their natural handicaps in manipulative skill, have been seen to devise a tool: Brown and Norris (1956) reported a dolphin, having tried to get a moray eel to come out of its crevice and play, went off and killed a scorpionfish, then used the spiny body to poke at the eel. However, single, isolated cases of object manipulation give little confidence that the perpetrators have a general understanding of cause-and-effect relations among objects; a wider repertoire of tool use, showing some flexibility, would point more clearly to intelligent usage.

This picture is not just true of birds, it is general of mammals, including most primates (Beck 1980). The closest that any of these animals get to showing a *repertoire* of tool-using skills is probably seen in the sea otter (*Enhydra lutris*). Sea otters use rocks, which they pick up on the sea bottom in one hand, carry to the surface and support on their wide tummies as they swim on their backs; then they can crack open a hard crab or an abalone (which has to be held in the other hand while getting the rock) with some ease, using the rock as an anvil. Some otters specialize on abalones, others on crabs, and it seems that the best rock for the purpose varies between the two tasks (bigger and flatter rocks are better for molluscs). Daughters of otters that specialize in using one type of rock for one type of food grow up to do the same as their mother; yet both crabs and abalones are found commonly in all these otters' ranges (Riedman *et al.* 1989). Even though the basic ability is characteristic of all sea otters and presumably genetically specified, social learning must be important in acquiring the details of otter tool use, and appropriate tools are used for the different jobs. Nevertheless, the sea otter's ability to use tools to solve problems is severely restricted; the 'repertoire' is not present in any one individual animal.

Among a few species of primates, a very different picture emerges: of animals that can learn to use a range of tools for a range of purposes, animals that can choose between methods. This suggests real intelligence, and has been a focus of much investigation. The primates in question consist of every one of the great apes when kept in captivity, but only the common chimpanzee in the wild, and in addition one monkey, the South American capuchin (*Cebus* sp.). This last fact, that a genus of platyrrhine monkey should show skills found in apes but lacking in other monkeys, is particularly intriguing. Capuchins use sticks as tools spontaneously for several purposes: as rakes for food, as probes for liquids, as weapons against other monkeys and—the only case of capuchin tool use in the wild—in killing a snake. This catalogue suggests strongly that capuchins have a cause-and-effect understanding of the functional properties and uses of tools—or, at least, sticks as-tools.

Until recently, this conclusion was unquestioned. Now, Elisabetta Visalberghi has carefully analysed the errors made by tool-using capuchins, and made a very different interpretation. Visalberghi and Trinca (1987) gave capuchins access to peanuts inside a rigid and fixed horizontal transparent tube (Fig. 7.1). The nuts could not be reached by the fingers, and the tube was too thin for a whole arm, but a variety of sticks was available. Most capuchins, after an hour or two of trying other methods and manipulating sticks in various ways, found out how to use a stick to push the food out. Then, each of the successful monkeys was tested with the same task and a range of sticks, many of which were blatantly unsuitable for pushing a peanut out of the tube. These might be too short (in this case, putting one stick after another into the same end would serve to push the food out); too thick to go into the tube, or tied up in a bundle (here, untying the bundle or breaking the thick stick would make thinner pieces available for use); or a stick with fixed cross-pieces close to each end (but pulling out a cross-piece

Figure 7.1 Visalberghi found that capuchin monkeys were readily able to use tools to solve problems in the laboratory. This one is in the process of succesfully pushing a peanut out of a horizontal plastic tube (photo by E. Visalberghi).

would allow the stick to be used). Each monkey solved these problems in a few minutes, but the errors they made along the way raise doubts as to what they really understand about a tool. Capuchins inserted little splinters when a perfectly good stick was lying there in front of them. They inserted short sticks on both sides of the peanut, then repeatedly took the two sticks out and put them back again in the same places, still with the peanut sandwiched in the middle of the tube. They pulled out one cross-piece, but then tried to put the other end—still blocked by a cross-piece—into the tube. Time and time again they would try with sticks far too thick to enter the tube, with sticks much too short to reach the clearly visible food, and even with a flexible piece of rubber. All these errors are hard to explain in an animal with any understanding of *why* a stick works as a probe to push out a peanut. A stick's thickness relative to the tube, its length relative to the tube, and the property of rigidity, are the elements of sticks that matter. In representational terms, an intelligent tool-user must notice and remember those aspects of a successful tool and relate them to the corresponding properties of tools that fail.

Next Visalberghi made the same task a bit more difficult—the plexiglass tube was given a closed well or trap in its centre, a hole in which the peanut would fall and be lost if it were pushed that way (Visalberghi and Limongelli 1994). Only one monkey learnt to solve this problem, always pushing the peanut in the opposite direction to the hole. However, if the tube were rotated, so that the 'trap' was upwards and no nut could fall into it (Fig. 7.2), the monkey still studiously avoided pushing a peanut in that direction. There was no comprehension of *why* a trap is a trap—because things fall into it under gravity. Finally, a test with an opaque tube with no trap showed that this monkey's strategy was to insert a probe always at the end furthest from the peanut; with a centrally placed trap, this works effectively, but to continue using the strategy when there is no trap shows the basic lack of understanding. The various errors that Visalberghi's monkeys made show that all their successes were based on trying to get the peanut out in every way that a stick could be manipulated, and sooner or later one way worked. Capuchins are quick-moving animals and devoted to peanuts, so 'later' was only a few minutes.

One possibility is that capuchins may be handicapped in complicated tasks by their style of dealing with the world. Visalberghi had found earlier that behavioural style is an important determiner of whether a monkey is successful on a certain task. Titi monkeys (*Callicebus moloch*) and squirrel monkeys (*Saimiri sciureus*) were compared on a range of tasks (Visalberghi and Mason 1983). Where speed in approaching the problem, vigour, and enthusiasm were useful in solving tasks, squirrel monkeys won hands down over titis, especially on the hardest version of each task. However, squirrel monkeys frequently solved the problems not in the organized ways envisaged by the researchers, but by breaking or upsetting the apparatus, gaining the food as a side-effect. Titis are quite different in style, looking for longer

(a)

(b)

Figure 7.2 When Visalberghi changed the task in various ways, capuchins showed that their learnt skill was not based on any real understanding of the situation. (a) The monkeys do eventually learn to deal with a 'trap' in the horizontal tube, by pushing from the side opposite to the peanut (this one is making an error); but when the tube is inverted (b), so the trap cannot function, they persist 'superstitiously' in their old strategy. (Photos by E. Visalberghi.)

before touching anything at all, and always touching less and more gently. Only one problem absolutely required a precise, specific response for its solution: getting marshmallow from a piece of macaroni after the macaroni had first been retrieved. On this task, titis were no worse than squirrel monkeys. Perhaps, if even more precise and delicate tasks had been set to both monkeys, the gentle explorative style of the titis might eventually have proved superior to the bull-in-a-china-shop approach of squirrel monkeys.

Capuchins, like squirrel monkeys, have a vigourous approach to life. The foraging of a troop of capuchins has been likened to the progress of an invading army, smashing and killing everything in its path; debris rains down from their branch-breaking and bark-tearing; birds that sometimes mob them as predators (which they are) are grabbed, killed, and eaten. Capuchin foraging has its own technical term: 'destructive foraging' (Terborgh 1983). Perhaps this style of approaching problems—break them—though efficient in capuchins' natural environment, may be an impediment with some of the tasks that researchers have set them in the laboratory. Clearly, we again risk drawing conclusions that are not species-fair until a wide range of tasks has been investigated as cleverly and thoroughly as Visalberghi has explored the probe task.

It also has to be pointed out that careful calculation on the basis of deep and sophisticated knowledge is not always the *best* strategy, even for people. The problem-solving tactics used by skilled electronics experts who are called in to 'troubleshoot' faults in the nuclear power industry of Denmark give an example where the opposite approach is better. Instead of diagnosing a fault on the basis of the pattern of symptoms, they prefer to carry out a whole series of simple, routine tests of the key components (Rasmussen and Jensen 1974). The psychologists were much surprised, and asked the experts why: they agreed that they *could* have used their electronics theory to avoid the need for tests, but tests were infallible and they knew their thinking was not, and saw no reason not to use the 'quick and dirty' approach. If this had been a case of animal problem-solving in the laboratory, psychologists would have been liable to conclude that the animals were forced to use task-specific tricks to solve the problems, because they were too unintelligent to think. Perhaps 'intelligent' tool use seldom pays for monkeys.

Nevertheless, on the available evidence, capuchin monkeys cannot be claimed to have shown any 'insight' into *why* an object is a useful tool. There is no doubt that their enthusiastic and manipulative style is an ideal device for learning trial-and-error solutions to problems, and we have no strong reason for suspecting that they have any greater understanding than they have yet shown. Real comprehension of mechanical relations may be restricted among animals to the great apes. This would be consistent with what we have already seen of their representation of objects in problem-solving; that chimpanzees can generalize uses of an object between play and a problem-task suggests an appreciation of object properties and relations at a rather abstract and symbolic level.

A high level of understanding of needs and ends is confirmed by data from chimpanzee tool use in the wild. Chimpanzees use many different kinds of objects as tools, and for many different purposes (Fig. 7.3). Thin, bendy lianas or grass stems are inserted as probes in *Macrotermes* termite

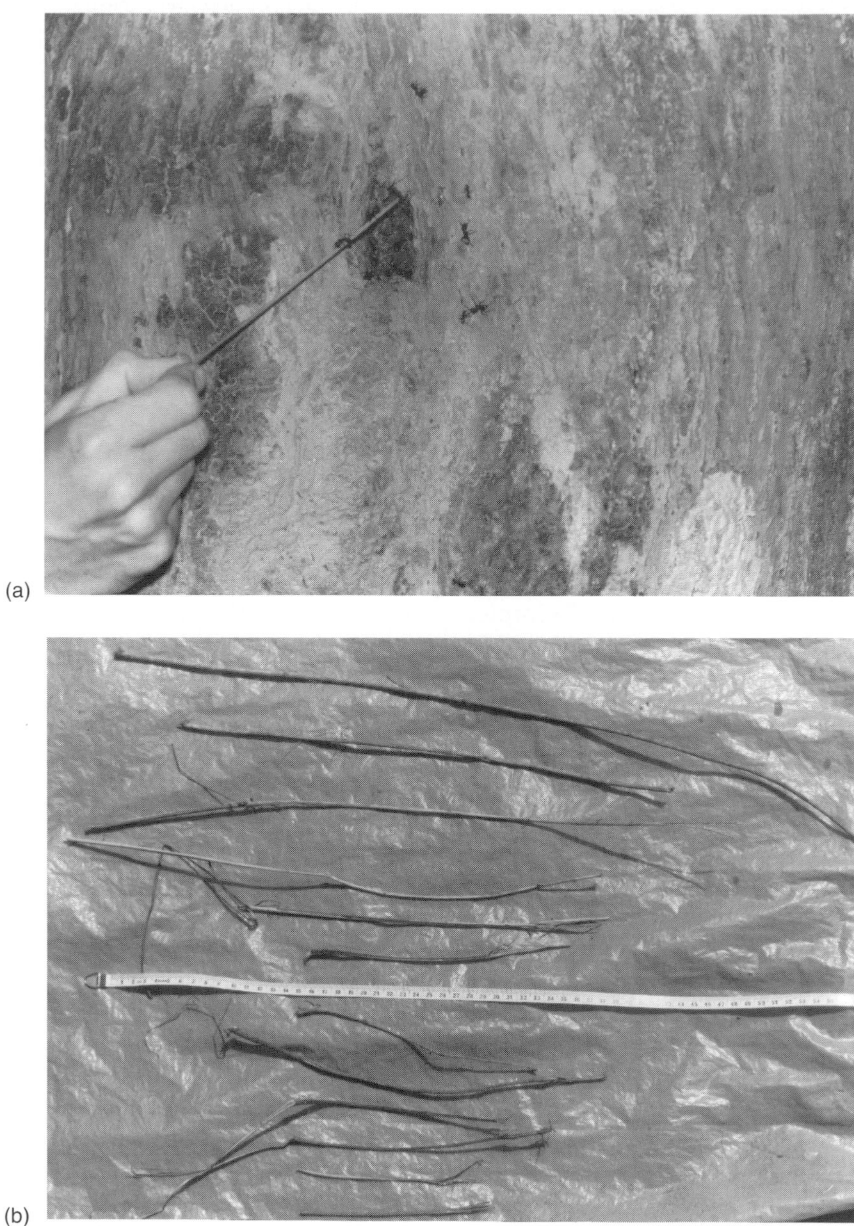

Figure 7.3 Probing for insects is not as difficult as it is sometimes claimed to be: (a) two *Campanotus* ants have attached themselves to my own amateur effort at a tool. (b) Some real chimpanzee stick tools, collected at Mt. Assirik, Senegal. The larger five are wands used for 'dipping' into *Dorylus* ant swarms, the smaller seven are the more flexible probes, used here for extracting *Macrotermes* termites.

Figure 7.4 A female chimpanzee at Mahale, Tanzania, probes the nest of *Campanotus* ants with a slender tool made from a grass stem.

hills or *Campanotus* ant nests inside trees; the guard insects attack the probe and by gently pulling it out the chimpanzee is able to pick the insects off with its lips (Fig. 7.4). Long, whippy wands are dipped into the moving columns of the formidable armies of *Dorylus* ants that march through African woodlands and savannahs; the aggressive soldier ants swarm up the wand like moving hair, and when nearly at the chimpanzee's hand it will sweep a cupped hand along the wand and stuff the struggling mass of ants into its mouth—and chew fast. A different type of stick again is used for digging out nests of wild bees to eat honey, or to extract marrow from bones: strong rods for levering. Bunches of leaves are chewed till they are reduced to a spongy wad, and the wad dipped into small holes to soak up water that is then squeezed into the chimpanzee's mouth. Large rocks are placed carefully on the forest floor, a hard *Panda* or *Coula* nut is oriented in the right way on its surface and held there, so that a round pebble can be smashed down to break the nut (Fig. 7.5). Banana leaves are picked and used as umbrellas in heavy rain. A small grass fire is investigated gingerly with a stick (Fig. 12.6). Leaves are used to wipe blood from a wound, or faeces from the individual's bottom. Captive chimpanzees have used poles as ladders, and short sticks as pitons, to aid their efforts to cease being captive. The list could run on and on even with current data, and it would be unwise to close off the catalogue of objects they use, and purposes

Figure 7.5 A 2-year-old male chimpanzee inspects a shell of a *Coula edulis* nut, cracked by his mother, while she holds the nut's kernel between her lips. She has used the 4–5 kg stone hammer that she still holds in her left foot. (Photo by C. Boesch.)

to which these objects are put. The fact is that chimpanzees tend to solve problems by the use of objects as tools.

Many of these objects are 'found objects'; that is, the animal selects an existing object for specific use as a tool. The selection of only certain objects to try shows that the tool's functional properties are specified in the chimpanzee's understanding of the needed tool. For instance, those chimpanzees that use hammer and anvil stones to crack nuts (the habit is only found in West African populations) are very fussy about which rocks to use—probably for good reason, as it is a difficult skill only mastered in late adolescence.

Other chimpanzee tools are not 'found objects', but *made* by the chimpanzees by removing parts of the natural material. An ant-dipping wand is fashioned by snapping off a thin, tough stem of several feet in length, breaking off the leafy top and stripping off all the side leaves. A termite-fishing tool is made by pulling off a grass stem or thin vine, biting the tip to make a clean end, and removing enough leaves to allow insertion into the small tunnels of the insects. Unlike human tools, the range of methods chimpanzees use in tool manufacture is limited: no tools have been recorded made by addition of one item to another, and no tool has been made in the wild whose sole function is to make another tool. However, the observation of an individual which carefully positioned a sliver as a *wedge* below a loosely seated anvil stone to make it level, before starting to crack nuts with a hammer stone, comes quite close (Matsuzawa 1991).

Just like the the careful selection of found objects, the modification of inadequate material until it meets the requirements of a tool shows that chimpanzees, unlike capuchin monkeys, have a mental representation of what a tool needs to be for a certain job. Often the modification is subtraction of parts, which also shows that chimpanzees can identify a potential tool 'embedded' in a larger, non-tool object. Tools are made in advance, and seldom need to be modified once the job is begun; sometimes fishing tools are even made many yards from the site at which they will be used, and carried in the mouth to the termite mound. This forethought shows that these chimpanzees are not solving each specific problem by trial and error, as capuchins seem to be doing, but already have a mental representation of a tool which would be adequate for the task—the problem is simply to find something that matches the representation, or to make it. Of course, the original mechanism of acquisition of the mental representation might have been by trial-and-error learning; what is important is that chimpanzees learn what is needed of a tool, as a functional description of its properties: a 'schematic anticipation'.

The more complex manifestations of tool use in wild chimpanzees (nut-cracking, ant-dipping, and insect-fishing) are not easy to compare with the tool use displayed by other species of ape in captivity, since each of these three skills has a component of social tradition. Not every chimpanzee population performs each activity. Nut-cracking, with hammer and anvil, is found in all populations studied in a wide area of West Africa, and is totally absent in East and Central Africa; the hard nuts, and suitable rocks to crack them with, are equally available at these sites. This pattern suggests diffusion by 'traditional' transmission from an original point of inception, as in human cultural spread. Most techniques, however, are erratically spread among chimpanzee populations. For instance, ant-dipping is regular in Tanzania at Gombe, not found 130 km away at Mahale, yet it does happen often at Mt. Assirik, thousands of miles away in Senegal. This more erratic distribution implies either that all chimpanzee populations have these skills, but some display them so infrequently that they have yet to be reported, or that the skills have been invented several times in different populations—which also means that they are supported by a strong underlying tendency to do that sort of thing. But in none of these cases is it possible that each individual chimpanzee invents the techniques for itself: some sort of traditional transmission is certain.

Tool uses by other captive ape species, in contrast, concern individual solutions to problems. All captive apes readily take to artificial 'termite mounds' in zoos: concrete mounds, ready-prepared with holes in which honey is placed, obtainable with the appropriate stick. The animals have to choose and modify the branches they are provided with, but in other ways the task is a far simpler one than insect-fishing in the wild. Knowing where insects are found, even—in the case of *Macrotermes*—having to locate an unopened emergence tunnel and pick the mud off with a fingernail, and the slow and delicate withdrawal of the implement, are aspects not simulated by the crude poking of a pool of honey.

Far more impressive are the abilities to make stone tools, shown by an orang-utan and recently by a pygmy chimpanzee. Wright (1972) first allowed a 5½-year-old orang-utan, Abang, to learn how to cut a cord with a stone flake in order to open a box for a food reward. Wright repeatedly demonstrated sawing through the cord, and there is now independent evidence that an orang-utan should be able to impersonate an action (see Chapter 6); but sawing is an action that orang-utans use naturally and Abang may simply have acquired the knack by trial and error. Once he was proficient, Abang was instead given only a flint core and a hammerstone. The technique, used by early man to 'knap' flint, was demonstrated for him: striking the core in a certain way causes a flake to be split off. To make this task, which even people do not find easy to copy, a little easier for him, the core was fixed down to a board with a leather strap and a base of modelling clay. In early trials, the tiny chips Abang managed to detach were too small to use as tools, but he did try several times to use them on the cord. After seven demonstrations, and $1\frac{1}{2}$ hours of cumulative exposure to the task, Abang succeeded in striking off a flint flake; he failed to cut the cord with this flake, but by then he had the idea and after a couple more flakes he was able to get to the food. While Abang's performance may not have depended on impersonation, it shows clearly that he was capable of organizing the complex task, program-level imitation. Currently, Nicholas Toth is working with a pygmy chimpanzee, Kanzi (whose language competence is now famous, see Chapter 11), on a similar task (Toth *et al.* 1993). Without any instruction or demonstration, Kanzi has learned to produce useable stone cutting tools. The technique he prefers, throwing the rock down at a hard surface, may well have been in regular use by the hominids who made Oldowan tools 1.5 My ago, and some of Kanzi's tools would be classified 'Oldowan' (N. Toth, personal communication).

To summarize the findings of this chapter, all the great apes, but probably no other animals, can comprehend the simple cause-and-effect relationships that govern the use of objects to solve problems: this requires that they have symbolic representations of objects. The mental and manual capabilities of these animals evidently support tool-using and tool-making under certain circumstances. Although other species sometimes use objects as tools, there is reason to think that their abilities are supported instead by genetic tendencies or trial-and-error learning, without any understanding of how things work.

Why should all great apes have these abilities, yet only common chimpanzees profit from tool use in the wild? A shared descent from a toolmaking ancestor is one possibility, but it may also be that tool use and an ability to understand object properties are a by-product of other abilities—abilities all great apes rely on. For instance, a gorilla's ability to learn a structured, several-stage task which includes highly specific elements, such as folding nettle leaves to minimize the number of painful stings it receives, may depend on just the same understanding of how the physical world works, although it requires no tool use. Our understanding of the techniques used in feeding on plants by apes and monkeys lags far behind our knowledge of tool use, so it is too early to say if these techniques were the evolutionary stimulus for monkey/ape differences in insight.* Another possibility is that cause-and-effect comprehension is a by-product of a much more global change in mental capacities, having a different evolutionary origin. To see what this might involve, we must move to other senses of 'insight' in the following chapters.

Further reading

Tool use among animals is nicely described in B. B. Beck (1980) *Animal tool behaviour* (Garland Press, New York). W. C. McGrew (1992) *Chimpanzee material culture* (Cambridge University Press, Cambridge), which compares the special abilities of chimpanzees against anthropological criteria, is now the 'bible' for tool use in this species. The relationship of tool use to intelligence and especially language is extensively covered in Gibson and Ingold (1993). See especially the chapter on capuchins by Visalberghi; those by Gibson, Lock, Parker and Milbrath, which use Piagetian theory to analyse animal abilities; and Reynolds, who suggests that human tool use differs crucially from chimpanzees' in the making of 'polyliths', joined combinations of objects that stay together without gravitational support.

*Baboons roll prickly pear (*Opuntia*) fruits in sand, breaking off the unpleasant spines (Robert Barton, personal communication). However, rolling is a motor action found in many cercopithecine monkeys, so acquisition without insight is very possible, and no organizational complexity is shown.

8
Understanding minds: doing and seeing, knowing and thinking

Humans show another sort of insight, quite different from their understanding of the everyday mechanics of objects—an understanding of other people. We assume that other individuals, just like ourselves, are animate causal agents with minds, and we treat them as having mental states—beliefs, feelings, intentions, and so on. Furthermore, this 'works', in the sense that on the basis of what we think other people are thinking, we can predict what they are going to do—not all the time, but much better than just guessing.

As part of this predictive process, we assume that the nature of other peoples' mental states is very like our own—that their elation feels like our elation, that red to them looks as it does to us. Philosophers are quick to point out that we have no evidence for this, and we can never get any, so we may be quite wrong to make such assumptions. The everyday example of the very many people who are red–green colourblind shows clearly what the philosophers are getting at. 'Colourblind' people are happy to talk about red and green as separate colours; they just find them rather similar to each other, as the rest of the population find mauve and purple. They might say, for instance, 'the red berries on a holly tree are not very obvious, but, yes, they *are* red, not green like grass'. Evidently when colourblind people see red it is not the same red: but we might not have realized that fact by just talking to each other, and could then have had endless arguments about colour preferences and conspicuousness. The fact that we *do* have endless arguments about other mental states, such as consciousness, should serve to warn that we may be talking at cross purposes. Even within our own species, understanding mental states of others is not easy; when we ask about mental states of other species, life gets tough indeed. Certainly as humans we can never hope to know much about the private *minds* of other species; we will never know what it would feel like to be an ape or a lizard.

However, we *can* ask whether animals, like us, treat other individuals as *if they* have mental states, because if they do so, it would make an observable difference to their behaviour. Any animal that did act as if other individuals have mental states would then be said to have a *theory of mind* (Premack and Woodruff 1978); when I assume you have particular thoughts and fears, I am using my theory of mind. Most animals lack a theory of mind—as scientists have always believed, since they saw no evidence of the diagnostic behaviour. But increasingly some primates *are* providing positive evidence. Having a theory of mind has always been considered central to ethical status as a 'person', so any evidence for it in other species has moral implications far beyond the scope of this book. What follows is only a brief summary—each topic deserves a book, and most of them are being written. Theory of mind is a very vague and all-encompassing term, and it will be simpler if we sort out a few of the possible components of it by using evidence from people, before looking at the evidence from primates. (Although in fact the term was invented by primatologists, needing a label for how a chimpanzee could manage to solve a task that depended on realizing another individual's intentions.)

To start with, imagine playing this game with a 10-year-old child. (A smart child, who has been playing the flute and was enjoying programming a computer before he breaks off to play with you.) Three distinctive boxes are put on the table between you and the child. Your helper, another adult, says 'I must go out for a few minutes, but I will put my money in this round red box for safe keeping. I'll be back soon.' She places a coin in the box and goes out. You say to the child, in a conspiratorial tone, 'Let's play a little trick on her: we'll move the coin from that red box to the long, green one!' Gleefully, obviously enjoying such games with adults, the child helps move the coin. Your helper does not return immediately, and in the interim you ask the child, 'Did you see which box she put her coin in?' The child has no doubts: 'Yes! The red one!' Then you say, 'And where is it now?' Again, there is no confusion: 'The long, green one!' Finally, you ask, 'Well, when she comes back, where will she look for her coin?' The answer is immediate and positive: 'In the long, green box!' No, that is not a typographical error, that is the exact response that some children give. They are autistic. Autism is usually associated with some developmental retardation, but the 10-year-old in my example had a mental age of 5 years, well above the age at which every normal child will say 'The red box!' in answer to the question, and consider it a very obvious test they've been set. Uta Frith, Alan Leslie, and Simon Baron-Cohen adapted this little game as a task to set to autistic children, because they suspected that autism might cause a deficit in theory of mind (Baron-Cohen *et al.* 1985; the task was originally invented by Wimmer and Perner (1983) for use with normal children, who make the same errors as autistics up to about 3½ years of age). Mothers of autistic children consistently report that their child does not understand jokes or games properly, even though they seem very intelligent in other ways. Jokes often rely on someone being fooled into a false belief, and games require players to pretend to believe something they know not to be true, really. Perhaps, Frith and her colleagues wondered, autistic children cannot understand situations where belief and reality do not accord.

Alan Leslie (1987) proposes this most formally, suggesting that the underlying deficit in autism is an inability to hold in memory two sets of mutually contradictory information at the same time. As adults, we do this all the time: our minds are full of untrue facts that we are well aware of. We know the 'fact' that the Sun revolves around the Earth; and we attach to this the marker that people used to believe this before Galileo, but that it is false. We know that we are invisible; from the viewpoint of the friend we are playing hide-and-seek with, whereas of course we are quite visible from where we are crouched. We know that we are innocent; that is, innocent as far as the taxman knows, whereas in fact we know that we were meant to declare those holiday earnings. And so on. Keeping separate what *we* believe, from what we know *another* person believes, or from what we *want* them to come to believe, or from what we know *used* to be true but isn't now, or from what we *pretend* to believe in the game, is so routine for most people that we seldom consider what we are doing. If we were unable to do any of these things, the consequences would be more far-reaching than failure to enjoy 'let's pretend' games, make jokes, or defraud taxmen. The automatic way in which we take account of the different views, background, emotions, and aptitudes of other people—sometimes called empathy—is fundamental to real communication and interpersonal understanding. And this is just where autistic children are apparently handicapped, often so at variance with their evident high intelligence in other spheres.

The autistic child's deficit is very specific to understanding people. (I should point out that the definition of autism is difficult, and many children diagnosed as autistic have very major problems with using language or in relating to people; this is not true of the children studied in the experiments discussed here.) In another study, the same team looked at the children's ability to put pictures in order, so they told a story (Baron-Cohen *et al.* 1986). If the story was based on physical cause and effect (e.g. a man next to a rock on top of a hill; a man on top of a hill pushing a rock; a man on top of a hill and a rock halfway down; and so on) then normal and autistic children were equally good at sequencing a muddled set of pictures. Some interpersonal sequences, for instance ones connected by visible conflict and subsequent distress, did not present a problem: the distress could be seen. But some sequences depicted people getting the wrong belief or failing to realize facts. When understanding this was essential to getting the correct sequence, autistic children had difficulty. For instance, the following sequence requires empathy to understand the distress: a child putting her doll down and turning to a flower; a child picking a flower with a doll behind her on the ground; a child sniffing a picked flower with another child taking up the doll behind her back; a child crying, holding a flower but with no doll to be seen. Here, autistic children fail.

Causal agency

In evaluating animal abilities to understand other individuals' thoughts, we have to be careful in ways that may seem pedantic at first sight. For

Figure 8.1 Gomez has shown that when very young, a gorilla wanting to gain an out-of-reach reward will *push* a human (or an inanimate object) to the place and climb up. At a later age, it will instead gently *lead* the human to the place and push the human's hand towards the task needing to be done, as here. (Drawing by P. Barrett, from description in Gomez 1991.)

instance, understanding of an individual as a causal agent is not the same as understanding their mental states, although in everyday life we usually equate mental wants with goal-directed actions. Realizing that other individuals are causal agents would be a great boon to a social animal, such as many monkeys and apes.

The development of comprehension of causal agency has been studied by Juan Carlos Gomez in a female infant gorilla, as she dealt with everyday examples of the problem of getting to out-of-reach objects (Gomez 1991). Köhler had originally set this sort of task to his chimpanzees, along with stick-raking tasks. He noted that he had to be very careful to prevent the chimpanzees using him as a tool to help them—apparently the natural approach for a chimpanzee with such a problem. Gomez' young gorilla was just the same. At first, she solved the problem by pushing a chair or convenient human into position and climbing up it. Later, at about 18 months, she began instead to request the human's help by the use of eye contact and leading by the hand, moving the person's hand towards the task she wanted them to do (Fig. 8.1). This shows the development of a practical understanding of the human as causal agent, but we cannot assume that the gorilla necessarily attributed any mental states to the people that she got to help her.

Visual perspective-taking: appreciation of geometry

In normal life, seeing is believing. However, strictly speaking, there is an intervening step: if we know that someone has seen an event, we deduce that they know it happened. At first sight this seems a hair-thin distinction to make. Yet it turns out that when autistic children are given a test of what someone else can *see*, they are no different to any other children. For instance, if the experimenter puts a number of large toys around the room and asks 'What am I looking at?' the autistic child has no trouble replying accurately, even though the child is not looking in the same direction as the experimenter (Baron-Cohen 1991). Yet we know that the same child will systematically fail tasks that require understanding of what someone else *knows*—knowledge that results from what the person has been able to see. So we have to recognize that it is possible to understand that an object is in full view of a person and yet not appreciate what that person will know about it as a consequence. We must therefore be careful to distinguish in the evidence from animals, between evidence for an ability to understand another individual's visual perspective, and ability to understand their knowledge and mental perspective.

The need for perspective-taking in some kinds of imitation has already been mentioned, in Chapter 6. Without some understanding of viewpoint, simple acts would be mirror-reversed when copied, and even rats do not make this reversal error; complex copying would be a shambles. There is no theoretical need for a theory of mind (*mental* perspective-taking) in order to imitate, although this is often claimed. Certainly, having an understanding of the goals and knowledge of another individual would encourage an animal to imitate useful aspects of their behaviour. But only an ability to take the visual perspective of others is absolutely crucial for imitation. So while we cannot be sure that great apes take mental perspectives into account on the basis of their imitative ability, we can be reasonably confident that they understand visual perspective.

There is also evidence that several species of monkey are able to work out what can be seen from another's viewpoint—even when this differs from what they can see themselves—from certain records of deception (primate deception is described more fully in Chapter 9). For instance, Nelly Ménard has described the reaction of nervous, only partly habituated Barbary macaques (*Macaca sylvana*) in the Atlas mountains of Algeria, to suddenly finding themselves close to her: 'They initially had a barely perceptible reaction of surprise, then continued to walk in an apparently unconcerned manner in the original direction. They would then pass behind a tree but did not re-appear on the other side. After several minutes I realized that they had disappeared. I found them sometimes 25–30 m away in a direction given by a line between three points: observer, tree and macaque'. She gradually discovered that what the monkeys were doing was sneaking off directly down the narrow cone of invisibility behind a tree. Their behaviour was too precise for them to have arrived at the tactic by using a simple rule, such as 'only retreat when the person is invisible'. Mosquitoes, homing in on a body to bite, follow a rule as simple as that. They travel down the cone of warm, damp air rising from the body by changing direction each time they enter cool, dry air, as if they were bouncing down the sides of a tube. But there is no sign in the actions of Ménard's monkeys of the characteristic error-corrections such a rule would lead to: blundering out of the cone of invisibility, seeing the person again, changing direction again, and so on. The monkeys' behaviour looks much more like a result of their calculation of interpersonal geometry (which may be a quite unconscious process for them).

A similar rudimentary geometric appreciation is shown in this description of baboons (*Papio hamadryas*) watched by Hans Kummer (in Byrne and Whiten 1990) in Ethiopia (Fig. 8.2):

(a)

(b)

Figure 8.2 Two cartoons, both illustrating Hans Kummer's observation of a female hamadryas baboon grooming secretly (see text). Each assumes that the female attributes mental states to the male – for which there is no good evidence. In (a) she attributes his physical view of the situation, with no other baboon to be seen; in (b) she attributes to him a belief that no other baboon is present, an even stronger claim. (Drawings by D. Bygott.)

An adult female spent 20 min in gradually shifting in a seated position over a distance of about 2 m to a place behind a rock about 50 cm high where she began to groom the subadult male follower of the group—an interaction not tolerated by the adult male. As I was observing from a cliff slightly above [the animals] I could judge that the adult male leader could, from his resting position, see the tail, back and crown of the female's head, but not her front, arms and face: the subadult male sat in a bent position while being groomed and was also invisible to the leader. The leader could thus see that she was present, but probably not that she groomed. The only aspect that made me doubt the arrangement was accidental was the exceptionally slow, inch by inch shifting of the female.

In both these records, the animals may very well have learnt, by trial and error, that certain configurations have useful properties—in permitting desired but difficult actions. However, to learn these tactics (even by trial and error) it is essential that the *configurations* be recognizable: and they are only recognizable by virtue of their geometry. Individuals incapable of understanding the projection of a straight line through space (a line of sight) could never learn tactics that work by preventing line of sight vision. This is a very simple sense of the term 'geometry', to be sure, but it is still a degree of sophistication beyond association learning. Without this sophistication, the best a female in the predicament of Kummer's hamadryas baboon could do would be to groom the forbidden follower male only when the leader male was invisible to her: 'if the leader is out of sight it is safe to groom subordinates'. Most secretive behaviour of primates and other animals can, in fact, be accounted for by rule-learning as simple as this; but records like Ménard's and Kummer's suggest that monkeys as well as apes can perform simple geometrical calculation of what other individuals can see.

Joint role comprehension

Common chimpanzees show an understanding of others' perspectives that goes rather beyond a purely visual transformation. They can take either role in a co-operative task, when they have learnt only one of the two roles necessary for joint success. Daniel Povinelli has devised a task in which one individual could see which of two handles would give food rewards when pulled, but could not reach the handle (Povinelli *et al.* 1992*a*). To succeed at the task, this individual had to indicate the correct choice to a second individual, who could reach the handle but not see if it was correct—both thereby gained food rewards (Fig. 8.3). Chimpanzees succeeded in learning either role. More importantly, they were able—without further training—to assume the other's role when they were reversed. Monkeys, by contrast, showed no such immediate comprehension of their new role (Povinelli *et al.* 1992*b*). The chimpanzees' performance implies that they understand the logical organization of the (joint) task, including

Figure 8.3 A rhesus monkey tested in Povinelli, *et al.*'s (1992*b*) role-reversal experiment, pointing for a naïve human informant. (Photo by D. Povinelli, courtesy of University of Massachusetts Primate Library.)

co-ordination of the two roles—a similar sort of insight into behavioural organization to that involved in program-level imitation. What is more, it strongly suggests that they understand what the other needs to *know* in order to succeed—hinting that chimpanzees can represent the knowledge of other individuals. The next section pursues this theme, examining evidence for knowing about knowledge, as a first step towards a full theory of mind—which would also include knowing about emotion, about false belief, and consciousness of self.

Knowing about knowledge

In the game used to illustrate the theory of mind deficit in autism, the child failed to understand a false belief ('she believes that X, whereas I believe X is false'). To understand another's false belief is more complicated than just knowing that they know something that you don't. Understanding of relative knowledge or ignorance is also easier to test in animals.

The ability to comprehend what another individual knows (because it is able to see something invisible to oneself), has been specifically tested in rhesus monkeys and chimpanzees (Premack 1988; Povinelli *et al.* 1990, 1991). In these tests, the primate could choose the advice of one of two

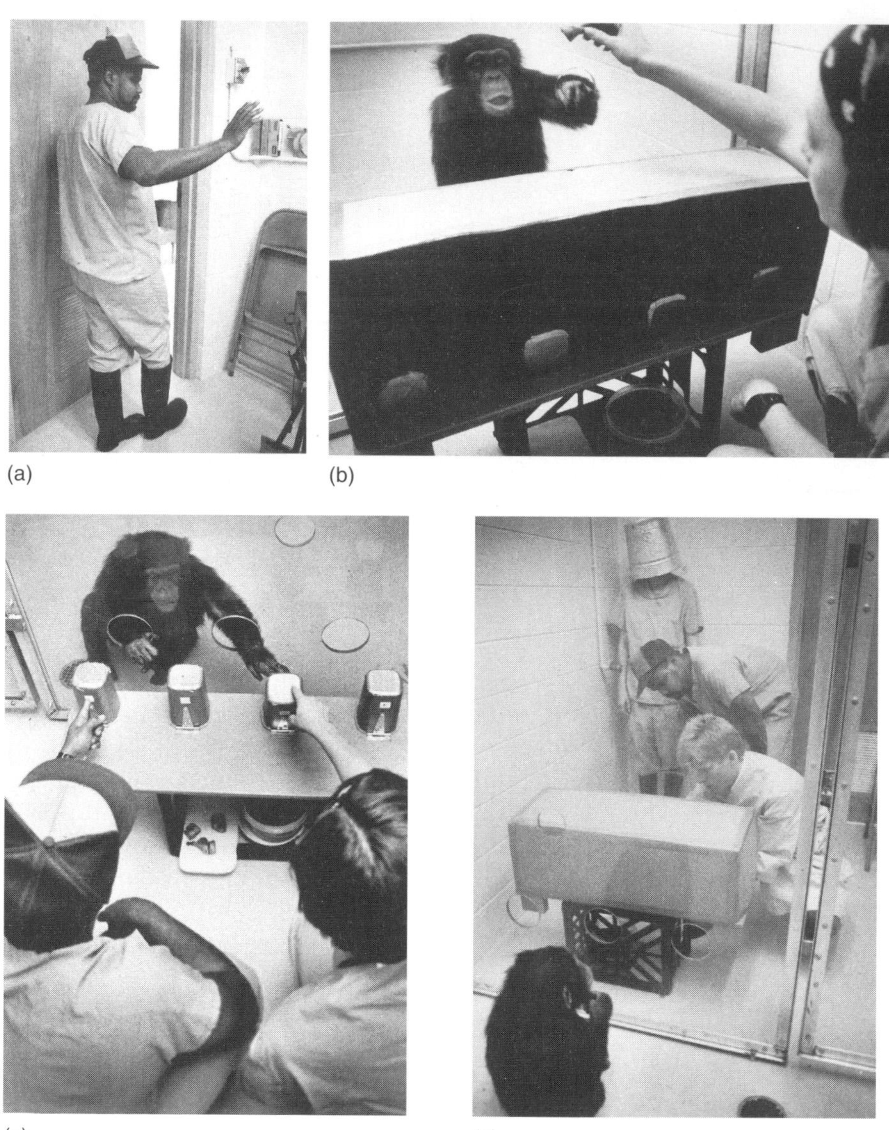

(a) (b) (c) (d)

Figure 8.4 Do chimpanzees understand the connection between seeing and knowing? (a) The 'guesser' (see text) leaves the room, as the chimpanzee watches; (b) the 'knower' then hides food under one cup; (c) the guesser returns and both simultaneously point to a different cup; (d) a transfer procedure with vision of the guesser obscured by a bucket over the head. (From Povinelli, *et al.* 1994; photos by Donna Bierschwale, courtesy of University of Southwestern Lousiana New Iberia Research Center.)

human helpers in deciding which container was baited with food (Fig. 8.4). The act of baiting was hidden from the primate, but visible to one of the humans. The other human was prevented from seeing by a screen in the way, by being out of the room or by pulling a paper bag or other cover over the head at the crucial time, in different versions. Some, though not all, chimpanzees can reliably pick the helper who would be expected to know the right answer. Rhesus monkeys failed to pick the correct helper even after a long series of trials; however, negative results are always hard to interpret. Monkeys do not naturally point or spontaneously learn to do so in captivity. They do not as infants play extensively with objects like paper bags, even if given the chance. And they interpret a stare at another individual as a threat. None of these characteristics would aid learning in the task, and none applies to apes like the chimpanzee. Just as in human intelligence testing it is very difficult to devise a 'culture-fair' test, in animal work it is hard to find a test that is 'species-fair'. The chimpanzees, on the other hand, succeed on the task: does this prove that chimpanzees can understand the difference between the mental states of ignorance and knowledge? Almost. No one experiment or observational study, however clever it is, is going to 'prove' such a crucial point, on its own. In this particular case, it is still possible that the chimpanzees succeeded in a way that does not depend on knowing about knowledge. For instance, they might have learnt to rely more on people who stay nearby rather than leave the room, or never to trust anyone who puts a bag over his or her head! The suggestions sound silly, but that is only because we, as normal humans, find it hard to imagine *not* being able to understand another's mental viewpoint. The alternative accounts would require very rapid trial-and-error learning, but haplorhine primates may well be adapted to just such rapid learning in social situations (as we will see in Chapter 13). *Immediate* comprehension would increase our confidence in the chimpanzee's results being due to insight into others' knowledge, but a trial-by-trial analysis was not published. Nevertheless, the fact is that this ingenious study is *not* an isolated one, but part of a growing body of evidence converging on the idea that great apes can take into account other individuals' knowledge—a first small step towards discovering whether any animals can be said to 'think'.

Understanding intentions and accidents

A further aspect of understanding other people concerns their goals and intentions, and how these differ from our own. Can an animal realize that others' goals may be different from its own, and can it appreciate the difference between deliberate and accidental actions? The ability of chimpanzees to switch roles in a two-partner co-operative task, without training for the new role, already suggests that chimpanzees might understand intentions. This has also been tested directly. A captive chimpanzee was presented with a series of short film clips, each of which depicted a human with a problem (Premack and Woodruff 1978). For instance, a shivering man was seen in a bare room with an oil heater, but no matches with which to light it. The ape was given no formal training, but merely shown several photographs, and spontaneously chose the photograph of the object

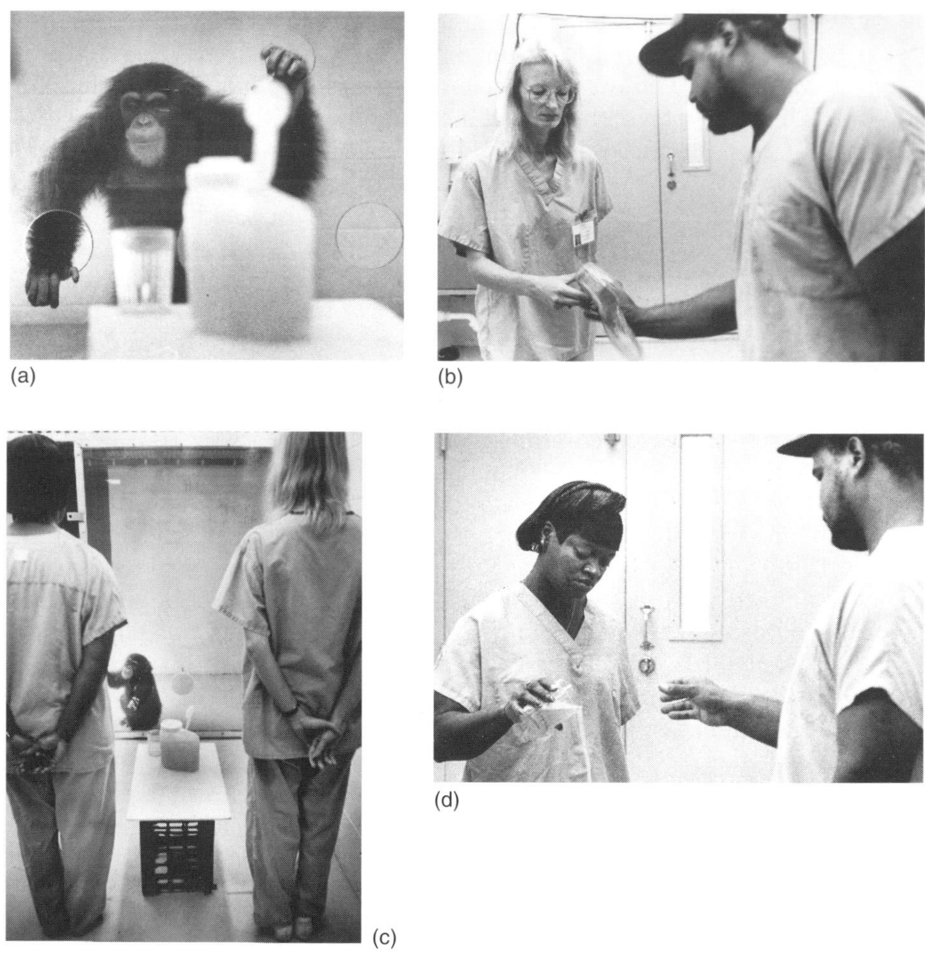

Figure 8.5 Do chimpanzees understand the difference between accidental and deliberate harm? (a) The chimpanzee points to an actor (previously unfamiliar to the chimpanzee) who is holding juice, requesting it be given, and watches carefully what happens. (b) One actor accidentally spills juice while passing it to the trainer; (d) the other deliberately pours it away. (c) Afterwards, the chimpanzee is given a choice between the actors: will it avoid the 'malicious' and pick the 'clumsy' one? (From D.J. Povinelli, and H.K. Perilloux, H.K. (unpublished manuscript.) 'A preliminary note on chimpanzees' reactions to intentional and accidental behavior with equivalent outcomes'. Photos by Donna Bierschwale, courtesy of University of Southwestern Lousiana New Iberia Research Center.)

that would solve the problem, in the example given, a box of matches. The researchers termed this empathic understanding of the needs of another individual 'theory of mind', the origin of the term; however, it is not impossible that the chimpanzee's success was based on non-empathic means (for instance, associating matches with fires).

Understanding of the difference between accident and deliberate malice has also been shown experimentally in a chimpanzee, who was deprived of a valued drink, in circumstances engineered by the researcher, Daniel Povinelli (Fig. 8.5). On one occasion, the loss was through an 'obvious accident' by an apparently well-intentioned human, who tripped. On another, a different person brought the drink but then deliberately poured it on the ground in front of the chimpanzee. Afterward, the animal consistently chose the 'clumsy' person for its drink requests (Povinelli 1991). Both these fascinating experiments are in need of replication, as both were carried out on only one subject, and with fewer controls than would now be expected. For instance, the non-verbal communication accompanying the deliberate pouring away of a drink is almost bound to be more threatening than that shown when a drink is offered; chimpanzees are highly sensitive to such signals, which are almost exactly the same in chimpanzee and human communication. Nevertheless, the balance of evidence at present would credit the chimpanzee with an ability to judge intentions and needs—at least of humans in experiments, and so presumably of other chimpanzees in nature. No evidence has ever been offered that chimpanzees share another aspect of empathy, an understanding of (and sometimes sympathy with) the emotions of others.

Reflecting on oneself

Another facet of the process of coming to understand the distinction between other and self is the ability to 'see ourselves as others see us'—literally. Once we have the ability to represent how things look to others, with their different knowledge and experience, one thing that we might think about is how we look to them. How behaviour and appearance will be construed by others is an important consideration to most humans. This opens the possibility of learning how we actually look to others—through the use of modern devices like reflective mirrors and closed-circuit TV, or older ones like the still surfaces of ponds. Can animals understand their reflections?

Most animals, when confronted with a mirror in which they can see themselves, give a reaction appropriate to a strange member of their species and sex (Fig. 8.6). For instance, a male shore bird, finding a mirror placed in its breeding territory, will display aggressively at the 'interloping male' in the mirror. Some animals will subsequently habituate, or get bored, and show no further reaction to mirrors. Domestic kittens and puppies first threaten the 'animal' in the mirror, then try and investigate by pawing behind the glass, and gradually come to avoid or ignore mirrors altogether. Most adult domestic cats and dogs therefore ignore mirrors.

Monkeys are unusual, in that they can learn to *use* mirrors, for instance to see round a corner and identify another monkey there (Anderson 1984; Fig. 8.7). This supports the evidence from cases of deception, that monkeys

Figure 8.6 Monkeys and apes often make inappropriate 'social' responses to seeing their reflections: (a) a gorilla stares at and threatens his reflection in a forest pool; (b) a rhesus macaque threatens her mirror reflection with an open mouth display (photo by J. Anderson).

can work out simple, everyday geometry. But they still systematically fail to understand their *own* reflection in a mirror, and continue to react to it as if it were a stranger (Fig. 8.6). How do we know? There are many ways an animal might show that it knew that a reflection was itself, for instance

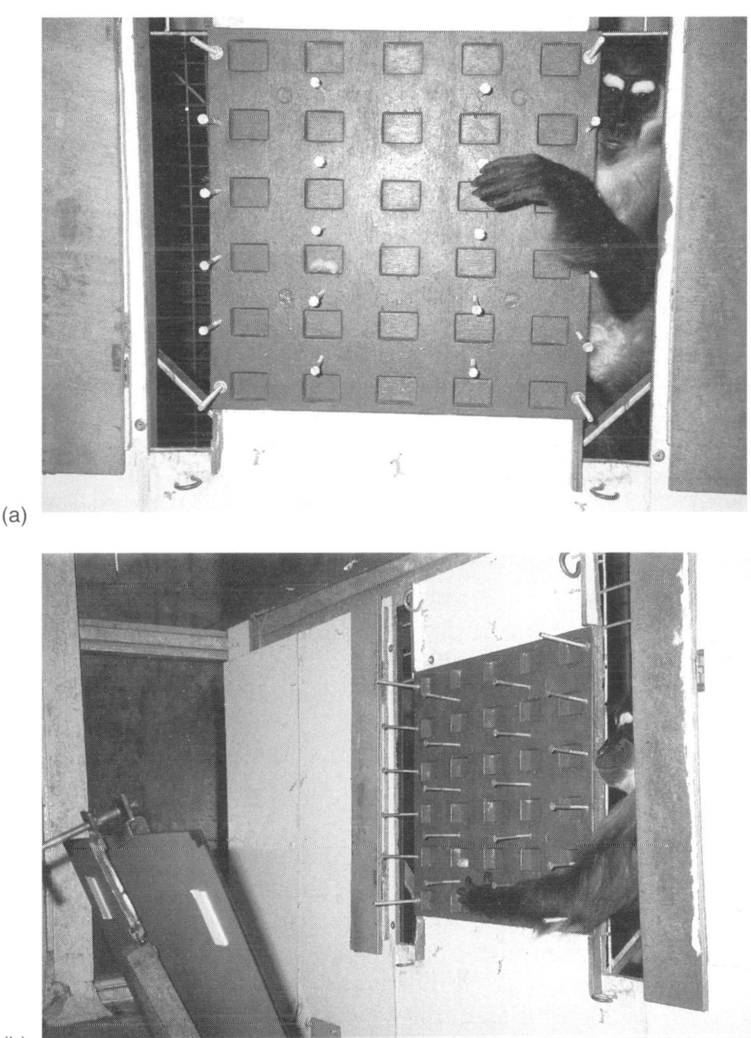

(a)

(b)

Figure 8.7 After prolonged experience, monkeys are able to solve problems by using mirrors to see out-of-view objects. (a) In an experiment designed by Heather McKiggan, a mangabey *Cercocebus torquatus* reaches through a narrow slit to grope for a peanut; the task is difficult because spikes prevent sweeping searches of many holes at once; (b) the mangabeys learned to use a mirror to guide their hand. (Photos by H. McKiggan.)

using it to explore parts of its body only visible in a mirror or watching the reflection while it systematically changed its expression (Fig. 8.8). Some of these signs may not be fully diagnostic, but Gordon Gallup has devised a strong test of whether an animal realizes that a reflection is itself. First, the animal must be given plenty of time to get used to mirrors and see reflections of the world, including itself, in the mirror. (Even adult humans cannot understand what a mirror is doing if they lack prior experience of mirrors altogether, as was dramatically illustrated when the first contacts were made earlier this century with several New Guinean tribes, still living in a stone-age economy. They reacted with fear and incomprehension to the 'people in the glass', until the device was demonstrated clearly to them.) Then, under anaesthetic, an odourless and smooth paint spot is applied to some part of the animal's body, for instance high on its forehead or on the back of its hand. When it recovers, its behaviour is watched closely—and the mirror left nearby. Monkeys immediately notice spots of paint on their hands and investigate them, trying to get the paint off. However, when they walk full in front of a large mirror and glance at their reflection, they show no sign of surprise at the vivid paint mark on their brow, nor any attempt to touch it. They simply ignore it.

Gordon Gallup (1970) has shown that, in complete contrast, chimpanzees and orang-utans are generally able to interpret their reflection in a mirror correctly. When they recover from anaesthetic, they at first show no indication of knowing they have been marked, but as soon as they catch sight of their face in a mirror they immediately reach and touch the spot, just as we would do. Oddly, several gorillas tested in this way have failed. However, the reactions of one captive gorilla, Koko, show that she does recognize herself in a mirror (Patterson and Cohn 1994). Instead of the rather drastic procedure of anaesthetic, the researchers used the trick of wiping Koko's brow with a cloth. She got used to this gentle and unthreatening manoeuvre; usually the cloth was just slightly damp with water. Then, occasionally, a harmless water-based paint was hidden on the cloth, and a large coloured mark thus placed above her eyebrows so that she could not see it directly. (I should explain that Koko is no ordinary gorilla, but has been raised much like a human and also taught the symbols of American sign language, a topic to which we will return.) Again she paid no attention, until a few minutes later she caught sight of herself in a mirror—and jumped in comical 'double take', proceeding to investigate the mark while carefully looking at her reflection all the while. This did not particularly surprise those who work with Koko, since she had already discovered a black pigment spot in her mouth with the aid of a mirror, and would readily reply 'Me, Koko' in sign language if asked what her reflection was (Fig. 8.9).

Is Koko 'special' because she has been taught a sort of language, or because she has been brought up like a human; why should she succeed and other gorillas fail? Certainly, there is plenty of individual variation in

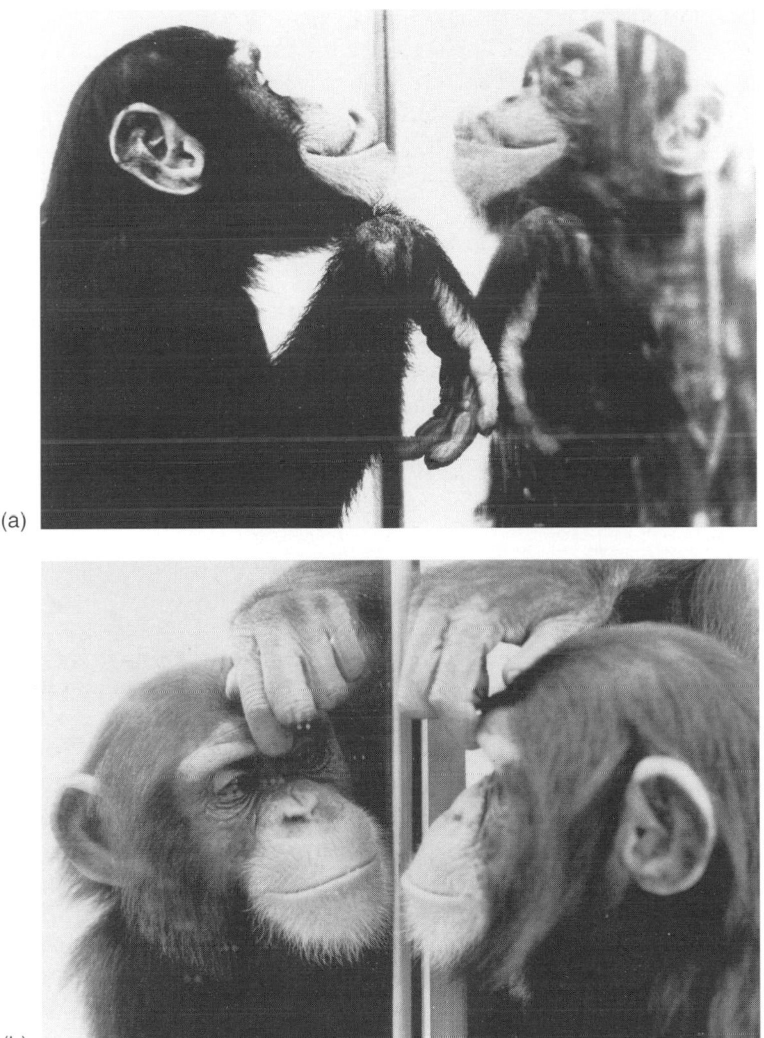

Figure 8.8 Chimpanzees readily learn to use a mirror in ways that show understanding of their own reflection, for example (a) examining the underside of the tongue, or (b) picking at a part of the brow ridge the animal could not otherwise see (photos by Donna Bierschwale, courtesy of University of Southwestern Lousiana New Iberia Research Center.)

mirror self-recognition even in chimpanzees. Some individuals fail to pass the mirror test, especially animals that were very old when they had their first experience with mirrors (Swartz and Evans 1991; Povinelli *et al.* 1993). It is possible that particular developmental circumstances are needed to bring out the latent potential of self-recognition. (Unsurprisingly,

Figure 8.9 Other species of ape also learn to react appropriately to their reflection in a mirror. The gorilla Koko contorts her face to see a spot on her cheek better in the mirror. (Photo by F. G. Patterson and R. H. Cohn.)

very young chimpanzees also fail; in humans, self-recognition develops gradually, young children behaving just like non-primates at first.) Furthermore, the mark-test may be a very conservative measure of ability; passing it is reliably associated with using mirrors for bodily self-exploration, but some apes which do the latter still fail the mark test. Another possibility is to do with the behavioural styles of different species of apes: gorillas are gentle in their investigation and tend to 'look but not touch', whereas orang-utans and especially chimpanzees are enthusiastic and often destructive in their actions (very reminiscent of the titi/squirrel monkey difference explored by Visalberghi and Mason, Chapter 7). This may make many gorillas, but not those with the extra confidence given by very special treatment, rather disengaged from apparatus such as mirrors put in their cages. They therefore may not learn the properties of mirrors after experiences that would have been quite sufficient for another species of ape. For the moment, then, I will assume that all great apes, but no monkeys, have the potential to understand whether reflections in mirrors are of themselves.

What does this mean? Gallup has used mirror self-recognition as an indication that an animal has a self-concept. He argues that with no 'I-concept' to label, we would not be able to understand exactly what was on the mirror surface when we looked into it, and the task of interpreting our own face reflected in a mirror would become impossible. If monkeys could not understand *anything* reflected in mirrors, as is true of most animals, several other interpretations would be possible. Jim Anderson's discovery (1984) that monkeys can guide their actions with a mirror makes their failure at mirror self-recognition all the more striking, and supports Gallup's theory.

How do mirror-self-recognizing organisms make the intuitive leap to treating self and other as equivalent in mind? There are two possibilities. A concept of self might be acquired by learning first that mental states are useful concepts in predicting the behaviour of others; then, by taking the others' point of view, the self, too, is viewed as having similar mental attributes. Or, an intuitive understanding of self may come first, and later the individual finds it useful to attribute similar mental states to others—the better to understand their mind and behaviour—a view defended by Nicholas Humphrey (1983). In essence, his idea is that we treat others as different versions of our own self, and therefore endow them with similar properties—knowledge, intentions, and so on. On either theory, there is a necessary connection between mirror self-recognition and attribution of mental states to others.

However, great apes do not carry out the full range of behaviours that a human would do in front of a mirror, so their idea of 'self' probably differs from a human one. They certainly remove material that defaces their appearance, and occasionally try out the effect of adding things to their image in a playful way: Gallup (1975) noted a chimpanzee stick celery leaves up her nose and swat at them! But there is no evidence of modifying the image in a way to change or conform to the views of other individuals (Mitchell 1993). Nothing in great ape mirror-use matches the way we comb hair or put on make-up or jewellery, whereas human adornment is a universal trait.

In summary, there are a number of lines of evidence that converge on a strong suggestion of a monkey/ape difference in the way other individuals can be understood, and how their (different) viewpoints can be represented. Most experiments have shown chimpanzees successful, and some show rhesus monkeys failing, at tasks which require some understanding of another individual's mental states as well as visual perspective. None of these tasks go as far as to show understanding of false belief, which young children of 4–5 years old age certainly have, whereas much younger children (and autistic children) do not. On most tasks, the other great apes have not been tested, but if mirror self-recognition depends on the same underlying ability then all great apes have the potential ability to understand some mental states. Most of the demonstrations we have seen have been in more or less artificial circumstances, giving us little appreciation of what the ability to attribute mental states to others might be good for. What actual use is it to have a theory of mind? There are several possibilities, which form the subject of the next chapter.

Further reading

Many of the issues of animal understanding in this chapter are taken up in A. Whiten (ed.) (1991) *Natural theories of mind* (Basil Blackwell, Oxford), although the book is oriented towards developmental psychology; see especially chapters by Gomez, Leslie, Baron-Cohen, and Whiten and Byrne. There is an enormous literature on mirror self-recognition, but many recent advances are described in S. Parker, M. Boccia and R. Mitchell (1994) *Comparative reflections on self-awareness in animals and humans* (Cambridge University Press, Cambridge).

9
What use is a theory of mind?

The great apes, especially the chimpanzee, evidently do have some understanding of other individuals, as intentional agents with knowledge and desires different to their own. To some extent, great apes can attribute mental states: they have a 'theory of mind'. In some of the cases we saw in Chapter 8, the demonstrated achievement appears very unlikely to be what originally favoured evolution of the underlying competence. For instance, an individual great ape can sometimes predict how another individual might solve a problem, react sensibly to its own face reflected in a mirror, and efficiently take over another's role in a co-operative task. In the wild state, these skills seem useless, yet there is no doubt that mental-state attribution did evolve. Can we put forward any more plausible benefit that theory of mind might confer, as a possible candidate for its original selective advantage?

The clue may lie in the other set of abilities in which we have seen evidence that great apes can understand other individuals: their ability to distinguish between malevolent and benign intentions, and between ignorance and possession of knowledge. These distinctions could be useful in a number of ways, all of which involve altering other individuals' beliefs. The alteration may be with ill intent, in the manipulation of others' behaviour for one's own ends and avoiding being manipulated in turn—deceit. Or the intent may be benign, in realizing that one's offspring or friend would benefit from knowing a particular fact—teaching. It would aid in both these spheres to be capable of understanding that others know or believe different information to oneself. What evidence exists, then, that any animals deceive or teach each other?

The intentionality problem

The question is not as straightforward as it seems. There is often ambiguity, in our everyday usage, as to whether we mean 'deception' and 'teaching' to apply only to *intentional* deception and *intentional* teaching. As humans, we tend to assume intention when we see a directed action which leads to profit by manipulating another's knowledge; if it were *us* doing the action, we'd certainly have intended the manipulation! But this may not always be so, and the implications for an animal's mind would then be very different. Only when we deceive or teach intentionally do we use our understanding of other individuals' mental states, our theory of mind. The *profits* from deception and teaching, however, accrue regardless of the psychological mechanisms involved. Can deception and teaching be achieved functionally, without intent to manipulate mental states? First, consider deception.

Intentionality in deception

In an act of deception, someone has to be misled into believing something that is inaccurate, by the actions of another (call them *dupe* and *agent*). If the dupe is misled by a sheer accident of the agent's behaviour, we would quite rightly not claim it was deception. This is true even if the dupe, as a direct consequence of its error, does something which causes the agent to profit. We would instead say that the agent received a windfall gain from its actions, which had accidentally misled the dupe. However, suppose the agent, after one or two lucky coincidences of this kind, was able to *notice the connection* between its action and the subsequent profit, and repeated the action in similar circumstances. Then, its act is certainly 'intentional' behaviour in one sense: it is directed towards obtaining a particular goal. However, if the agent does this because it has made a mental connection *only between an action and a result*, the behaviour is not 'intentional' in the normal sense that people mean by intentional deception. Yes, the agent intended a free lunch, but it did not intend deception as such. Unless the agent knows that the *mechanism* of its free lunch was that it *made the dupe believe something untrue*, it could not even be said to understand its act of deception, let alone intend it. Nevertheless, it has carried out a deceptive act.

This distinction, between an act's consequence and its intention, is basic in human legal systems: between manslaughter and murder, for instance. Examples of the unintentional sort of 'deception' are found in some people's domestic cats. Cats much enjoy a soft chair next to a warm fire; their owners imagine they enjoy prowling outside on dark, wet nights, but kindly owners are often reluctant to ruthlessly disturb an obviously happily settled pussycat. Some cats have discovered a trick. When they see that the favoured chair is occupied, they go to an outside door and mew loudly. Their owner leaps to his feet and goes to open the door, and then looks round for the cat. The cat is asleep on the warm chair, and obviously completely settled! I do not believe that the cat necessarily realizes how this trick succeeds (i.e. that the owner has been made to believe the cat needs urgently to go outside). Much more likely, the cats have simply made the association between their behaviour and the desired result. Cats, like all other animals, are well-equipped to record such associations, by the system called operant conditioning. Any reward contingent on an action of the cat will tend to 'reinforce' that action; warm chairs and the like will automatically reward cats that mew at outside doors, so they will do so again in the same circumstances.

An act of deception may not even be intentional in the weaker sense. The performance might have been coupled to the reception of certain releasing stimuli by evolution; the animal would then not even necessarily intend a profit (i.e. represent a goal), but might be acting purely mechanically. Eyed hawk-moths react to rapidly looming objects by flicking open their hindwings. The spot patterns on the wings give a very passable imitation of a fierce pair of eyes belonging to a large hawk. As a consequence, predators which loom up on eyed hawk-moths are suddenly confronted by a pair of eyes, apparently belonging to a much larger predator! They often desist, quickly. This sort of behaviour is treated as 'deception' in biology textbooks, but no biologist has ever meant to imply that eyed hawk-moths intend to cause predators to believe they have seen large hawks. (Discussion of intentionality is a major part of philosophy; philosophers say 'intend X', whereas cognitive psychologists say 'mentally represent the goal of X', but they mean the same.) Most biologists would assume that the moth's behaviour is reflex, and that the moth does not even intend to escape predation—although this is somewhat a matter of faith as only a moth could really tell us. The moth's 'eyes' are a fixed part of its body, the deception *strategic* in the sense that the moth is committed to the one method, by its very anatomy. Strategic deception is not the only sort of non-intentional deception found in nature: *tactical deception* can occur, where a behaviour can be switched from honest to deceptive usage. The domestic cat's trick for gaining comfy chairs is a case of tactical deception, but it is not only mammals that show such behaviour. An example in invertebrates comes from the behaviour of stomatopod shrimps (Adams and Caldwell 1990). These crustaceans fight with one arm modified as a club, often inflicting serious damage on an opponent. However, when they moult their outer skeleton, as happens regularly, the new club is soft and useless for some time. However, they do not retreat in every encounter until it hardens; they bluff, posturing just as if their club were fully functional, and often the opponent retreats. Their deception is not rigid and inflexible: if the opponent does not retreat, they quickly and invariably retreat, whereas normally they would often fight. However, Adams and Caldwell could detect no evidence of learning, and concluded the tactic was 'hard-wired' in the shrimp nervous system by genetic programming.

Intentionality in teaching

The same set of options confront us when we consider teaching. Young animals can learn from others, including their parents. The mechanism of their learning can be of several kinds, as we have already seen. Evolution will favour individuals that happen to perform acts in front of their offspring, causing them to learn survival techniques more quickly than otherwise. This is true regardless of any intention or lack of it on the parent's part. The parent's actions might still be described as teaching, in a sense.

But they would not be intentional, any more than the response of the eyed hawk-moth to looming objects or the bluffing of a soft stomatopod.

Alternatively, parents might have learnt that their offspring more quickly show the behaviours they want them to show, if they themselves perform the behaviours conspicuously in front of their offspring. If so, the parents would be intending a change in their offspring's behaviour. This could also be called teaching, with greater justification. But the parents would still not need to understand anything about why their offspring's behaviour actually changed in the desired way. Their intention is to change or encourage *behaviour* not knowledge. This parallels the example of the cat's trick of gaining access to warm, comfy chairs, and could equally be learnt by reinforcement without understanding. Finally, a parent might *understand a deficiency of knowledge* in its offspring. As a consequence of this understanding, it might try to remedy the knowledge gap: intentionally teaching the youngster what it needs to know. This final sense of teaching is what we usually mean by the term.

Levels of intentionality

It is worth emphasizing that these distinctions are easily forgotten once one comes to talk about specific cases of deception or teaching, and it is important to keep them in mind. The problem is that people are very intentional animals, so it is hard for us to empathize with creatures that are not. Humans show few behaviours which function to deceive or teach *without* their having at least an intent to achieve the profit. There are some exceptions: I have already put forward the 'babytalk' spoken to infants, as a wholly unintentional way of teaching grammar; the way we present ourselves in social situations might similarly be argued to function at a deeper level than we intend consciously. But even in the few cases that can be offered, the very fact that the real function—the true 'goal'—remains unconscious, ensures we do not get much practice at discriminating function from intention, to help us interpret other animals' actions. Of course, plenty of human behaviour is intentional only in the weak sense, where there is an intention to change behaviour but no full understanding of the mental changes that are the mechanism of the manipulation. However, humans (with certain exceptions) *can* routinely understand the intentions and knowledge of others, so we readily jump to the fully intentional level of understanding. Even where we learn a trick by a history of reinforcement similar to that I envisaged for the cat, we can easily realize how it worked afterward. The cat probably cannot, any more than it can 'understand every word I say'.

These distinctions all depend on *intentionality*, not an easy idea to bring into biology. And, as I hope will be becoming clear, this idea of intentions all depends on attributing mental states. The philosopher Daniel Dennett (1983) has introduced a nice way of looking at the different sorts of intention that may be involved. The eyed hawk-moth, flicking open its wings in response to a looming stimulus, is showing 'zero-order intentionality'—the intentionality of a simple machine, like a cash dispenser. (When sufficiently frustrated by cash dispensers, we may attribute to them much deeper and machiavellian sorts of intentionality, however!) The cat, manipulating its gullible owner into leaving the warm chair (assuming my scepticism about cats' understanding of their owners' minds is justified), is showing 'first-order intentionality'—it *does* intend (represent the goal of) gaining the chair. If it spoke English, it might grudgingly admit 'I want to sit on that chair' but I doubt if it would say 'so I'll make him believe I need the toilet and want to go outside'. And, regardless of the fact that a cat does not speak, its behaviour must have been caused by its intention (goal representation): a first-order intention, in Dennett's terms. Dennett's 'second-order intentionality' is reserved for cases when the behaviour shows that the agent has an intention that in English would be expressed 'I want him to think X' (i.e. mentally representing another's mental state). If the agent also believes 'X is not the case', then its action is (second-order) intentional deception. In the case of (second-order) intentional teaching, the agent instead believes 'X will be useful for him to know'.

Species bias and attribution

With deception or teaching that is not (second-order) intentional, it is impossible in practice to be sure if the intention is really first-order or zero-order. There is a long tradition, from Descartes onwards and especially represented in the American 'behaviourism' of Watson and Hull, that tries to explain as much as possible of animal behaviour (and usually that means 'all') as machine-like, with zero-order intentionality. The radical extreme of this tradition, following B. F. Skinner, also tries to do the same for human behaviour—which is at least fair! Too often, the behaviourist approach instead turns out to be yet another attempt to justify human uniqueness: 'animals are just like machines, humans are incomparably different'. In hard fact, there is no test for first-order intentionality. It could be that the eyed hawk-moth really does intend to deter its potential predator, and *we would never know*. Of course, it could also be that the moth intends the potential predator to believe that it has seen a big hawk, but here we can point to the complete lack of diagnostic signs of any such intent. Moths react to looming cardboard squares and to looming animals that could eat them, alike; they expose their huge 'eyes' to small animals, that might plausibly be frightened by hawks, and to big ones, including real hawks. So we have real reason to doubt that they understand about the mental states of predators.

By contrast, there are no observable differences that we can expect between zero and first-order intentions. In practice, people are all too ready to attribute first-order intentions to mammals, especially if the behavioural tactic is one the animal has learnt. People are unwilling to give the same benefit of the doubt to insects or shrimps, especially if they seem to have a tactic genetically hard-wired. But we cannot know. To avoid these unanswerable conundrums, I propose to roll together Dennett's zero- and first-order intentionality, even though they are logically distinct, and call them for short '*unintentional*', as in 'unintentional deception' and 'unintentional teaching'. Only second-order intentional behaviour forces the animal to attribute mental states to others, and I will call these '*intentional*', as in 'intentional deception' and 'intentional teaching'.

Notice that from the victim or pupil's point of view, what matters is not the possible intentionality of the treatment it receives, it is whether the treatment works. Unintentional deception and teaching are biologically just as important, if they work. We will sidle round to the big question of whether there is any evidence for intentional behaviour, by first taking a look at the evidence for both intentional and unintentional actions together, asking only:

(1) does an animal carry out a behaviour in appropriate circumstances (i.e. when it will profit from causing another's error, or when a relative or friend will profit from gaining knowledge, respectively); and

(2) does this have the appropriate functional consequence (of deception or teaching, respectively)?

Tactical deception

Since this was my own introduction to the tough problems that arise when one tries to decide the intentionality of animal behaviour, I will explain in detail. While studying the foraging of baboons, *Papio ursinus*, I was surprised to see deception. The sort of thing I saw was the device one young baboon used to gain food from a larger, adult animal (Fig. 9.1). The juvenile, named Paul, came across an adult female, Mel, just finishing the laborious process of digging up a corm. These were major sources of nutrition at that very dry, cold time of year, but difficult to obtain from the hard ground; Paul was probably unable to dig his own. He looked round, seeing no other baboon, and screamed loudly. His mother, who was higher ranking than Mel, ran into view grunting aggressively and immediately pursued Mel. When they had both left the immediate area, Paul ate the corm. According to the literature at that time, only chimpanzees (to be precise, only those chimpanzees at one field site and one zoo) ever indulged in deception like this. Beginning to doubt my eyes, I was relieved to find that my colleague, Andrew Whiten, had also seen similar tactics. We saw Paul use this tactic three times in several weeks, but never when the manipulated animal (his mother, or the leading male) was in clear view of the 'cause' of his scream. There seemed no doubt that Paul was not really hurt

Figure 9.1 An interpretation of deceptive behaviour; the letters A and T label the agent and target in the deception. The juvenile baboon Paul (A), screams when confronted with adult Mel (T) in possession of a coveted food; the 'thinks' bubble implies that he believes his mother (the social TOOL) will falsely imagine he has been attacked, an interpretation argued against in the text. (Drawing by D. Bygott.)

or frightened, and no doubt that the animal running to his aid believed the contrary: in this population, mothers did not generally come to the aid of weaned offspring having feeding conflicts.

Not all the deception we saw worked the same way: the tactic used by an adolescent male to avoid punishment, for instance (Fig. 9.2). This male, Melton, had played too roughly with an infant, who screamed in distress. Several adults, presumably including its mother, rushed to the scene and chased Melton. Instead of running away, he jumped to his hindlegs and stared, as these baboons typically do if they have seen a distant predator or another baboon troop and need to see better over the long grass. The pursuing animals stopped and also looked in the same direction as Melton, and the chase was not resumed; it was clear they all thought there was something to be seen. I, too, was at first deceived, but careful search with binoculars revealed that in fact there was no possible cause for alarm, just a rocky hillside. Baboons have sharp eyesight, but without any artificial aid to their vision, they presumably remained convinced there had been good cause for alarm.

In both examples, the behaviours were 'tactics' in the sense that the agent's behaviour was deployed in just such a way that another animal, the target, would do something to the agent's advantage (and often to the target's disadvantage). The tactics were 'deception' in the sense that they

Figure 9.2 The adolescent baboon Melton (A), pursued by an adult (T), stands and stares, aborting the chase; the 'thinks' bubble suggests that he realizes the target has been led to believe he saw a predator. (Drawing by D. Bygott.)

could not have worked unless another animal, sometimes the target, was duped into an erroneous belief. We coined the term *tactical deception* to capture a range of tricks like these, used by animals to manipulate their fellow group members (Byrne and Whiten 1985). Not knowing how much the agent understood about what it was doing, we kept intention out of our definition, but we wanted to exclude rigid and inflexible 'strategic' sorts of deception to which an animal is committed for life or at least for long periods. Our definition of *tactical deception* was a functional one: 'acts from the normal repertoire of the agent, deployed such that another individual is likely to misinterpret what the acts signify, to the advantage of the agent' (Fig. 9.3).

Acts of tactical deception involve other individuals: as *objects* to be manipulated, as *social tools* to manipulate others, or even sometimes as the *resource* to be gained. Where these animals are long-lived and spend their lives in proximity to each other as baboons do, they may have long memories, and they certainly have the ability to retaliate. There is therefore greater potential for complexity in tactical deception than in manipulations of physical objects. At first we imagined our baboons were very special in having this ability, but our fellow primatologists soon disabused us of that, when we talked to them in bars after conferences. Many we spoke to said they had seen behaviours 'just like those'. Why had they not published these fascinating data? Because they had seen only a couple of

Figure 9.3 Tactical deception is used by female mountain gorillas to avoid the mating restrictions imposed by their group leader. (a) Female Papoose solicits Titus, a non-leader silverback, with sideways glances and head movements; the couple then typically mate silently. (b) Leader males often appear justifiably suspicious of their females' absences, and will sometimes search for them. (c) In this instance the leader male Beetsme has just interrupted the pair *in flagrante*.

cases, and science is not built on anecdotes; one could get a very bad reputation by publishing such things. However, this coyness could cause a real problem. Suppose tactical deception *is* an important part of animal behaviour. A given tactic could not be used very often without counter measures developing against it, as in the famous legend of the boy who cried 'Wolf!' Tactical deception would therefore have to be frequency-dependent. Used too much, it would cause counterdeceptive tactics; used too little, and it would have no selective advantage to the user. What 'too much' and 'too little' are in practice will depend on the costs and benefits of the situation: a tactic that causes little hurt to its targets, but great gain to its agent, might perhaps become fairly frequent, especially if it were subtle and the fraud hard to detect, and especially if individuals of the species had poor memory. From its very nature, tactical deception in primates (which have excellent memories) should be infrequent, very subtle, or both. If primatologists saw it all the time, there would have to be some mistake. The reality was just what we would expect: many primatologists had seen tactical deception but only rarely. Yet this rarity was leading to *nothing* being published: a vicious circle.

Who deceives?

We tackled the problem of under-reporting by making a broad survey of all the behavioural scientists that we could contact who might have relevant observations, asking them to report cases of behaviour that matched our definition or our examples. An initial attempt, writing to those primatologists that we happened to know were in a good position to record subtle primate behaviours, showed the phenomenon to be both widespread and interesting in primates (Whiten and Byrne 1988). (In fact, although we did not know it at the time, we were not alone in our interest: Bob Mitchell was already busy working on animal deception in 1985. The fact that the analysis of deception he, quite independently and earlier, devised (Mitchell 1986) is so similar to our own is encouraging, although for years afterwards the 'rival camps' distrusted each other!) Our first survey showed that a more extensive one would be worthwhile, so we devised a more systematic strategy for finding informants, enlisting the help of the main international societies of primatologists and animal behaviourists to canvass all their members. This reached a far wider pool of potential respondents, but despite our efforts it was essentially only primate researchers who had anything to report. *Domestic* cats and dogs use tactical deception frequently (we have received many convincing observations), but it seems to be a rarity in the wild among non-primates.

Our compilation of primate records (Byrne and Whiten 1990) contains 253 accounts of behaviour that look like tactical deception. All are described carefully by skilled, respected primatologists; they are not 'anecdotes' in the usual derogatory sense of stories with doubtful pedigree, or the causal observations of untrained people. But, all the same, there are many difficulties in interpreting survey information. Maybe a record of 'deception' was just an accidental windfall from mere coincidence, a coincidence only noticed by the scientist not the animal. It is less exciting to report negative data: maybe some primatologists had seen nothing of the kind in years of close observation, and had not bothered to write in and tell us (although we had strongly urged them to). Subtle deceptions will be harder for people to detect, too: maybe the collection was representative for conspicuous cases of deception, but the really common types are too subtle to have been noticed. And certainly some primate species have been studied more than others, so have had more chance to prove their deceptiveness! There are plenty of problems, but we believed that it was better to grasp the nettle and accept the difficulties inherent in the messy data, rather than allow the potential insights into the evolution of intelligence to be ignored. But we were just as keen as the next primatologist not to be thought soft-headed and naïve, so we were determined to approach the data with special caution and a degree of scepticism.

For every record, we asked 'can we account for what was seen without involving tactical deception?'. Was there a deliberate act to produce a result, or could it have been a coincidence that stuck in the observer's memory and notebook by its striking nature? Is there evidence that some animal was actually led to believe something untrue, or could the tactic have worked by some other means of manipulation? Were the communicative patterns used by the animals well-enough understood by scientists to be sure one was used in an unusual, deceptive manner? Only when we were convinced that the answers were 'yes', 'yes', and 'yes' did we label the record as tactical deception. This cut the number down to only 117, 49 of these from field studies and the rest from captivity (Fig. 9.4). Our harsh procedure no doubt threw out many babies with all that bathwater, and

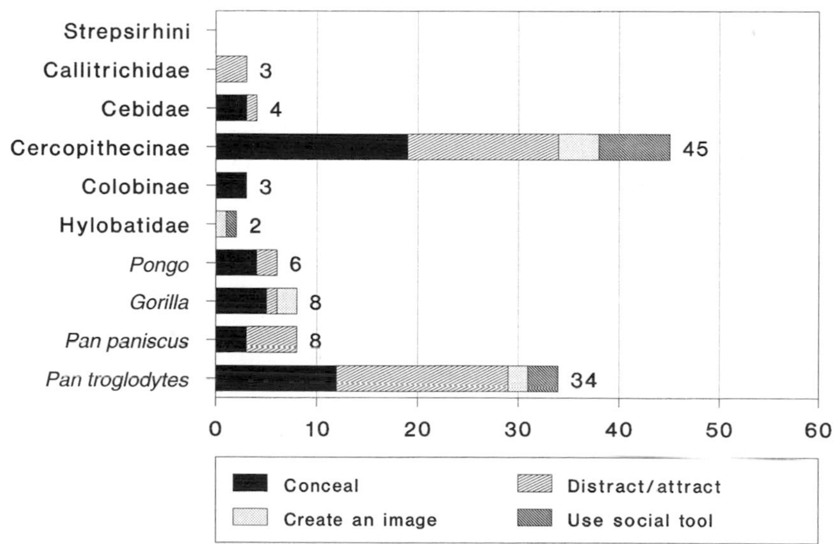

Figure 9.4 The distribution of tactical deception among primates. All records where the manoeuvre functioned by deceiving another individual are included.

perhaps offended a few observers who were convinced that their report was of true deception, but we wanted to err on the side of caution.

To make a correction for the amount of time each species had been studied (not a perfect correction, which may be impossible), we compared the frequency of deception records with the frequency of studies, for each taxonomic group of primates. They were significantly different: some primates evidently use deception more than others (Byrne and Whiten 1992). The most obvious differences were the complete lack of fully convincing cases of deception in strepsirhine primates, and the large amount perpetrated by chimpanzees and baboons. That baboons stand out is interesting, since their close relatives the macaques are, if anything, more well studied, and have certainly been a focus of an immense amount of careful and close-range observation. Yet they do not stand out from other primates in how much deception they have been seen to employ. This gave us some faith that the data were due to differences in the animals rather than the people who watch them!

Does this mean that monkeys and apes are better endowed with genetically encoded trickery, are better at learning, or are able to understand the minds of their fellow primates? The first option is unlikely. In almost every case, the tactics are not used by *every* individual of the species that is given the opportunity, they are only seen in a few animals. Nothing else in the behavioural repertoire of monkeys would lead one to expect their elaborate and flexible behaviour patterns to be tightly channelled genetically.

Learning is much more likely as an explanation. How might the young baboon, Paul, have learnt to obtain food by screaming? Suppose that in the past, he has several times approached too close to an adult or larger juvenile feeding on a desirable resource, and been threatened. As an infant or young juvenile, he would scream in real fear in such a circumstance, and his mother would run to his aid. Suppose also that on some of these occasions he gained (as an accidental windfall) a food reward, like a nutritious underground corm. Given these events, the food reward would automatically serve to reinforce his screaming in future, similar cases: he would have acquired the tactic by conditioning alone. Is this little scenario at all likely? The answer is surely 'yes'. However, more would be needed to condition the behaviour pattern as we observed it, since Paul did not scream when he met just the same situation but with his potential helper nearby or in full view. A more prolonged or fortunate history of events would be required to 'shape' the precise eliciting pattern of food-held-by-animal-subordinate-to-available-helper-who-is-itself-out-of-visual-contact. The unlikelihood of such a history occurring very often suggests that baboons possess an ability to learn rapidly in social situations. Later we will see some evidence that supports this suggestion. In the case of the cat's tactic for manipulating its owner, a much less specific reinforcement history would be required. Suppose only that the cat, in the past, genuinely wanted to go outside, but not as much as it wanted to sleep by the fire. Thwarted of its priority goal, it switched to the second alternative, and mewed at the door. However, just then, the chair became vacant (which we, but not the cat, realize was because the owner believed the cat needed urgently to go outside, and got up to help), and the cat was able to revert to its major aim. This highly plausible history would serve to condition the cat's future use of the tactic. In general, interactions with loving humans in a built environment give ample opportunities for trial-and-error learning to proceed from lucky coincidences, explaining why domestic carnivores seem more deceptive than their wild relatives.

Intentional tactical deception

It is much harder to determine whether an animal's learning a tactic is preceded or accompanied by having insight into the beliefs of the victim (that is, insight into the mechanism of the tactic). It is not, however, impossible. There are several ways that an animal could, in principle, show us that it was capable of attributing intentions to others. Andrew Whiten and I were surprised to find that some primates *did* give strong indication of this. (Remember that our study was published before the evidence of Chapter 8 was known, and at a time when few scientists believed that (second-order) intentional behaviour in animals was possible.) How could an animal show intentional understanding?

Most obviously, it might show *righteous indignation*: not simply frustration or anger at losing a prize, but a reaction specific to understanding that it had been deceived. Something like this was noticed by the Dutch developmental psychologist, Frans Plooij, while studying infant behaviour in Jane Goodall's famous chimpanzees at Gombe. These animals are so used to humans that they often try to make physical contact, which might be dangerous (especially for the chimpanzees, who can catch any human disease) and so is discouraged. On one occasion an infant chimpanzee began to groom Plooij. Any direct pushing away might easily be seen as threatening by the mother chimpanzee. Instead, Plooij tricked the youngster by acting as if he had seen a distant object of interest. He suddenly stared keenly into the bushes. The ruse worked, and the young chimpanzee went off to investigate. When she found nothing, she 'walked over to me, hit me over the head with her hand and ignored me for the rest of the day'.

Understanding what others are thinking allows us sometimes to anticipate their behaviour: so evidence of *countering the anticipated behaviour* of another animal before it could happen and so become a nuisance would be a sign of insight. The Japanese zoologist Toshisada Nishida who, like Jane Goodall, has set up and directed a major study of chimpanzees for many years in Tanzania, describes a case of counterdeception that relies on anticipation of another's behaviour. He watched Chausiku, a mother chimpanzee, reject her son Katabi's attempts to suckle by covering her nipples. This did not stop Katabi trying to gain her comfort in a subtle way. Nishida describes how 'Katabi came towards me, and began to screech/scream loudly, reaching his hand towards me (as if pointing). Then, he went round me repeatedly screech/screaming loudly, while still reaching a hand to me. Chausiku and her male consort at once glanced at me, with hair erect. I retreated a little bit away from Katabi.' Nishida was sure that the adults believed (falsely) that he had threatened or teased the infant. And the infant was, as a result, then allowed to suckle. Six months later, Katabi did just the same, but this time with a conspecific instead of a human as 'fall guy'—an older adolescent male, Masisa. Masisa showed immediate nervousness, displayed submissively at the adult male present, and left Katabi. Nishida comments that this was 'the same reaction as I did' and that 'Masisa completely understood the dangerous situation'.

The use of tactics of *counterdeception*, with no possible opportunity to learn these counters by trial and error, can be good evidence of intentional planning. A particularly compelling impression of insight into another's thoughts is given by a behavioural 'arms-race' of deception and counterdeception. This was seen during one of the American psychologist Emil Menzel's well-known experiments on spatial knowlege (1974). One chimpanzee, Belle, was shown food hidden in the middle of a large, open enclosure, while the rest of the group of young chimpanzees was locked up out of sight. She was then replaced in the group, and all the chimpanzees let out into the enclosure. Belle usually led the group to the well-hidden site, and all shared the food. However, Rock, who was stronger than her, began to refuse to share and he monopolized the reward.

Belle accordingly stopped uncovering the food if Rock was close. She sat on it until Rock left. Rock, however, soon learned this, and when she sat in one place for more than a few seconds, he came over, shoved her aside, searched her sitting place, and got the food. Belle next stopped going all the way. Rock, however, countered by steadily expanding the area of his search through the grass near where Belle had sat. Eventually Belle sat farther and farther away, waiting until Rock looked in the opposite direction before she moved toward the food at all, and Rock in turn seemed to look away until Belle started to move somewhere. On some occasions Rock started to wander off, only to wheel round suddenly precisely as Belle was about to uncover some food. Often Rock found even carefully hidden food that was 30 ft or more from Belle, and he oriented repeatedly at Belle and adjusted his place of search appropriately if she showed any signs of moving or orienting in a given direction. If Rock got very close to the food, Belle invariably gave the game away by a 'nervous' increase in movement. However, on a few trials she actually started off a trial by leading the group in the opposite direction from the food, and then, while Rock was engaged in his search, she doubled back rapidly and got some food. In other trials when we hid an extra piece of food about 10 ft away from the large pile, Belle led Rock to the single piece, and while he took it she raced for the pile. When Rock started to ignore the single piece of food to keep his watch on Belle, Belle had temper tantrums.

Is it that countering deception with deception is always compelling evidence of intentional deception? Surely not, since if tactics which are deceptive can be linked to problem situations by the 'short-cut' of operant conditioning, without need for understanding of other animals' mental states, then why should not tactics of counterdeception be learnt in the same way? Rock's first three tactics can in fact all be accounted for in learning theory terms. Only when he begins to feign disinterest, then suddenly wheels round to catch sight of Belle's action, does the evidence start to become more compelling. Rock's looking away and suddenly wheeling round is an *unusual* chimpanzee behaviour: his appropriate use of a rare action to thwart deception is the combination that convinces us that Rock understood Belle's (deceptive) intentions and can anticipate her thoughts. Menzel's evidence is especially valuable, since his chimpanzees were under continuous observation in the open field set-up, so there is known to have been *no previous opportunity for trial-and-error learning*, beyond that which could occur in the experiments.

Use of a *novel behaviour* is equally strong evidence against explanation by the 'short-cut' of reinforcement learning without intentional understanding. This is seen in another record of chimpanzee behaviour observed by Frans Plooij (Fig. 9.5). At the time of the observation, Gombe chimpanzees were only fed bananas occasionally, on a strict rota. A human-

Figure 9.5 A cartoon based on Frans Plooij's observation of a chimpanzee using the 'hide-and-peek' strategy to unmask the deception of a lower rank individual (withholding its attention from a source of food). Here, there *is* reason to think the cartoon is correct in suggesting that the chimpanzees understand some of each other's mental states. (Drawing by D. Bygott.)

operated feeding box was remotely opened when any chimpanzee whose 'turn' it was for feeding entered the clearing. The probability was low that it would be any particular chimpanzees' turn when it entered the clearing. However, one male arrived and was lucky—the box's lock was released, making a distinctive click. Just at that moment, another male also appeared, dominant to the first. The first individual did not open the box, and instead acted unconcerned. This was not unexpected: Jane Goodall has long noted that some chimpanzees are able to inhibit their interest in a food object if a dominant is present, and so gain the food later. The dominant male left the clearing, but 'as soon as he was out of sight, he hid behind a tree and peered at the individual'. Thus he was able to see the box being opened, and quickly relieved the other of his prize. The novelty of an adult chimpanzee hiding and peeping out implies that this tactic could not have been learnt by reinforcement: only actions that have some finite probability of occurring can be selectively reinforced by contingent rewards. Chimpanzees simply do not do that sort of thing, so reinforcement has nothing to work on.

In all, we identified 18 cases where it seemed to us that the balance of evidence was strongly in favour of intentional deception by a primate. In many other cases, although the actions matched what in humans we would assume to be intentional deception, it was also possible plausibly to account for the tactic's acquisition by reinforcement without invoking an understanding of another's intentions: in these cases, we will never know for sure what the animal understood. But unless there is strong evidence against it, we assumed that learning was *not* accompanied by understanding, because it was so unlikely in the first place that animals should have (second-order) intentions and understand mental states. For the 18 cases that seem intentional, any one of them can still be challenged and an explanation devised that is based on a hypothetical series of coincidences in the past that might have given rise to learning by association. However, as the hypothesized coincidences become more and more far-fetched, and the histories of possible events that just might have reinforced these tactics grew longer and longer, we decided at some point it was simpler to accept that some primates can understand intentions. This conclusion has now received support from other lines of work, as we saw in Chapter 8.

These 18 cases are not randomly distributed among monkeys and apes, nor are they distributed in the same way as tactical deception in general (Fig. 9.6). For instance, none of the many baboon records of deception were at all convincing of intentionality. Instead, the intentional records overwhelmingly point to great apes: chimpanzees of both species, gorillas, and orang-utans. As with the monkey data, in all the many cases of tactical deception in domestic dogs and cats that I know of, there is no evidence of intentional understanding. It seems that great apes, but not other animals, are able to carry out their social manipulations aided by a real appreciation of what other animals can know or be led to think.

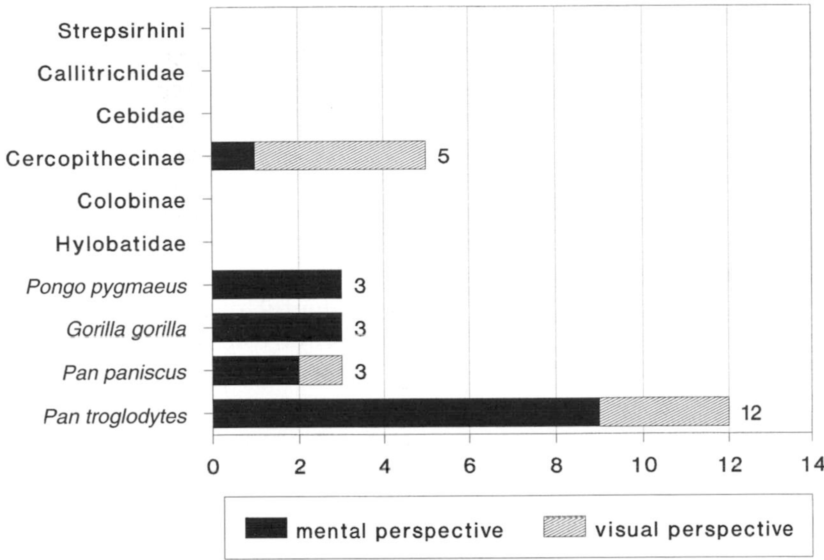

Figure 9.6 A numerical summary of those cases of tactical deception that imply taking account of another individual's perspective—both visual perspective-taking or mental-state attribution. Note that only a single case suggests mental-state attribution in a monkey; unless and until this is supported by further records or independent evidence, it is safest to regard this as a 'rogue' observation.

This does not necessarily lead to *more* deception happening in great apes. The agents and the targets of deception in these species are equally well able to anticipate the mental states of others. Indeed, this may lead to some of the deceptive tactics that are used often by monkeys being of little use to apes. There is, for instance, a strange absence of 'triadic' forms of tactical deception in great apes, where a third party is used as a social tool in some way to manipulate a target animal. The baboon that used its mother to displace an adult food competitor was using her as a social tool, in a triadic interaction; using another animal as a social tool is common in baboons. Dyadic forms of deception are equally recorded in baboons and great apes (*Papio* 23, Pongids 34), whereas social tool use is almost confined to baboons (*Papio* 7, Pongids 1). The single exception, the case described by Nishida, failed in its goal as the chimpanzee target was *not* deceived. The other kind of triadic deception used by monkeys and apes is where aggression is diverted to an innocent 'fall-guy', and in the only instance we know of where an ape has used this, the intended dupe was a human. In this case, a chimpanzee called Lucy, trained in sign language, had deposited faeces on the carpet of the scientist caring for her, Roger Fouts. When asked 'Whose dirty, dirty?' (the accepted sign for faeces) she replied 'Sue's'. Challenged by 'It's not Sue's. Whose is it?' she then tried

'Roger's'. Challenged again, she finally signed 'Sorry Lucy'. Charming as this account is, there is a serious possibility that apes may be too intelligent to be deceived by such ploys, and thus seldom use them under natural circumstances. Thus, having the ability to attribute intentions may cause overt deception to become rarer as well as more subtle.

If the deceptive tactics of monkeys lack the ape's insight into what the victim is thinking, and are learnt by mechanisms general in animals, as I have argued, why do non-primates not often show deceptive tactics under natural conditions? My belief is that, since the circumstances that could serve to condition deceptive tactics by coincidental reward are rare, only animals that learn very quickly will ever acquire much of this nature. Monkeys must be quick learners (at least under social circumstances). The rapidity of learning necessary for opportunistic acquisition of deceptive tactics by trial and error is very clearly revealed in recent experimental work of Sabine Coussi-Korbel (Fig. 9.7). She arranged for a group of mangabeys, *Cercocebus torquatus* (a forest relative of baboons), to have access to a large run in which there were many hiding places; a small amount of a preferred food would be placed in one of them. On some trials, one animal, called Rapide, was allowed to watch as the box was baited. Then Rapide was reunited with the group before all of them were let out. The problem for Rapide was the top ranking male, the aptly named Boss, who would seize any preferred item from the finder. This work was inspired by Emil

Figure 9.7 A mangabey retrieves and eats a hidden peanut after opening the slide-lid of the box, in Coussi-Korbel's experimental study (photo by S. Coussi-Korbel).

Menzel's studies with chimpanzees that we have already met; Coussi-Korbel was interested in how a monkey dealt with the task. On the first such trial, Rapide went to the food, and Boss followed and immediately took it from him. On the second trial, Rapide hung back, and the food was discovered by another animal while Boss remained near Rapide. On the third trial, Rapide again showed reluctance to go to the hidden food, and even moved a bit the other way; however, when Boss again followed him, Rapide saw his chance and ran for the food, managing to eat it before Boss arrived. This was clearly a windfall, from an opportunity created by the inhibition of Rapide's original enthusiasm. But on the very next trial, Rapide confidently set off in the wrong direction, and as soon as he was clearly being followed by Boss, he doubled back smartly and again got the food. He used this tactic several times afterwards. Thus only four trials were necessary to add a tactic of deception to Rapide's repertoire, yet the only mechanism was trial-and-error learning. In laboratory studies of learning with rats and pigeons, many hundreds or even thousands of trials are routinely used to inculcate habits that resemble insightful behaviour. In a mangabey, only four experiences with the task were necessary. The power of rapid learning to mimic insight and understanding of mental states is dramatic.

Deception in play?

Before leaving the subject of deception, we should consider the deception that may take place in play. Much children's playing involves pretending that something is true, when it is not: this would apparently need a theory of mind. However, studies of children's development suggest that much pretence may *not* require a full understanding of other peoples' belief. In a range of tasks that depend on understanding belief, 3-year-old children fail. For instance, in appearance–reality games, where children are shown an object which is really something else—such as a 'rock' made of painted sponge—4-year-old children have no difficulty explaining the deceit. However, 3-year-olds tend to equate appearance and reality, answering that it is a sponge and it looks like a sponge. Yet there is no doubt that 3-year-olds do pretend. For instance, they have no trouble understanding that someone is 'only pretending' to be a dog. Also, they can distinguish reliably between dreams, images and thoughts, on the one hand, and reality, on the other. It would seem that 3-year-old children can see the difference between frivolities that have no relation to reality, and reality itself; but serious thoughts about the world are seen as always true, with no possibility of error or misinformation.

Sorting out the mental underpinnings of play becomes even more tricky when we turn to animals (Fig. 9.8). Kittens chase balls of wool as if pretending that they were prey. This may not be at all the same thing as children's pretence, although it certainly looks like it. As an alternative which

Figure 9.8 When wild primates play, it is often difficult to know if pretence is involved. Here, a subadult male mountain gorilla, Cantsbee, has invented a game: he leans forward so that his high crown and forehead dip into a pool of water; as he sits upright, the water drains over his face into his mouth where he licks it. None of this routine helped him to drink, but he spent many minutes engrossed in it.

meshes better with the rest of cat behaviour, it could be explained by saying that the characteristics of the object elicit a hunting response, because of an overlap in features between the appearance of an unwinding ball of wool and an escaping mouse. By contrast, not all of children's pretend play *can* be 'explained away' in this way, because quite often the *consequences* of the pretence are elaborated and used in the play. For instance, a child may pretend to be a doctor and then give 'medicines' to her playmates. Alan Leslie (1987) has argued that this elaborated type of pretence requires the holding of simultaneous mental representations of two conflicting sets of knowledge or belief: in this case, something like 'I am a doctor' and 'I am Sally playing with my friends'. If so, the ability is logically equivalent to knowing that another individual's knowledge or belief is different to one's own—a theory of mind. Two mutually contradictory databases have to be held concurrently in memory, without the two becoming confused or conglomerated. (Some doubt is cast on this, however, by the early age at which elaborated pretence is first seen in children.)

Several apes have shown pretend play of this level of sophistication, in which consequences of the pretence are elaborated (Fig. 9.9). The classic example comes from the home-reared chimpanzee, Viki. She not only acted as if she was trailing a pull toy on a string but showed consternation and

(a)

(b)

Figure 9.9 Apes reared in human environments, especially if they have been taught some sign languge, often give better evidence of pretence. (a) The gorilla, Koko, signs 'drink' as she puts a toy alligator to nurse at her breast. (b) As she drinks from an empty cup, she makes exaggerated, loud sipping noises. (Photos by F. G. Patterson and R. H. Cohn.)

appropriate strategies to free the toy when it became snagged on a (real) object! Other chimpanzees have apparently invented imaginary monsters with which to frighten their conspecifics, and publicly available film of these individuals also shows them eating imaginary food and having their fingers bitten by a child's doll (see Savage-Rumbaugh 1986). Kanzi, a captive pygmy chimpanzee, often acts as if he was holding an object which does not exist: he may hide this invisible object and retrieve it later, all as if it were real (Savage-Rumbaugh and McDonald 1988). Frans de Waal (1989*b*) has recorded pygmy chimpanzees apparently playing the game of 'blind man's buff'. One individual covered its eyes and blundered after the others in the group, as if it could not see! In gorillas too, there are data of a similar kind. The home-reared Koko has used signs to refer to a rubber hose as an elephant's trunk, apparently as a joke (and see Fig. 9.9). And a wild mountain gorilla, Maggie, was watched pulling up a mass of soft moss, holding it under her chest as she walked to an open area, where she built a nest for herself and sat as if nursing the moss bundle, cuddling and fussing over her imaginary baby for many minutes. Whether she was pretending that the object was a baby (while realizing at the same time that it was not, really) is, however, not proven; it is possible she was merely triggered into her maternal mode by the baby-like properties of the moss, like a kitten's hunting tactics are triggered by a rolling ball (and see Fig. 10.2). Nothing as elaborate as this has been recorded in monkeys, although a young rhesus monkey was once seen to carry a half-coconut clasped to its belly, just like its mother clasped her new infant. It seems as if, once again, ape abilities greatly exceed those of monkeys in behaviour that depends on understanding others' beliefs. However, we must be guarded in use of this data, because of the controversy within developmental psychology as to whether elaborated pretence really implies a theory of mind, when it occurs earlier than any other indicators of mental-state attribution.

Play is a fascinating topic, and it is tempting to pursue the various play behaviours of animals for what they might imply about the animal mind. Other instances of mental state attribution in childrens' play could be cited (for example, teasing and joking), and possible animal parallels found; but often it is impossible to gather genuinely comparable data from non-verbal animals, and always interpretive problems remain. Even in humans it is difficult to evaluate the extent of bluff and posture in childrens' behaviour. Until these problems can be overcome, it is safer to leave play out of the evidence for the evolution of cognitive ability.

Teaching

Tim Caro and Marc Hauser have recently taken a functional approach to animal teaching, directly comparable to the one Whiten and I took with deception (Caro and Hauser 1992). They also used a wide definition, requiring only that 'an animal modify its behaviour, to no immediate benefit to itself, only in the presence of a naïve observer, and with the result that the observer gains knowledge or learns a skill with greater efficiency than otherwise'. This rules out most cases of learning aided by stimulus enhancement, response facilitation, or imitation—where the animal whose behaviour is copied takes no account of whether it is watched or not. It also excludes certain ambiguous cases, like weaning or fighting. In these, an animal may learn that it should feed for itself or not challenge dominant individuals, but since there is definitely an immediate benefit to the 'teacher', we can never be sure that this is not sufficient reason for the behaviour, with no necessary function as teaching. Nevertheless, Caro and Hauser find a number of cases meet their criterion for teaching, in two orders of mammals and one of birds: carnivores, primates and raptors. (And suggestive observations in sealions (*Zalophus californianus*) and orcas (*Orcinus orca*) suggest that teaching may be more widespread, though hard to observe.)

Domestic cats are well known for their habit of releasing prey they have caught, often injured, and sometimes catching the prey again; feral cats do not usually show this behaviour, presumably because they are less well fed. However, feral cats do bring back and release live prey when their kittens are of an age to be mobile. Behaviour of this kind has also been recorded in tigers (*Panthera tigris*), lions (*Panthera leo*), cheetah (*Acinonyx jubatus*), and other carnivores, such as otters (*Lutra canadensis*). Caro himself studied cheetah families in detail, finding that mothers' behaviour changed strikingly when cubs were about 3 months old. Before this time, a mother would normally kill prey herself, but when cubs are around 3 months mothers begin to release live prey in front of them. The cubs chase the prey, but rarely kill it, and after 10–15 minutes the mother intervenes and kills the prey. As the cubs grow older, mothers release up to one-third of prey, and cubs begin to suffocate and kill the animals themselves. Later, mothers gradually cease releasing prey for their cubs. This behaviour was selective: neonate gazelles, which cubs can catch quite easily, are usually released, whereas adult gazelles are not, and fast-running hares are significantly more likely to be maimed before release than the young gazelles. And it was not free of cost: quite apart from delaying the mother's own feeding, animals such as hares often escaped from the cubs, and the food was lost. It is difficult for these observations alone to show that the experience resulted in faster learning or more skilled performance, since all mother cheetahs do the same, but with domestic cats Caro (1980) used experiments to check this. He found that kittens were more skilful in killing mice at 6 months of age if their mother has been present when they encountered mice during their early weeks of life. However, it is not clear that mothers of cats or cheetahs are sensitive to their offspring's skills—their changing sequence of behaviour might be under genetic control, unfolding as the kittens grow up, regardless of what the kitten actually does. There is nothing, therefore, to tell us whether the teaching is intentional.

A very similar pattern is widely reported for raptorial birds, although here there has been no systematic collection of observations comparable to Caro's work with cats. Raptors, such as sparrowhawks (*Accipiter nisus*) or peregrines (*Falco peregrinus*), typically switch from presenting their offspring with dead prey, when they are young, to releasing the prey in the air (sometimes alive) when they are older. An extraordinary account, by Colonel Meinertzhagen (the soldier in charge of covert operations in Palestine during the First World War, and later the discoverer—by shooting—of the giant forest hog, *Hylochoerus meinertzhageni*), describes diligent parental encouragement in a family of ospreys (*Pandion haliaetus*). The parent birds refused to give fish to their young until they left the nest on the first day; then until they caught the fish in mid-air on the second; then until they took the dead fish from a water surface on the fifth. This procedure was apparently adhered to strictly with each young bird (Meinertzhagen 1954). Ospreys are world-wide in their distribution and often common, so it is strange that nothing of the sort has been reported before or since; and scientific fraud is not unknown!

For primates, Caro and Hauser found many cases of 'maybe' teaching, but the evidence was seldom conclusive. Infants of several species have been recorded to be 'encouraged' to walk by their mothers: the mother moves a little, looks back, if the infant moves the mother goes on a little further, and so on. But whether this ever advances an infant's walking skills is unknown, and the mothers may simply be torn between wishing to move and not wishing to leave their infants trailing behind. Adults which have knowledge of a danger, such as a poisonous fruit, have been seen to threaten naïve individuals that approach the danger, in several species. The naïve individuals have sometimes been shown to learn avoidance. However, avoidance might not have been a consequence of the threats, it might have been learnt directly by observing the knowledgeable adult's own avoidance. In a study of young vervet monkeys' vocal development, Hauser himself found no clear evidence of teaching. Infant vervets make many errors in the animals to which they give specific predator-alarm calls; gradually their rather vague appreciation of the calls' normal referents narrows down to the adults' very specific usage (Seyfarth and Cheney 1986). Adults often 'echo' an infant's correct call, just afterward. They may not be trying to influence the infant: inevitably, adults that call just after an infant are more likely to give an alarm call matching the infant's if the infant has used the appropriate call. All the same, this might serve to 'encourage' or shape the infant's responses to match the adult usage. But in 14 cases, where Hauser observed an infant's next use of a alarm call subsequent to just such possible encouragement, the proportion of calls given appropriately was no more than before; no learning seemed to have occurred. Only one record suggested that adults' calling can have an effect on infant usage. An infant gave a leopard-alarm in error to a herd of stampeding elephants. In fact, a real leopard was spotted at much the same time by the dominant male, who therefore gave the same type of call. The next four times the infant saw elephants on the move, it gave leopard-alarm calls, an unusual persistence of such an error. Apparent punishment was also seen in four cases: in each, a mother returned and bit or slapped her infant which had caused her to flee by giving an inappropriate alarm call. Unfortunately, there is no evidence that infants learnt anything from this treatment.

Mother primates of several species pull their infants away from novel objects (two species of macaque), or remove foods from infants if the food is not part of the diet (chimpanzee). Caro and Hauser suggest that the latter might be 'accidental', but having seen it happen in gorillas, I doubt this (Anne Russon, who has noted the same in orang-utans, shares my scepticism). An infant was fiddling with and chewing at a leaf (of a species not normally eaten), facing away from the mother who was eating herself, when the mother broke off her feeding, reached over the infant's head and took the leaf, dropping it well out of the infant's reach. In the case of a chimpanzee watched by Mariko Hiraiwa-Hasegawa (1986), the mother not only did the same, but systematically picked every other leaf of the same species in the infant's reach and placed her foot firmly on the pile of leaves! But in any of these cases, the function is unclear: does the behaviour serve to *teach,* or simply to remove infants from danger? Getting evidence on this matter would be very difficult.

Only two records of primate behaviour fully satsify Caro and Hauser's functional definition of teaching, and in each case there is also reason to suppose the teaching was intentional. In both cases, the primates were chimpanzees.

After the death of her own baby, Washoe, a chimpanzee taught to sign American Sign Language, was given an infant chimp, which she adopted. The human caretakers did not teach the infant Loulis to sign, and indeed they stopped signing at all in her presence. Washoe used both demonstration (with careful attention to Loulis' gaze direction) and moulding of Loulis' hands to teach him to sign (Fouts *et al.* 1989). Washoe herself had been taught by humans, who sometimes moulded her hands into the correct configuration and put the hands through the necessary movement; this is what she did several times with the infant Loulis. The direct effect of Washoe's demonstration and moulding is hard to measure, but certainly Loulis learnt many signs during the years in which he saw no human sign and got no human encouragement for doing so: after 5 years he reliably used 51 signs, often in two-sign combinations like 'person come'.

Recently, wild chimpanzees have also been seen teaching their infants, in this case imparting the tool-using technique of cracking hard nuts using a hammerstone, with another stone as an anvil. This is evidently difficult for chimpanzees to learn (Fig. 9.10); Sugiyama *et al.* (1992) found that some chimpanzees take more than 14 years to acquire the technique. Christoph Boesch observed that mothers sometimes demonstrate the skill for their offspring: they perform the actions slowly and in full view, paying

Figure 9.10 Nut-cracking is slow and difficult for chimpanzees to learn. This 3-year-old female uses her mother's wooden hammer, but has failed to position the nut on an anvil: she will fail to crack it. (Photo by C. Boesch.)

close attention to the eye-gaze of the youngster and only continuing when it is watching (Boesch 1991*a*); normally, a skilled adult moves her hands so quickly that it is hard for the human eye to follow the movements. Mothers have also been twice recorded doing what is called 'scaffolding' in human developmental psychology: setting up the physical situation so that the child is able to achieve the final goal easily, at a stage of development when it could not perform all the necessary constituent acts or sequence them correctly. Once, after a juvenile male had already put a nut on the anvil, the mother took it off, cleaned the anvil, and repositioned the nut in a more favourable orientation. In another case, a mother reoriented the hammer for her juvenile daughter. In both cases, the offspring were then able to break the nuts. (In addition, mother chimpanzees often leave their hammers or their accumulated nuts handy, and allow their young to take them over—whereas adults normally eat all the nuts they gather and often carry their hammers with them.)

The techniques of demonstration, moulding, and scaffolding imply teaching in the intentional as well as the functional sense: an understanding of the specific lack of knowledge of the young animals which are being taught. The finding of (second-order) intentional teaching in a great ape, the chimpanzee, is consistent with what we have already seen of the species' ability to attribute mental states, in several other areas. Interestingly, there is now evidence suggestive of teaching in bottlenose dolphins (*Tursiops truncatus*), another species for which we have already seen evidence of theory of mind capabilities. Female dolphins remain in the natal group, so need to acquire a different whistle to their mothers, whereas males, which leave at adolescence, copy and retain their mother's signature whistle. Sayich *et al.* (1993) report a mother switching her signature whistle to a new 'tune' for several months after a female infant's birth; once the infant had learnt the mother's whistle and adopted it as her own, the mother reverted to her original one.

The data of this chapter have supported the hypothesis that the great apes, which in artificial laboratory tasks give evidence of having a theory of mind (mental-state attribution), use this capability also functionally, in natural circumstances. This does not result in a plethora of socially complex behaviours in apes, compared with other simian primates. Deception is actually commoner in some monkeys, but all these cases can be explained by rapid trial-and-error learning; the sophistication of ape deception marks it out. Teaching is similarly restricted among primates to apes (in fact to the common chimpanzee, on current evidence), but may also occur in dolphins, consistent with other evidence that they, too, have a theory of mind. It remains unexplained why such an apparently valuable technique should be used so minimally by animals apparently capable of understanding its benefit. Either much teaching in great apes is being missed by observers, or teaching is not the great gift that our educational establishment believes it to be, or apes only partly understand their fellows' understanding and knowledge. The last alternative is perfectly possible, but, if so, we have as yet no idea of where their deficiency lies.

Further reading

The most appropriate extracts from Dennett's original proposal of levels of intentionality are combined with his experiences in trying to apply the ideas to real primates, in his chapter in Byrne and Whiten (1988*b*). This book also has several chapters on tactical deception in primates and children, including Menzel's pioneering work; and Mitchell and Thompson (1986) contains a wealth of interesting data on animal deception. But for the most recent analyses of deception and teaching, the best sources are Byrne and Whiten (1991, 1992), and Caro and Hauser (1992), respectively.

10
Planning and thinking ahead

From the evidence of the Chapters 8 and 9, great apes are certainly 'special' in some way to do with mentally representing the minds of others. It seems that the great apes, especially the common chimpanzee, can attribute mental states to other individuals; but no other group of animals can do so—apart from ourselves, and perhaps cetaceans. What does this underlying competence consist of, that we have seen put to use in intentional deception and intentional teaching? And is it related to great apes' (equally special) abilities to understand how things work? To attempt an answer, we must temporarily leave the realm of facts about animals, and venture into speculation and theory: about what brains do, the nature of computation, and what 'thinking' really is. With this grounding, some of the results we have already seen will be viewed in a different light.

Prediction machines

Before an animal could be expected to *devise* tactics, to exploit differing beliefs in others, or to endeavour to create those beliefs by deceit or teaching, it must first know the likely consequences of a new set of beliefs. It must be able to predict what another individual would do *if* its beliefs were changed. Now, the extent to which orang-utans, gorillas, and chimpanzees comprehend others' knowledge may well not be the same as our own, in either quantity or exact nature. But *any* representation of the contents of other minds, however limited, could allow improved prediction of others' future behaviour: behaviour that follows logically from a starting point of different goals and beliefs to one's own. Predicting the likely consequences of deficiency or error in knowledge is the starting point: reaching it could in turn lead to devising ways to remedy the knowledge deficiencies of dependants or friends (intentional teaching), and to create deficiencies or errors of knowledge in competitors (intentional deception). Additionally, realizing that competitors may be doing just this to oneself, and taking appropriate action, brings a further layer of understanding (Dennett's third-order intentionality, e.g. 'he wants me to think that he doesn't know where the food is hidden', 'she wants me to realize that she knows more about this than me'). Arms-races of second-guessing, and true co-operative pedagogy, can begin to happen.

Working out consequences, from premises other than current reality, is what in humans we would call *planning* or *simulation*. Many years ago, Kenneth Craik suggested that conscious thought had the function of testing out plans of action before embarking on them (Craik 1943). His analogy was to the test-bed simulations of engineers, in which scale models are tried out to find their capabilities and weaknesses, before the expense and risk of constructing real structures or machines is contemplated. If human thought, he reasoned, allows us to model or simulate aspects of the world that might prove dangerous or unfortunate, then we could avoid much risk to ourselves. Kenneth Craik envisaged the brain as a prediction machine. In 1943, few people imagined the possibility of computing the solutions to quite arbitrary problems (bridge design, the next sentence in a conversation, a chess move) on a single machine. With no tangible 'model' to use as analogy, Craik's suggestion that thinking was a simulation of reality must have seemed very vague and improbable. But as the idea of a computational machine was transformed from a dream of one or two people to a reality, the full power of Craik's idea began to be appreciated. When first developed, computers were used only for solving tediously large numerical calculations ('number crunching'). 'General purpose' computing—designing programs to solve a whole range of problems, *any* problem sufficiently well understood to be posed in exact form—had become a reality by about 1955. Miller *et al.*'s *Plans and the structure of behavior* (1960) was the first non-technical exploration of the consequences. Nowadays, the rather linear and more-or-less logical steps of our conscious thinking are currently best understood by analogy with digital computing.

Computation

'Computing' is often used in a general way to mean any calculation, and this was its original meaning. However, it has also come to be used in a very specific sense, and it is this sense that I mean by talking about 'general purpose computing'. In the 1930s, a young mathematician named Alan Turing was involved in some abstruse problems of pure mathematics. These related to the question of the solvability, in principle, of well-defined problems. A proof in geometry or formal logic, or finding the shortest route home, are familiar examples of well-defined problems; deciding who to marry or what career to follow are ill-defined, in that a correct solution is hard to recognize even when you have it. It had been shown that any well-defined and completely definite problem or solution could be expressed as a number. (Well, I did say 'abstruse'! The idea of encoding a problem as a number is a strange one, but in fact every program encoded in a modern desktop computer is stored as a number, and some of these *do* solve problems.) The question was, could procedures exist in principle for solving all well-defined problems: could all the appropriate numbers be found? Or were there some problems, not vague ones but definite and clear problems, that could never be solved by a mechanical step-by-step process? Pure mathematicians like Turing had no interest in actually solving the problems, only in whether the concept of 'solvability' could be made precise: his was by no stretch of the imagination the sort of practical enterprise that is easily understood by the general public or research-funding agencies! Turing imagined a 'machine' that could read numbers from an unlimited memory (such as a very long strip of paper), and had the ability to move to a new place along the strip, and erase or write a number according to what it had read, and nothing more. The numbers that Turing's 'machine' could derive, he called 'computable numbers', and he showed that these include all the step-by-step proofs that can be achieved by a definite, mechanical process. From there it was a small step to the conclusion, wholly irrelevant to everyday life, that there are certain numbers that are not computable, thus certain well-defined problems whose answers cannot be found by a step-by-step procedure.

'So what?', one might well ask. Indeed, few people read Turing's great paper (Turing 1937). However, as a mathematician, Turing became engaged in secret wartime work that led to deciphering the German coding system called 'Enigma'. The Enigma coding machines had a series of discs, each with fixed but random letter–letter conversions: A went in, P came out, and so on. Each disc meshed with the next, so the P was fed into another random conversion, producing B, say. There were three discs, so the B became, say, L. The result, L, was then written wherever an A occured in the original text; all letters and spaces were encoded in the same fashion. The three discs could be rotated, and every few days the discs of every machine used by the Nazi naval intelligence service were rotated to new positions: then As no longer became Ls, but something else. As long as the disc positions in which a message was encoded were known, deciphering was just a matter of running the process in reverse. Without a machine and information on how the discs are positioned, deciphering seems impossible. Nevertheless, only a random coding process is truly impossible to break, and in the case of Enigma there was a non-random constraint on the process of encoding. The discs were rigid, so if one letter-converter moved six places, so did all the others. This slight constraint, combined with the known spelling rules and letter frequencies of the original language, made the job of deciphering the output, without knowing the machine's settings, possible—just. (Luckily the basic design and principles of operation of the system were known.) Turing supervised the building of machines that, using early electronic technology, explored the contingencies between letters in the coded strings, and ruled out possible disc settings, one by one, till the current code could be broken.

These machines were not general-purpose computers, having only a highly specific function. But in working with the new technology, Turing realized that his original *imaginary* 'computer' could actually be built, and could function fast enough to produce results in reasonable time. This meant that any problem that could be posed in the form of a number (which meant any clear, well-defined problem, such as the performance of a bridge under stress, or a chess move, or even perhaps the next sentence in a conversation), could be solved—in principle. Instead of a long paper strip, there would be a huge array of valves recording the binary states; pulses of electricity could 'read' and 'write' to these electronic memory units. Only the series of steps to be taken then had to be worked out before the machine could solve the problem in hand. An appropriate series of small logical steps became known in time as the 'program', and the job of fashioning it 'programming'.

Unfortunately for Turing, only a brilliant mathematician or someone who had worked on the Enigma decoding project, and would therefore have to keep silent, under the Official Secrets Act, could appreciate the correctness of his vision. British science funding was too scarce for such abstruse stuff, and it was left to one of the few people who had read, and understood, Turing's paper, John von Neumann, to develop the first computer in America. Even then it was years before computer scientists caught up with what Turing in the late 1940s could see would follow: general-purpose computing. All the early computers were used for numerical computation, but this is not an intrinsic restriction on a digital computer. As Turing had originally shown, *any* definite problem can be converted to a series of logical steps and hence converted into a number, and then solved. The breakthrough, as far as psychology was concerned, came with the 'Logic Theorist' program of Newell, *et al.* (1958): a program that solved the taxing puzzles of formal logic in a fashion sufficiently similar to the fumblings of philosophy students to demonstrate that it was a feasible 'model' of what people were doing when thinking.

Just as it makes no difference to a 'Turing machine' whether its memory is a long paper strip, an array of valves, or, as most often now, an array of transistors on a silicon chip, it would make no difference if the machine was entirely built out of biological material. Indeed, the all-or-nothing electrochemical impulses that travel along neurones in the brain, and the intricate and vast network of interconnections, seem much like what a biological Turing machine would look like. This idea, that the brain is a biological machine that can solve general problems by computation, has been the view of the brain that has dominated cognitive psychology and neuroscience since 1960. Whether the brain is always linear and serial (like the machines von Neumann built); sometimes more parallel in operation (with *several* computations occurring at the same time, as part of the solution to the same problem, as Turing himself envisaged); or even a 'connectionist' network (with the process distributed over a network by means of altered strengths of connection between network units), is controversial. But in each case the brain would still be, mathematically, a Turing machine.* The previously mysterious process we call 'thinking' can, after all, be understood in a mechanical and definite way.

Mental simulation of intentional action: imagination

This insight is relevant to Craik's original vision of thinking as mental simulation of possible future outcomes: if the brain is a sort of computer, then prediction and simulation is just what we'd expect it to be doing. It also means we have some hope of understanding it, by analogy with mechanisms that we can actually build. We can also extend his idea to the social sphere; thinking then corresponds to *mental simulation of intentional action*. Instead of a database of tensile strengths, material thicknesses and lengths, forces, and tolerances—which would allow simulation of the future performance of a bridge—a social predictor's 'database' would contain (among other things) beliefs about other individuals and their limited or incorrect knowledge. The calculations applied to this database would be the same as those normally used by the individual for calculating its *own* future actions on the basis of what it really believes to be true. The results, however, would inform it of likely moves of competitors or allies, or likely problems for dependants and friends.

With this perspective, the special abilities, that we have already seen great apes to have, suggest that they (like humans) are able mentally to simulate actions. To the extent that great apes can select or make tools appropriate for the job, in advance of feedback from the the task itself (Chapter 7; see also later in this chapter), or structure skilled behaviour without trial-and-error learning (Chapter 6), they are simulating physical action. To the extent that they intentionally deceive and teach, and solve the various more artificial tests of intentional understanding (Chapters 8 and 9), great apes are simulating social action. What the data show, therefore, is that in a limited way *great apes can think*.

It remains to be seen whether all great apes are equal in their understanding of mind and physics. Only the common chimpanzee has produced more-or-less convincing evidence in all spheres; for other apes the story is less convincing. Whether it is a coincidence that the chimpanzee is also the one animal that routinely makes tools and has the most complex social life in the wild, must be left as an interesting unsolved question for the moment. We simply cannot rule out the possibility that the common chim-

*Roger Penrose has recently suggested that humans can solve certain non-computable problems. Some of his examples are hard for non-mathematicians to evaluate, such as tiling a plane with an irregular tile, forming a non-repeating pattern; others are simple, such as realizing that A × B is always the same as B × A, by seeing that geometrically both form a rectangle of the same dimensions—but in this simple case a computer capable of representing two dimensions would seem able to solve it after all. No coherent alternative to operating as a Turing machine has yet been proposed for what the brain might be doing during thought.

panzee's apparent superiority to other great apes is merely a matter of ecological differences resulting in different demands on this species—or even sampling bias, when chimpanzees have been so much more studied than any of the other apes. Equally, variations across the apes, in the basic ability to represent the intentions of other individuals, and to understand how things work, cannot be ruled out. If present, this variation could tell us how and when the ability to think developed in our evolution, and perhaps how social understanding is related to object-world comprehension. Clarifying exactly which ape species are capable of which skills—something we can hope to see achieved in the next few years—will be essential to reconstruct the detailed evolution of the early stages of human thinking.

Thinking in animals

There is thus some evidence in both the social and mechanical spheres that, if thinking involves simulating or computing outcomes without performing them, then great apes may be able to think. Could this ability be more widely used, to imagine future states of the world in general? To deceive or teach intentionally, for instance, an animal must already have some ability to hold at one time databases of mutually conflicting information (its own knowledge, versus that of others), and to operate on each independently. Why should the independent databases not include *future* possible realities, as well as current variations from truth in other individuals?

The ability to imagine other possible worlds than the current perceived truth is what has led to so much human endeavour: 'All men dream. Most men dream only at night, and their dreams dissolve in the realities of day. But the dreamers of the day are dangerous men, for they will strive to turn their dreams into very truth' (Lawrence 1926/35). Is there supportive evidence for ape thought: and how much separates a chimpanzee from Lawrence's 'dreamers of the day'? Evidence for thinking in animals is understandably slight, in view of the practical difficulties of obtaining it. Several interpretations of thinking are possible:

Thinking as problem-solving: learning set

In general, problem-solving in animals is difficult to study, but one artificial task that relies on seeing the logical connection between different problems does exist. This is called 'learning set'. In it, an animal is given a series of problems to solve by trial and error, but the solutions are related by a rule, such as 'odd one out' or 'match the sample' (Harlow 1949). The swiftest performance will come from generalizing across the details of individual problems, realizing that the rule is the same. To notice such rules, animals must characterize the rewarded stimuli in abstract terms, as we do when we write the rules in English: 'odd one out' rather than just 'red ball' Learning set therefore tests the ability of animals to make somewhat abstract generalizations. The learning set paradigm has been used extensively, and Passingham (1982), reviewing this work, has pointed out that primates learn these rules quicker than non-primates such as rats, cats or squirrels. Furthermore, rhesus monkeys far outperform small New World species like marmosets, and rhesus themselves are outclassed by chimpanzees. Passingham reviews other rule-learning tasks, showing that chimpanzees, rhesus monkeys, cebus monkeys, squirrel monkeys and marmosets, and finally strepsirhine primates, such as the ring-tailed lemur, can all learn rules; but their facility to do so decreases in that order.

Thinking as mental concatenation of disparate facts

In a most minimal sense, 'thinking' could be said to mean the derivation of novel solutions, or novel uses of old solutions, by mental operations. This would not necessarily involve any mechanism with the power of a Turing machine. To what extent do animals show this basic sort of thinking? At its simplest, this would involve concatenating knowledge learnt in two previous circumstances, in order to deal with a third, novel circumstance. In this sense of thinking, even laboratory rats qualify: they exhibit concatenation of pieces of knowledge learnt separately (Dickinson 1980). Having learnt to find a particular food in a hopper after a tone sounded, rats then experience illness (actually the experimenter causes this by other means) after eating this particular food. When the tone next sounds, they do not approach the hopper: they have put the two pieces of knowledge together. Getting evidence beyond this minimal sense of 'thinking' has yet to be done in laboratory experiments.

A source of evidence less powerful than direct experimentation, but still valuable, is the case where no learning history for acquisition of a behaviour is plausible, yet the behaviour is made up of two components, each learnable. Cases of this sort suggest greater complexity in chimpanzee mental computations, as might be expected. One example comes from their unusual activity called 'border patrols'. Border patrols are not simply territorial defence behaviour. Unlike any other species of animal, chimpanzees at times deliberately seek out and kill males, and sometimes older females, of neighbouring communities (Goodall *et al.* 1979). Single animals encountered on border patrols are murdered by the excited chimpanzees, predominantly males, with bare hands and teeth. Young females are instead coerced, and sometimes follow the aggressors for a time. This has several times resulted in one powerful community gaining land and young females from their neighbours. The pattern is chillingly similar to the intercommunity raids of Yanomamö people of the Amazon, described by Chagnon

(1974): male-led raids, deliberate murder of males in neighbouring communities, female capture, territorial enlargement. Chimpanzees are uncharacteristically silent and show cautious and skilful bushcraft when on these dangerous patrols into the ranges of other communities (Goodall 1986). Infants are occasionally present and if they become distressed they are immediately comforted; when adults (or a human observer) are carelessly noisy they are threatened. These behaviours imply that the connection between noisiness of a party member and potential danger is well understood. Yet border patrols are quite rare events, and so risky that the 'punishment' for error may well be death. Reinforcement learning thus seems unlikely to underlie the chimpanzees' knowledge. Instead, it is perhaps more likely that the connection is derived mentally.

Thinking as abstract generalization

Sultan, Köhler's chimpanzee, is often said to have suddenly found his effective solution to the raking problem after a pause, and his insight is thus implied to result from thinking. However, inactivity does not necessarily imply thought; and, since play with the sticks filled the pause, the sudden solution was more *noticed* in his hands than thought out, as we saw earlier. This cautions that much human 'thinking' may be no different to Sultan's, a matter of realizing that the answer is in front of us. The chimpanzee who realizes that a tactic in his play will serve to gain a food reward, and the person who realizes that a dancing ring of snakes in his dream will solve the structure of benzene (as Kekulé is said to have done), are both generalizing from one situation to another. Generalization is a very basic tendency in animal behaviour: a pigeon taught to peck a red key for food, will 'generalize' this response to similar-looking keys, such as orange or purple ones, while avoiding very dissimilar colours such as white or blue. However, the nature of the generalization varies. In the case of generalizing from dancing snakes in a dream to molecular bonding, the generalization is very *abstract*, whereas the pigeon's generalization to colours nearby in the colour chart is making a *concrete* generalization.

This abstract/concrete distinction simply means that the hierarchical level of description at which the two things are 'the same' is at a different level. Dancing snakes and imagined bonds are only very loosely similar in appearance, the same only at a high level of conceptual organization, whereas Sultan's generalization was only from play actions to real-life actions, the same but for the context. Nevertheless, even this smaller level of abstraction shows a degree of flexibility, where solutions are not bound to their original context and experience is not rigidly compartmentalized. The level of abstraction at which generalization can occur may therefore be an interesting component of intelligence.

The pattern of these various results from possible diagnostics of animal thought, does not suggest any 'Rubicon' between monkey and ape. Instead, some capability for rule-learning, concatenation of knowledge, and generalization out of immediate context, seems present in many animals. There is a gradual change in usefulness and impressiveness of these basic abilities, with monkeys more prominent than strepsirhines and many non-primates, and the larger Old World monkeys and apes (and perhaps cetaceans) most impressive of all. This contrasts with the findings on understanding of beliefs, attribution of intentions, and how things work—where a sharp discontinuity is implied between great apes and all other animals. Abstract generalization, rule-learning, and mental concatenation of separate pieces of knowledge seem to be part of the pre-ape cognitive endowment. But there is no clear sign of directed, computational thought outside the social manoeuvrings and technical skills of chimpanzees and other great apes—the first glimmerings of analytical thought and imagination.

If apes can genuinely think, we would expect them routinely to imagine and plan for future possibilities, and would expect to see behavioural evidence of this planning in their everyday behaviour. The next section examines whether this is so.

Anticipating the future

The big problem with studying 'anticipatory planning' is knowing what it might *look* like in non-verbal animals. Most signs that humans give of planning for the future come in their verbal and written acts.

Certainly, great apes have shown convincingly that their behaviour is not entirely driven by currently observable stimuli. When making tools for food-processing, chimpanzees sometimes fabricate or carefully select the tool in advance and out of sight of the food. Termite-fishing probes may be carried a few hundred metres; hammer-stones may be taken much further to sources of nuts. Chimpanzees anticipate in time as well as in space. Termite-fishing is possible for only a limited season each year; when the reproductive, winged alates are preparing to emerge from tubes that will be opened in the mound, the mound surface is softer than normal and can be picked open with a fingernail. The very fact that at the start of this season chimpanzees begin to travel to and inspect the mounds—which they have previously ignored for months, and which are still often showing no sign of winged alates' emergence—shows that they anticipate (Goodall 1986). Similarly, mountain gorillas show that they anticipate the seasonal availability and local distribution of plant foods. Bamboo shoots are a favourite food, but only emerge at one time of year, in one zone. As that time approaches, gorilla groups make major detours, rapidly and without feeding much on the way, to inspect the bamboo groves. When no shoots are found, they return to their previous zone of feeding with equal rapidity, leaving aged gorillas, juveniles, and less-fit researchers trailing behind. In Zaire, Grauer's gorillas (*G. g. graueri*), which also feed on bamboo, make even greater detours to areas of bamboo as the season approaches, and sometimes go so far as to dig invisible shoots from underground (Goodall 1977). Orang-utans similarly take detours off their route, moving directly to a particular tree, checking it for fruit availability, then returning to their previous route if the fruit is unripe. Spatial anticipation may not be restricted to great apes. Some movement patterns of baboons are consistent with this sort of anticipatory checking of seasonal foods (Robert Barton, personal communication), and the evidence on cognitive maps in spider monkeys (Chapter 12) suggests the same.

However, all these signs of forethought concern items relevant to the animals' current motivational state, their current goal. Humans plan beyond their current needs and desires. Is there any evidence that great apes behave in ways inexplicable on the basis of their current motivation, but that make sense as signs of future plans? There are two possible candidates for anticipatory planning in apes.

First, as mentioned earlier, chimpanzees at several sites have 'waged wars' against neighbouring communities. Their regular border patrols into the no man's lands bordering their community territory have become what Christophe Boesch calls 'commando raids', and adult males of neighbouring communities have been systematically eliminated by brutal hand-to-hand fighting. The rewards are plain: in the end, females of depleted neighbouring communities transfer to that of the aggressors. However, these rewards are long-term. No immediate rewards accrue to the males who engage in the (presumably risky) activity; although females have sometimes been coerced towards the aggressors' territory, the real transfers have always been later, and no mating has been seen at the time of the violence. When males set out on border patrols or commando raids, their behaviour cannot reflect their current bodily needs; does it reflect their long-term plans? One critique of this view would suggest that the behaviour is genetically channelled, selected because it has functioned to perpetuate genes of animals with such tendencies. In support of this account, lone male gorillas also display at breeding groups, attacking females within them and sometimes killing their infants. The rewards are again long-term; females sometimes choose subsequently to transfer to the successful aggressor. Any regular, species-typical behaviour that has genetic benefits is, of course, subject to the suspicion that it is not planned (or learnt), but part of the genetically governed species' repertoire. However, the lack of any comparable behaviours in monkeys is perhaps interesting. (Many monkey species' basic organization is based on powerful female lineages, where such violence by males could not succeed, but even in 'non-female-bonded' monkey societies it does not occur.)

Less subject to genetic explanation, but based on a unique observation, is the response of Mahale chimpanzees to a baby leopard. Chimpanzees regularly display at leopards, which show a healthy fear of them. In some West African areas, chimpanzees use branches as weapons with which to attack leopards; even lions, much larger than leopards, are followed with interest and subject to aggressive display by chimpanzees. However, chimpanzees are sometimes killed and eaten by both leopards and lions. Display at and interest in predators is widespread in mammals and birds, and thought to be an entirely functional adaptation—no evidence of anticipatory planning.

Rather different is an event at Mahale that several researchers, including myself, witnessed (Hiraiwa-Hasegawa *et al.* 1986; Byrne and Byrne 1988): different both in the risks to the chimpanzees and the apparent goal of their actions. A group of adult males was already surrounding the group of rocks in which a mother and cub leopard was sheltering when we arrived on the scene. Most of the chimpanzee party, females and juveniles, were well off the ground in trees: they were screaming, showing fear-grins, and urinating. We sympathized with their behaviour, since the intermittent roars of the adult leopard were very loud and intimidating! The leopard was in a typical 'birth cave', a 3 m long fissure with a narrow, triangular mouth of under a metre across, the width of a single chimpanzee. The persistent males, which did not include the alpha-male but several old animals, closed in on the cave mouth, displaying loudly around and on the rocks, until the leopard roared, when they leapt back a few metres. This was repeated many times over 45 min, until finally one of the males went

Figure 10.1 An adult male chimpanzee pummels a dying leopard cub, after another male took the cub from the mother leopard within a narrow cave (photo by J. Byrne).

right inside the narrow cave. He emerged carrying a small cub, crying pitifully; we estimated it at 2–3 months, at which age it would not normally emerge from a birth cave. The other males clustered round, pummelling and pulling the cub, tossing it up in the air; one male bit it (Fig. 10.1). After a few minutes, they left it and we ascertained that it was dying. Other chimpanzees appeared fascinated with the body, and one adolescent female in particular carried it for hours, cuddling and tickling it in her day-bed (Fig. 10.2). However, the group of males that had killed it showed no further interest, instead going back to the cave for a while. We believe that they found no other cub, and they soon resumed normal ranging.

The adult female leopard did not emerge to challenge the chimpanzees, so their estimate of the risk was presumably a good one. All the same, to enter a narrow cave and remove a baby from a mother leopard must be highly dangerous. The chimpanzees' efforts were directed *at the cub* not the mother, and *towards its death*, rather than its possession and consumption. To what end? Humans might well carry out this action, with the

Figure 10.2 After the leopard cub died, the adult males lost interest but juveniles carried the body up into the trees and experimentally dropped it. Later a juvenile female carried it for hours, carrying it like an infant and holding it while she made and slept in a day-bed. (Photo by J. Byrne.)

ultimate ends of reducing the population of dangerous carnivores and deterring the mother from continuing to inhabit their particular range. It is not easy to account for the chimpanzees' actions without attributing similar goals to them, which implies long-term anticipatory planning. With only a single observation, little confidence can be put in this deduction; to use the ultimate researchers' cliché 'further data are necessary on this matter'.

Ape mentality: why not more?

The evidence for cognitive abilities reminiscent of those of humans is patchy in apes, even for the well-studied chimpanzee. Although all great apes make and use a range of tools in captivity, and appear to understand the cause-and-effect logic of their use, only chimpanzees regularly make tools for several purposes in the wild. Only gorillas have so far been shown to use complex, hierarchical task organization in their normal environment. Certainly, most great apes can understand their reflection in a mirror, but they do not use the image to adorn themselves for the benefit of others. Great apes can impersonate actions, but this has only been shown clearly in home-reared individuals, not in the wild. Occasionally great apes show pretence, but this is also largely in home-reared animals, and pretence anyway has an uncertain relationship to belief attribution. Experiments with single chimpanzees have suggested empathy with others' problems, and comprehension of accident versus design. Only twice has intentional teaching of infants been recorded convincingly in chimpanzees, never in other apes. All species of great ape sometimes show that they can attribute deceptive intentions to others, to judge from observational data. A few intriguing chimpanzee behaviours imply anticipatory planning for the future. This imperfect set of evidence has taken a lot of getting, partly because the diagnostic signs are intrinsically hard to observe, partly perhaps because most observers aren't looking for them.

But we are still confronted with a paradox: if cognitive abilities are so useful in social and other spheres, as we like to imagine they are, why aren't these demonstrations much, much more common and obvious in these animals which apparently can show the cognitive skills occasionally? Surely hierarchical task organization, impersonation of actions and teaching, for instance, would enable a chimpanzee to learn far more advanced crafts than ever seen in wild chimpanzees? Perhaps this intuition is simply wrong: perhaps only language, and experiences organized in a linguistic framework—as are the lives of the home-reared animals on which some of the current evidence rests—would take an ape much past what is currently seen in the wild. It is even very possible that researchers at present are systematically underestimating the cognitive complexity of what does go on. But it is also worth considering other explanations, which begin from the premise that wild apes do *not* realize their potential. One possibility is that ape abilities are more bound to their immediate sphere of use than we might expect, and what happened in later human evolution included a weakening of boundaries between these spheres. Another is that apes know so very much less than humans that even having the rudiments of human non-linguistic cognition does not produce much that we recognize as intelligent: a matter of sheer quantitative difference in what they have to think and plan *about*. Whether we shall ever know the answer for sure is a matter of conjecture.

Postscript: a double-standard for monkeys and apes?

Fully accepting the ape–monkey difference in their technical understanding and their intentionality has consequences that will worry some: a sort of 'double standard'. Consider a gorilla and a vervet monkey, both described as executing a sequence of actions that has the effect of socially manipulating a conspecific to the actor's advantage. The sequence has the same pattern, and in neither case is a full history of its ontogeny available (a normal problem with the rare observations we have of apparently intelligent behaviour in wild primates). Imagine that in both cases it is possible to construct an elaborate *post hoc* account in behaviourist terms—the social situation acted as a stimulus array controlling the behaviour, with no need to invoke intention attribution. But the accounts are so elaborate and seemingly contrived as to be dismissed by any social psychologist whose data was of *human* action. Then in the monkey case we should still accept the behaviourist account, but for the ape behaviour we would now use an intentional explanation, even though in the given case intention attribution was unprovable.

For a real example, consider what we should make of this observation of gorillas by Dian Fossey (Byrne and Whiten 1990):

> (May 1976) Majority of group were day-nesting within a 25 ft radius, with low-ranking Quince at the edge of the group. After intently gazing at Poppy [a 1-month-old infant, Effie's daughter; adolescent gorillas are strongly attracted to babies] from the side-lines, Quince stares in the opposite direction, circles and begins bending down branches for a nest. After momentarily sitting in the nest, Quince, with gaze averted from Poppy, gets up and moves a few feet closer to repeat the act of 'nest-building'. After roughly 40 minutes and 6 'nests' later, Quince was sitting next to the dominant female Effie and gazing directly at infant Poppy.

The account itself contributes no evidence of intention attribution, yet once it is accepted that gorillas *have* such an ability then a rather compelling intentional interpretation becomes possible (Fig. 10.3). Quince, adolescent and unrelated to the highest ranking female, Effie, could not simply walk up to Effie and sit down to gaze at her new infant: only Effie's own daughters can do such a thing (present tense, since Effie is still the highest

Figure 10.3 Dian Fossey described a juvenile gorilla, Quince, building day-beds in order to reach the infant of high-ranking Effie. It is hard to believe Effie misunderstands the juvenile's actions, yet the tactic was successful. (Drawing by D. Bygott.)

ranking female, of this group as I write, and is no more permissive with non-relatives than in 1976). Yet if at any point Effie had screamed in threat at this approaching female, the silverback leader who would rush to intervene would see that Quince had 'only been building a day-nest', and would be expected to intervene against Effie. The behaviour remained at all times ambiguous and liable to be misinterpreted—by anyone, that is, except Effie who could hardly have failed to realize what we call the 'true' motive.

If Quince had been an inarticulate and working-class adolescent, approaching a well-to-do lady's baby in an expensive pram but 'checking her shopping list' throughout, a similar interpretation of intended ambiguity would be uncontroversial. The girl *could* have been asked her motive for continual re-checking of the same list, of course; but would she have been honest in her reply, or even (since I described her as inarticulate) able to explain? In general we do not find it problematic that people cannot or will not explain what we consider to be their 'real' motives. Instead, gaining predictive power over their future behaviour is our everyday criterion of understanding. (If the well-to-do lady picked up her baby, smiled at the teenager, and offered her a chance to hold the child, we might predict that the girl would not afterward return to list-checking.) This is the same criterion as any behavioural scientist should adopt, and the issue is simply one of whether there are more cases where such intentional accounts make wrong predictions than there are with other theories. And with independent evidence that gorillas can attribute intentions, the apparently anthropomorphic account becomes the more parsimonious one.

Further reading

As it is a more speculative venture, there is less that can be followed up in this chapter. The best description of computing and Turing machines I know is in A. Hodges (1983) *Alan Turing: The enigma of intelligence* (Burnett Books, London). This is a biography of Alan Turing which also describes the fascinating story of the decipherment of the Enigma code. Dickinson (1980) gives the evidence for rudimentary 'thought' in rats—concatenation of evidence from separate experiences. Boundary patrols and chimpanzee warfare are described in Goodall (1986), along with a great wealth of behaviour that, if chimpanzees were accepted as having (second-order) intentional understanding, would be seen in mentalistic terms.

11
Apes and language

We have now seen a remarkable cognitive difference between great apes, especially the two species of chimpanzee, and monkeys. Among other things, apes appear to be able to take the mental states of other individuals into account. Working from the beliefs and intentions of other individuals, an ape is able sometimes to calculate profitable future actions to take itself. Mental-state attribution ('second-order intentionality') is also relevant to communication. Most theoretical linguists agree with the philosopher Grice in identifying mutual intentionality as the heart of linguistic communication: a speaker realizes that the hearer understands that the speaker intends the hearer to comprehend the speaker's utterences. If so, then an animal that could not take mental states into account could never communicate in this way; but since great apes *can*, perhaps what they lack is something less deep-rooted? Perhaps we could supply it artificially?

If this speculation were correct, it would imply that the underlying system of human language is, to a serious extent, *learned*, by every developing child. Of course, as emphasized in Chapter 4, this learning must certainly, in humans, be guided by behaviours (of both the infant and caretaking adults) that are genetically channelled, and therefore missing in other great apes. But could language really be a matter of learning—'software' rather than 'hardware' in human brains, to use modern computer jargon? The idea gains some credibility from the striking evidence (to which we return in Chapter 12) for a 'leap forward' in human cognitive achievement at the Upper Palaeolithic. The sudden appearance of cave painting, mass destruction of big game, cultural variation, and ocean travel, is evidence for a recent origin for language in anatomically modern humans, within the past 200 thousand years. This recent and sudden origin is more consistent with an invention than a product of gene selection, especially in a species with a long generation time.

Human linguistic behaviour has clear biological foundations, of course. In particular, there are many evolutionary specializations for speaking. The peripheral apparatus involved in speech is intricate and complex, and richly endowed with motor control from the brain, allowing exquisite programming of the musculature involved in speech in a way that would be impossible for another species to duplicate. Until recently, there was also concensus among neuropsychologists that structures in the left hemisphere of the human neocortex (Broca's area in the frontal lobe and Wernike's area in the temporal lobe) were essential for programming at a more abstract level, that of sentences. Damage to these areas, but not most others, results in speech deficits in humans; an elaborate theory was worked out, of how the two areas control grammar and lexicon, respectively, and communicate to build up whole utterances. The existence of neocortical structures dedicated to language would make it unlikely that any other ape, lacking these structures, could ever acquire any human-like communication. However, there are dangers in making strong claims that particular brain parts evolved 'for' language, and are dedicated to particular functions. The extent of localization of cortical function has always been exaggerated, perhaps a legacy of nineteenth century phrenology; in fact, great flexibility and plasticity exists in the cortex. For instance, although the left hemisphere is the site of linguistic processes in most humans, if this hemisphere is destroyed at birth language development is unimpaired: the right hemisphere can take over speech functions fully, giving instead some impairment of abilities normally associated with the *right* hemisphere. And it has been found recently that Broca's and Wernike's areas actually both control breathing, a completely different role to the traditional—mistaken—view of neuropsychology (Whitcombe 1994). Highly controlled breathing is certainly crucial for speech, and the ability is not fully mature untill 10 years of age, which is why children talk so differently to adults; but these areas are not pre-wired for language programming.

The evolution of human breathing control, along with precision motor control of tongue and supralaryngeal tract, uniquely allows humans to *speak*; but some form of *non-spoken language* might nevertheless be possible in other (intentional) species. Perhaps the underlying language system, as opposed to its implementation in speech, consists of a set of programmes that are learnt by every child during the first few years of life. In the same way that a computer can be given a new program to run, perhaps even a chimpanzee has sufficient brain hardware to 'run' the programmes necessary for language? The chimpanzee brain might of course simply not be big enough for all the new programmes; but if they could acquire even a basic set—perhaps those used by a 2-year-old child—it would be of major interest.

Cognitive foundations for language in animals

Can apes *use* language, even though they do not naturally acquire it? This fascinating idea was envisaged at least as early as the 1920s by Yerkes (who was well aware of ape–monkey differences in cognition, although his evidence was largely anecdotal and intuitive). He suggested that, as chimpanzees seem unable to modify their voices, sign language would be an appropriate method of approach. A project to do just this was begun in the 1960s and continues to this day, by Allen and Beatrix Gardner. Subsequently, two gorillas and two orang-utans have also been taught sign language (Fig. 11.1). In parallel, other projects were begun, using arbitrary visual symbols instead of hand configurations and movements to express words (Premack and Premack 1972; Rumbaugh *et al.* 1974). These projects have only used chimpanzees, but recently this has included the pygmy as well as the common chimpanzee. Fixed symbols have the advantage that rigorous controls and tests are more straightforward than with sign language, although all projects now use adequate controls and produce reliable results.

Many of these studies are long-term and detailed; their findings are complex and extensive. A whole book would be needed to do full justice to the conclusions, and in fact many books have been written on them

Figure 11.1 The gorilla, Michael, giving various signs in American sign language: (a) 'alligator' (a toy), (b) 'stink', (c) 'fruit', (d) 'lettuce/tree' (composite sign invented by gorilla, used to refer to bamboo), (e) 'lettuce', (f) 'hair'. (Photos by F. G. Patterson and R. H. Cohn.)

already. Here, only an outline of the achievements, particularly those most relevant to understanding the natural cognition of apes, will be attempted. Ape language work has generated heated controversy, resulting in extreme polarization of attitude among the rival researchers and their various detractors. Consequently, no summary will please all those closely involved in the work. However, at the risk of inspiring a lynch mob to explain my errors to me, I will attempt to give a version that seems to me a fair statement of what has been achieved by the apes, and what has not. I will not even try to be fair to the humans involved, because the identification of precedent in publication and the tracing of ideas and influences is a major undertaking, if it is even possible now.

With this aim in mind, I will begin with the work of Sue Savage-Rumbaugh and Duane Rumbaugh, rather than with the sign language work that was begun earlier. Starting here is convenient, because the basic findings (which I believe are now shown by all the major studies) are simpler to demonstrate using a language of fixed symbols than one of gestures. The Rumbaughs, working at the Yerkes Regional Primate Research Center, devised a vocabulary of arbitrary patterns, each a bit like a Chinese character. This analogy is a helpful one, for each token of 'Yerkish' stands for a word. In the early work, the chimpanzee was isolated in a room with a keyboard of Yerkish characters; all communication was via the keyboard. Learning by Lana, the pioneer chimpanzee, was much slower in this socially deprived environment than that of later chimpanzees who have been brought up more as children, and simply shown a board of Yerkish symbols that they and the people looking after them could point out. But even Lana showed that she could learn the differences between the many symbols and sequence them in short strings, to obtain rewards or to answer questions put to her. Subsequent chimpanzees were taught to ask for things that they wanted to look at, to use, or to eat, by using the Yerkish symbols. In this way, chimpanzees could be given problems that required them to ask for various tools or missing objects for success. They were able to do so, by pointing to the tool if it were present, or to the symbol if it were not. Generally, they only asked for things that they subsequently used: their requests were not random. Testing of their knowledge of what symbols referred to was regularly done 'blind'; that is, by an experimenter who did not know which symbols were being shown to the ape, so could not possibly give any clue as to the correct answer expected. When this tester occasionally made a mistake, unknowingly asking for an object not present, the chimpanzee showed distress but was most reluctant to guess. Outside the context of specific tasks, these chimpanzees routinely use Yerkish symbols to indicate their intended future actions, or their desires. This is clear, because they go on to do what they have announced, or to choose what they claimed to want if given a choice of attractive possibilities.

The chimpanzees' lives were made full of interest, and they were taught elaborate games just like children. Some of these relied on turn-taking and co-operation. For instance, one player sits with a board of appetizing foods and drinks on their lap. The other player has to ask for an item by pressing the appropriate Yerkish symbol; only then are both 'allowed' to eat the chosen items. The apes were, of course, taught this game with a human as the other player, but later they played it among themselves. The self-control of two young chimpanzees, with a tray of tasty goodies in front of them and no human in the room, when one of them fails to see the Yerkish request of the other and so refuses to allow eating to proceed, is a moving and impressive demonstration, recorded on videotape. Watching it leaves no doubt that common chimpanzees can learn turn-taking and understand the co-operative roles of others, confirming the experimental results we have seen already. Other games involved more complex co-operation, for instance when one player must help the other from an adjacent room, by passing a tool through a narrow opening; then, once the problem is solved, the reward is shared between them. Again, the young apes play this among themselves, though originally a human was the second player. In a test, the Yerkish symbols were experimentally denied to the chimpanzee who needed them for his request. His response was to improvise—for instance, using the picture on a label of a canned food as a symbol to reference what he needed. Although using only one 'word' at a time, this co-operation shows true communication: each participant taking account of a shared intention to exchange reliable information for a common purpose. Once again, this provides confirmation of the intentional abilities of chimpanzee deduced from observation and experiment.

The work of this project can now be used to settle two of the most hotly contested issues that were raised in the early days of 'ape language' studies. There is now no doubt that these apes can understand and use the concept of *reference*; that is, the fact that one thing, a word, can be made to stand for and refer to another thing, an object or a class of objects. Nor is there doubt that they are capable of using the words for real communication, requesting and offering new information when it is appropriate, as well as demanding things and commenting on performance.

These abilities were first claimed for chimpanzees on the basis of the behaviour of Washoe, the pioneer chimpanzee taught American sign language, and this led to controversy. The Gardners' early methods may have been less rigorous than the ideal, but their later work has repeatedly shown that their signing chimpanzees are using signs referentially and communicatively. Premack's early study was closer to the Rumbaugh's, in that the chimpanzee, Sarah, was taught the meanings of arbitrary symbols. In this study, metal tokens were placed on a magnetic board. Sarah was given no opportunity to use the tokens for normal communication, but set tasks which she had to perform, and only a small set of terms were taught. This led to suspicion that the chimpanzee was simply solving a complex puzzle, and had no conception of the possibility of real communication with the tokens, nor that they could reference objects in general.

Although this may well be correct, the arguments about whether chimpanzees can, if suitably taught, communicate referentially can now be laid to rest with the consistently positive evidence from recent work using good scientific controls.

None of the studies has found apes ready to acquire much in the way of syntax, or grammar. Following Chomsky (1957), grammar is often considered the hallmark of language. By 'grammar', I do not mean the prescriptions of fussy schoolteachers—insisting that infinitives are not to be split, that sentences are not to be started with 'but' or ended with prepositions, that some words must be called 'nouns' and others 'gerundives'. Unlike this (prescriptive) grammar, the (normative) grammar of linguistics is a matter of the structural relationships among the parts of real utterances: the often hidden rules that we must all be following if we can speak a language at all. Since the symbols of Yerkish and the tokens used by Sarah have no internal structure (like Chinese characters, each is a whole and is not built up from parts or dissected), the grammar most relevant to ape 'language' describes the structures formed by strings of words.

The logical structure in a sentence is not that of a string, even though this is how it is spoken. Much of the subject of theoretical linguistics is to do with how the underlying structure should best be described and regularized. To explain what I mean, take the sentence 'The yellow and black hornet was caught by the hairy spider.' Some groups of words belong more closely together than others, and sometimes the closest relationships are not even between adjacent words. Here is one simple analysis of its grammatical structure, based on Chomsky's work. For a start, words that all refer to single objects are more closely related than others, as are those that refer to a single action: (the yellow and black hornet) (was caught by) (the hairy spider). These groupings are often called phrases. Within a phrase, some words are more closely attached than others: 'yellow and black' is a unitary colour scheme, and this adjectival modifier narrows the class of objects referenced by the phrase, as does the other adjective, 'hairy': (the ((yellow and black) hornet)) (was caught by) (the (hairy spider)). 'The' cuts down the class of objects referenced by the noun to a single token, and suggests that exactly *which* one must already have been made clear before this sentence was produced (otherwise 'a' would have been used). Because the sentence is in the passive form (the active version is 'the hairy spider caught the yellow and black hornet'), the extra pair of words 'was ... by' are needed, to show that the spider was the agent of the action. 'Was' and 'by' belong together, although they are not adjacent in the string of words. Finally, the word 'caught' is really a composite of two functional units: a unit of meaning (called a morpheme) 'catch', and a past-tense marker. In some verbs, the composite nature would be made more obvious by the -ed form of the marker, but 'catched' is not the adult English form. Other analyses are possible, but no simpler: the logical structure of even an ordinary sentence is therefore quite complicated.

In English, most of the structure is signalled by the order of the words. In Latin, structure is almost entirely shown by the endings of words—their 'inflections' (other languages use prefixes as well as suffixes). Where we realize that 'yellow and black' belongs with 'hornet' by the word order, in Latin word order can be varied because the words for 'yellow' and 'black' have endings that specify which noun they must go with. These so-called 'case' endings indicate which is the agent and which the object of the action, so extra words like 'was ... by' are not needed, even if the order is juggled. The basic information will therefore be coded in different ways in different languages, but always there will be structural rules to relate 'surface structure'—the string of words—to their 'deep structure', closer to meaning. All languages are alike in having *some* way of pointing out syntactic structure: the logical relationships within sentences which make them mean more than simply 'adding together' the separate meanings of each word.

In sign languages, as in English, order is used to convey syntax, but some are also somewhat inflected, because the sign can be made in different ways: the *place* where it is made, and the *direction* in which it is taken, can be used to point out the agent and object of the action referred to by the sign. Sign languages, however, generally rely less on word order and inflections than spoken languages; often context is needed as well. For instance, Israeli sign language does not mark subject from object, although signers who are also Hebrew speakers will use its word order to remove all ambiguity (Schlesinger, 1971).

The most elaborate structural rules acquired by a 'language-using' ape are those of Premack's chimpanzee, Sarah. She was taught to respond to sentences like 'Sarah put banana pail apple bowl', putting the banana in the pail and the apple in the bowl. Both fruits would fit in both containers, so context was insufficient to show which belonged with which. Sarah had to, in effect, parse the sentence as PUT (banana, pail) and PUT (apple, bowl). This she could do successfully. Similarly, she learnt to use quantifiers like MORE or LESS, and conditional, IF–THEN, constructions effectively. However, doubts as to the real communicative nature of the system taught Sarah, noted above, make her complex 'grammar' suspect. Nothing of such complexity has been acquired by apes taught with more complete communication systems. In the main, 'two-word grammar' has been the limit of their syntactical structuring: regularities such as a verb or a WH-word (e.g. 'where', 'what', 'when') always coming before their object, not the reverse. Of course, even humans have to start somewhere, and the ape regularities of word order can be compared with the two-word stage of language development in children. Like children at this stage, apes taught American sign language are able to comprehend WH-word markers for the question form. Chimpanzees, like young children learning sign language, use the place and direction in which a sign is made to indicate agent and object cases. Nevertheless, some cognitive limitation must restrict the apes' abilities to the grammar of young children, since they—unlike children, even those learning sign language—go no further.

The Gardners' project, as well as being the pioneer attempt to circumvent chimpanzees' vocal deficiencies with visual means, has also gone further than any other in the direction of natural language usage. They, and later Roger Fouts and his associates, set up a small group of sign-language chimpanzees, and observed their spontaneous behaviour as well as test performances (and see Fig. 11.2). The chimpanzees' understanding of the usefulness of communication was clear in their use of the system among themselves, and in their evident frustration at encountering a chimpanzee that did not understand the system. Most striking of all, the researchers allowed a mother chimpanzee to teach sign language to her infant without any human help. When Washoe's own baby was stillborn, the Gardners urgently searched for a suitable infant for her to adopt. Finding one, they told Washoe—with signs, since in this project the researchers never spoke when they were with the animals—that she would have a baby again. Washoe's visible lethargy and depression evaporated, and she became animated. However, when she saw the baby she rejected it and again acted as if depressed; it seems that she had not fully understood that she had not been promised her *own* baby's return, only a substitute. Of course, the researchers had made no attempt to discuss the finality of

Figure 11.2 The gorilla, Koko, signs 'monkey' as she looks at a picture book about primates (photo by F. G. Patterson and R. H. Cohn).

death with Washoe, and her understandable misinterpretation is a moving indication of just how much Washoe *did* understand in normal communication. Luckily, she did accept the new baby after a few hours, and from that day for the next 5 years, the baby (and therefore to a large extent also Washoe) was allowed to see no human using American sign language. Nevertheless by 29 months the infant, Loulis, had acquired 17 signs (reliably identified 'blind' by observers), rising to 51 signs by 63 months, by which point the researchers felt Washoe's deprivation of all signing communication had become cruelty, and abandoned the restriction. Loulis was also showing reliable two-word orderings by 15 months. Washoe's use of the devices of moulding hands to the correct configuration, and demonstrating the signs for Loulis, were mentioned as evidence of intentional teaching in Chapter 9.

All these achievements have been taught to the chimpanzees originally by humans (even the techniques of teaching employed by Washoe). Yet normal language acquisition by children 'just comes naturally'. Naturally, that is, in the context of normal adult–child interaction. But mother–child interaction may itself include many patterns of behaviour well designed by evolution to teach (functionally, not intentionally) the essentials of language. Perhaps, it might be thought, researchers should have tried this simple approach with apes? In fact, they already had tried and failed. In two projects prior to the Gardners' work, chimpanzees were home reared in the hope that they would acquire language. (We have already met important evidence on imitation and pretence from one of these projects, the Hayes' work with the chimpanzee Viki.) It was spoken language that was hoped for, and the chimpanzees acquired only 3–4 words, and pronounced them very poorly at that. As we now know, the difficulty for the apes lies in lacking the neural apparatus for the complex motor actions of tongue, mouth, and breath control needed for speech.

Within the symbol and sign language work of recent years, it is certainly true that projects that have treated their animals more like children have experienced much quicker and more efficient learning (even if sometimes at the expense of greater difficulty in proving success to sceptics). In David Premack's study, and in Herbert Terrace's which used sign language but employed behaviourist, animal-training procedures, far less was learnt than in the Gardners' work. Even within a single project, the Rumbaughs', a gradual change to more child-appropriate treatment for the subjects has resulted in spectacularly faster learning.

This took a new turn when Sue Savage-Rumbaugh discovered by accident that young apes can learn symbols entirely by observation. In trying to teach an adult pygmy chimpanzee by conventional means (she learnt little), her offspring Kanzi, happening to be present, began to pick up knowledge of the symbols spontaneously. Savage-Rumbaugh and her co-workers immediately capitalized on this, and set up a regime in which caretakers did not insist on symbol production, they merely talked about what was happening and going to happen. Pointing to symbols at the same time, they chatted about daily routines, outings and events in his varied and interesting life. Kanzi, and subsequently two other pygmy chimpanzees and one common chimpanzee, picked up the meanings of symbols and acquired large vocabularies, all without being taught. Kanzi even acquired the meaning of *spoken* English words, whereas extensive testing with earlier (common chimpanzee) subjects had shown that they got nothing useful from the conversations to which they, too, had been exposed. When Kanzi was tested 'blind' (i.e. the experimenter did not know which words Kanzi was listening to on a pre-recorded tape), his comprehension was up to 150 spoken words by age 6, and he was accurate even when tested with word pairs that differed only in one phoneme (a 'letter' of spoken speech).

Kanzi was also found to use word order to decipher meaning correctly, for instance discriminating 'Make the doggie bite the snake' from 'Make the snake bite the doggie'. Further, he could understand embedding of a clause, as in answering 'Go get the tomato that's in the microwave'. Tomatoes were present in several locations, some much nearer and more obvious than the one in the microwave, yet typically he did not even glance at nearby objects, going straight to the appropriate location. But when given the control sentence 'Go to the microwave and get the tomato', he hesitated and seemed confused, as well he might, since this is ambiguous as to *which* tomato is being referenced. Like other apes, Kanzi also used word order in two-word combinations to express grammatical distinctions. Clearly, apes can even pick up simple syntax by observation alone.

Techniques of helping young apes to acquire human language are still being developed—sometimes with the help of the apes!—and we can hope for much more from these studies in the future. Thus it would be premature to draw a line and state 'this, and this only, is what a great ape can achieve'. However, at present it is striking that even the most proficient chimpanzee (the pygmy chimpanzee, Kanzi) has learnt language much slower than a human child. When Kanzi was already 8 years old, his abilities matched those of a 2-year-old girl, brought up in closely comparable circumstances by a mother who is one of Kanzi's caretakers. First language learning in humans must take place within a 'sensitive' period during the early years. Children deprived of a normal environment during the first few years of life (for instance, when brought up by wolves after abandonment by the mother, or when cruelly deprived by parents), cannot reach normal language competence. If chimpanzees, too, have a sensitive period for acquiring language, and the failure to teach Kanzi's own mother in adulthood suggests this may be so, then chimpanzee language can never approach that of adult humans, unless new methods are able to speed up their language acquisition. On present evidence, it would seem that the difference between their achievements and ours will always be most apparent in their restricted and simple syntax.

Trying to talk with other species

This work, and comparable projects with orang-utans and gorillas which have apparently achieved rather similar but more limited results, shows that great apes do possess the cognitive foundations on which language evolution can build. Of course, until similar, painstaking work is done with monkeys, we cannot argue that *only* apes have such abilities. But the evidence of the previous few chapters suggests that the result might be very disappointing, and no-one has yet risked the huge expenditure of time and money to find out.

Fascinatingly, the techniques have been modified for use with more distantly related species to ourselves, suspected to have advanced intelligence. Louis Herman has devised an artificial system—to be precise, two systems (see Herman 1986)—with which to give novel, complex commands to dolphins. One bottlenose dolphin, Phoenix, learnt to respond to auditorily presented commands with a linear order syntax: PIPE FETCH GATE means 'take the piece of pipe to the pool gate'. The other, Akeakamai, was instead given visual commands with an inverse syntax: CHANNEL FISH FETCH means 'take the fish to the channel connecting the pools'. Sentences could be three-word, as in these examples, or more complex, like SURFACE PIPE FETCH BOTTOM HOOP, 'take the pipe that's on the surface to the hoop that's on the bottom'. These grammars allow about 2000 sentences in all, only a few of which were explicitly taught. When tested with novel sentences, both dolphins performed at about 65 per cent accuracy (chance is only 4 per cent, in all cases). Overall, the dolphins' performance was similar for two- and three-word sentences (about 95 per cent), but the difficulty of the inverse grammar showed up for longer sentences, with Akeakamai only getting 66 per cent against Phoenix's 81 per cent. In both cases, however, they are massively above chance. In fact the task difficulty and performance levels are far above those of Premack's chimpanzee; although limited to comprehension (it is not obvious how dolphins could produce language for the benefit of humans), this is more like a real, natural language than the limited system taught to the chimpanzee. Particularly impressive is the dolphins' relaxed attitude to major novelty: when, untrained, conjoined sentences were suddenly introduced (e.g. PIPE TAIL-TOUCH PIPE OVER, meaning 'touch the pipe with your tail, then jump over it'), both dolphins generally responded correctly straight away. As well as extending the range of sentences comprehended (potentially without limit), this has the characteristics of real comprehension, not rigid training.

'Reception-only' languages have now been tried with other animals. Ronald Schusterman has shown that sealions (*Zalophus californianus*) are able to perform very like Herman's dolphins (e.g. Gisiner and Schusterman, 1992), although he emphasizes that prematurely describing the animals' competence in linguistic terms may be unhelpful. (This is not human chauvinism, a device to keep animals on the 'right' side of the linguistic Rubicon; rather, he suggests that we do not understand language well enough to make testable predictions, and starting 'bottom-up' with animal learning theory will eventually lead to a better dissection of language skill.) Now, Sally Boysen is starting language-reception work with a pot-bellied pig and a border collie dog. So far, the dog has shown rapid learning of gestures coding actions, but not those for objects; whereas the pig learns gestures coding objects more easily than those for actions (S. Boysen, personal communication.).

None of these species is able to respond in kind. Certain birds, such as large parrots, do readily talk back to humans, but it has always been assumed they could never understand their vocal imitation. Nevertheless, the 'acid test' of attempting to teach language to a parrot has recently been attempted—with success! Irene Pepperberg devised a novel training regime for her African grey parrot, Alex. One human acted as trainer, the other as trainee, both modelling for Alex what a 'good' answer would be, and setting up rivalry with Alex for the trainer's attention. The two humans often reversed their roles of trainer and trainee, showing Alex the speaker-hearer interchangeability of human language. Alex's reward for linguistically correct utterances to questions was usually the object mentioned in the sentence, which he would eat or destroy (whichever was appropriate) with relish. Alex can respond correctly in English to questions about objects and their properties ('What colour?', 'What shape?', How many?'), and he can compare and contrast the objects in a set ('What's same?', 'What's different?'), focusing on shared or odd-one-out properties (Pepperberg 1990). His use of numbers up to six is particularly striking. He was not fazed by transfer tests with novel arrangements of objects, so there is no possibility that he was simply memorizing old arrays of objects or the distinctive patterns that certain objects make (like the pattern that 5 is always given on playing cards). He was not even put out by arrays of completely novel objects, for which he knew no verbal label. When given mixed-object arrays (e.g. two hairclips and four bobbins), he could be asked about the number in each subset, or the total ('How many toys?'). It seems that Alex has really acquired the abstract concept of number, as well as the linguistic concepts of turn-taking and simple syntax.

The cognitive capacities that this kind of work has shown in a range of species are impressive, and no doubt more revelations are in store. However, this is a diversion from our main theme: the tracing of the evolutionary route of *human* cognition. If dolphins, parrots, or border collies share some of the array of abilities that make up the human specialization for intelligence, it is by evolutionary *convergence*, not common descent from a shared ancestor. This can help to pin-point the environmental factors that select for intelligence, but not flesh out the evolution of human cognition. In the next chapter, we return to the main theme, asking: what factors might have led to the evolutionary development of intelligence in simian primates?

Further reading

Two ape-language projects are the subject of recent books: the Gardners', described in Gardner *et al.* (1989), and the Rumbaughs' in Savage-Rumbaugh (1986). For other great apes, see Parker and Gibson (1990): Kanzi's more recent successes are described in the chapter by P. M. Greenfield and E. S. Savage-Rumbaugh, and Project Chantek—the orang-utan work—in the chapter by H. L. Miles. The achievements of the gorilla Koko are most easily accessible in F. G. Patterson and E. Linden *The education of Koko*, Holt, Rinehart and Winston, 1981.

Part 4

Evolutionary causes and consequences

12
Food for thought

Now that we have seen various ways in which certain animals can usefully be called 'intelligent', we turn to enquiring the reason for this. *Why* did some animals become intelligent? In evolutionary terms, this can be rephrased: what were the selection pressures that promoted intelligence? In the Darwinian evolutionary process of natural selection, a selection pressure is a condition in the natural environment which benefits individuals with certain characteristics but handicaps those without, thus naturally 'selecting' for those advantageous characters. Looking for the selection pressure is asking, in other words, 'What was intelligence good for?'

We might also ask: what are animals using it for now that confers biological advantage? If the set of skills we label intelligence were not *still* useful for survival and reproduction in the modern descendents of animals that earlier acquired it, the abilities would have been lost ('selected against') if they were at all costly; and large brains, as we shall see in Chapter 14, are very costly. Often the two questions amount to the same thing, although if intelligence is a general-purpose capability, as suggested by the Turing machine approach, then this is not necessarily so. An ability that evolved because of advantages it conferred in one way may be put to quite other uses once it is there.

Many plausible areas of potential 'challenge' in animal lives have been suggested that might have selected for increased intelligence. Most—until recently all—proposals centre on the problems met in dealing with the physical environment. For varied species of animal, the most critical environmental demands might concern avoidance of predators, finding food, heat stress, cold stress, diseases, and so on. But for simian primates, where intelligence is a particular specialization, the range is smaller. Numerically, most mammals are under 10 cm long, so very vulnerable to heat, cold, and predation. Simian primates are much larger, and most live in tropical environments with relatively predictable temperature regimes. So it is not surpising that theories about the environmental problems that most challenged and shaped monkey and ape intelligence have centred on efficiency in food acquisition.

It is reasonable to think that feeding is more intellectually demanding for primates than for other animals, because most primates are unspecialized vegetarians. Most other animals are either carnivores or herbivores. Carnivores, by eating other animals, obtain a diet that is automatically *balanced* in nutrients in just the right way for building bodies, as well as getting material for conversion to metabolic energy. The only carnivorous primates are the nocturnal insectivorous strepsirhines and tarsiers, not noted for intelligence (capturing large animals to eat, which some primates do to supplement their vegetarian diet, may require intellectual skill, a possibility to which we return below). Herbivores mostly have gut specializations, such as several stomachs, that enable them to eat low-quality vegetarian food rather unselectively. In effect, they are symbiotic with the bacteria of their intestines, as they rely on the nutrients that the bacteria are able to manufacture from coarse plant food. To a limited extent, any mammal can do this in its large intestine, even humans. Unspecialized browsing animals like elephants, rhinoceroses, and horses are large enough to be able to eat quite poor-quality browse; but to do so they require to forage for long periods, they sleep little and are nearly as active by night as by day, so they may not have too much problem getting an adequate diet. The non-insectivorous strepsirhines, such as most lemurs, all have long intestines despite their small bodies, and are often active by night as well as by day. But monkeys and apes have a problem: they are diurnal (except for one platyrrhine species, the night monkey *Aotus*) and generally not of large body size, they have simple stomachs (except for two genera, *Colobus* and *Presbytis*) yet they eat largely vegetarian matter.

Monkeys and apes have to balance their diet, which they do by wide ranging and yet selective eating; this is nicely illustrated by a study of Sri Lankan monkeys, *Macaca sinica*, by Marcel Hladik. By careful observation and quantification of their feeding, and phytochemical analysis of their food plants, he was able to show that for these 'frugivorous' monkeys, fruit was always more abundant than they could ever need. However, the monkeys had large day ranges and occupied a home range too large for efficient defence as a territory. Why? Their ranging was apparently a consequence of a need to eat fungi, rotten wood, insects, bark, shoots—a whole range of items that allowed them to make up the protein, vitamin, and mineral deficiences of the energy-rich ripe fruit (Hladik 1975). The need for a balanced diet forces many primates to eat items that are hard to find. In studying baboon ecology (Byrne *et al.* 1993), I was continually amazed at the subtle cues that they must use to identify some of their plant foods (Fig. 12.1); at the most harsh time of year, the main survival foods were all either underground, or tiny and inconspicuous (Fig. 12.2).

Because of their special nutritional needs, simian primates may well need to employ more skill in feeding than other animals. But what skills *are* useful in feeding? 'Feeding skill' amounts to two packages of ability: *finding* a source of food, and *obtaining* the food once it is located. In either case, the evidence that suggests a need for intelligence is normally the complexity of the task. We will examine each package in turn, using evidence from topics we met in earlier chapters as well as novel information.

Figure 12.1 Baboons in the mountains of South Africa often excavate food hidden below ground (a). The only visible cue to the presence of a nutritious corm of the orchid *Eulophia foliosa* is the dry stem uppermost on my knife blade (b), and this is the same colour as the dead grass.

Finding food

To find food requires learning which items are edible, and getting to sources of them in the known home range at the appropriate season, both of which would be helped by a good memory (and, to make matters worse, trees in tropical forests often fruit on a non-annual cycle). This sort of memorization is called, in human psychology, having a *cognitive map*.

(a) (b)

Figure 12.2 In the leanest season each year, all foods are potential problems. (a) The corm of the lily *Watsonia lepida* requires excavation from rock-hard soil. (b) The small, swollen stem bases of the grass *Sporobulus congoensis* can only be spotted by the slight hairiness of the leaves (right).

Cognitive maps in primates

Although many animal species probably have extensive spatial knowledge, the idea that the advantages of a better cognitive map selected for greater intelligence was first introduced to explain primate intelligence. John Mackinnon (1978) noticed that an orang-utan, when confronted with a poor crop yielded by its favourite fruit tree, chose a route through the featureless Bornean forest that took in a whole series of these trees. Its route was so economical in effort that Mackinnon reckoned he could only match it with the aid of a carefully recorded map. Independently, Katy Milton (1981) proposed mental mapping skill as the explanation for the large brain of the frugivorous spider monkey (*Ateles geoffroyi*) relative to that of the more folivorous howler monkey (*Alouatta palliata*). These two species are the same size in body, but in brain the spider monkey is nearly twice as large (we will return to the topic of brain size in Chapter 14, where it will become apparent that simple comparison of brain to body may, in fact, be misleading). Spider monkeys often split off from the group to forage, and Milton suggested that to navigate individually around the spider monkeys' range requires each individual to have an efficient cognitive map. She noticed that the spider monkeys often set off determinedly along straight-line routes through the forest, that terminated at a fine fruiting tree. The leaves that howler monkeys are able to feed on are more abundant and much less patchily distributed in the forest than the erratic bounty of ripe fruit. This enables them to forage as a cohesive group and manage with far smaller home ranges, so they have little need of efficient cognitive mapping skills.* In Guyana, Marc van Roosmalen (1988) has noticed that certain spider monkey males apparently *prospect* for good trees in advance. In late afternoon, when the group has already found a tree in which they will sleep the night, a dominant male will sometimes set off alone and visit several fruit trees without eating; next day, the group will head for the best one, apparently led by the prospector male. Spider monkey ranges are very large, so a large brain would give a selective advantage, if cognitive mapping is costly on brain tissue.

Subsequent evidence of cognitive maps in primates has been sparse, but interesting. As we have already seen, chimpanzees in West Africa use round stones as hammers, and larger flat stones as anvils, to break open tough *Panda* and *Coula* nuts. Christophe and Hedwig Boesch (1984) showed that these stones were in short supply. Rocks of the right properties are a rarity in the forest and locating one without trouble is important when a new source of nuts is found; often hammer stones had to be carried to the source of nuts. The routes that the chimpanzees took—occasionally up to a kilometre—were highly economical on effort. They went straight to the nearest stone of the right type far more often than chance, and took 'short cuts' rather than retracing their routes. This implies that they remembered where they had last seen each useful stone lying: a cognitive map of the forest, annotated with rock locations.

The problem of finding out whether animals' navigation is efficient and 'map-like' becomes more difficult when resources are more abundant: the animal's goal has to be inferred in advance by the primatologist, before efficiency can be tested. Two species of tamarin monkey studied by Paul Garber (*Saguinus mystax* and *S. fuscicollis*) conveniently relied on a small number of species of tree for their food. Garber was able to show that on over 70 per cent of moves between trees, the next tree selected was the nearest example of that species (Garber 1989). With the rarer trees, when an error would be more costly in terms of wasted travel, this proportion

*But it may be that howlers confront just as severe spatial memory problems on a more intricate scale. Howlers, unlike colobines, do not have special gut adaptations to neutralize the poisonous secondary compounds of mature leaves and unripe fruit in tropical forests, yet they eat both. Kenneth Glander (1978) has shown that they know exactly which individual trees have the lowest toxin levels and eat only from those, and they select fruit and leaves with great care and deliberation, eating only a little of each type at a time. Their strategy appears to be dicing with death by poisoning—Glander has seen an incautious howler drop to the floor, poisoned—and a good memory would be essential for survival.

rose to 90 per cent. Also, the tamarins' routes between trees showed few twists and turns—they travelled directly to the selected tree.

Hamadryas baboons (*Papio hamadryas*) have long been noticed to mill around on the open ground near the cliffs on which they sleep, before they set off in the mornings to forage: phalanxes of animals like 'arms' of an amoeba push out, only to collapse back into the mass, before finally the whole group pours out. Once out foraging, this group splits into much smaller parties, which rejoin later. Hans Sigg and Alex Stolba (1981) discovered that the 'arms', apparently thrown out haphazardly, function as communication, by *pointing* at a possible place to meet up again later. When one direction of departure is finally accepted and the baboons set off to wander as small bands, their subsequent movements have no correlation to each other's route or to the direction of their eventual meeting place. Nevertheless, the orientation of the 'arm' along which they set off predicts the place where the troop later rests in the heat of the day. Baboons not only have cognitive maps, but they can label other animals' knowledge of large-scale space without using verbal descriptions.

Chimpanzees also communicate about spatial directions, in different ways in the two species. Sometimes when a pygmy chimpanzee group is resting, some males will break off small trees and drag the branches through the forest for around 10 metres; the group will subsequently set off in just this direction (Ingmanson 1993). It seems the chimpanzees are using the branches as a tool to convey symbolic information. In common chimpanzees, Boesch (1991*b*) has found that drumming on tree root buttresses signals movement direction. If a particular male drums on two different trees in quick succession, the group generally begins moving, in the direction indicated by the two trees' relative locations; if he drums on the same tree, they generally rest, and if he combines these displays, then the group will first rest, then move off in the indicated direction.

These scattered revelations of the remarkable navigational skills of some monkeys and apes give credence to the 'cognitive-map hypothesis' of primate intellectual origins.

Planning arboreal travel

The need for a cognitive map applies equally to monkeys and apes. Bearing in mind the clear monkey/ape division in insightful understanding, any suggested challenge that applies to apes but not monkeys is particularly worthy of attention. Daniel Povinelli and John Cant (1992) have suggested that the locomotion of orang-utans presents intellectual complexity (Fig. 12.3). This is particularly significant, because the orang-utan is known to have changed little in morphology since *Sivapithecus*, close to the common ancestor of all modern great apes. Thus, intellectual adaptations for orang-utan locomotion could in principle explain cognitive abilities of other great apes. Orang-utans travel by swinging, interchangeably using hands and

Figure 12.3 Orang-utan arboreal locomotion has been proposed to select for the ability to view the self as an object, to solve the three-dimensional engineering problem of manoeuvring safely through an arboreal habitat (photo by A. Russon).

feet, and often they build up the back-and-forth oscillation of their tree until they can finally catch hold of the next tree. Even deciding a potential route through the tangle of vines and poles is no easy task, let alone following it. Povinelli and Cant's idea is that working out the appropriate moves of limbs is complex, and—since adult orang-utans, especially males, are so heavy that they would be seriously injured by any miscalculation resulting in a fall—that this selects for computational ability. (No other modern primate is both so heavy and so arboreal, and only species of other great apes ever were, as far as we know.) Povinelli and Cant believe that the crucial ability selected was the ability to envisage the self in three-dimensional space, as an engineering problem. The generalizations from this objective view of the self, to mirror self-recognition and an objective view of others as like self, are then straightforward. The only unfortunate part of this intriguing speculation is the difficulty of testing it.

Obtaining food

Several aspects of obtaining food have been suggested to require greater than average intelligence: the capture of prey by hunting; the skilled tool use shown in insect-fishing techniques; 'extractive' foraging on food that is hidden in a matrix or otherwise concealed; and using complex procedures for food processing. These proposals do not necessarily apply to the majority of simian primates, or even the majority of apes, and in several cases they are derived from attempts to understand the selective pressures on hominids that resulted in the unique intelligence of modern humans.

Hunting

Most hunters of the animal kingdom are, of course, not primates, and surprisingly little is known of any intellectual skills that carnivores use in hunting, although big-game hunters have always claimed them to be considerable. The problem is that hunting by several animals at the same time, each blocking a possible escape route or taking over a chase when another leaves off, *looks* like organized co-operation to human observers (and also to the prey animal) yet may be no more than an accidental consequence of individually chosen strategies. However, Stander (1992) found 40 per cent of lion hunts in Etosha, Namibia, to show co-operation that went beyond this. When fanning out and circling, prior to driving the prey into an ambush by other, waiting lions, he found that 'all lions appear to watch both the prey and other pride members during the stalk as if to orient their own movements'. Clearly their prey could equally benefit from skilled evasion techniques, and Jerison (1973) has suggested that just such an evolutionary 'arms race' between predator and prey underlies the observed increase in relative brain size of both carnivores and ungulates in the fossil record.

However, few primates hunt in any sense of the term, so the 'intelligent hunter' cannot be a general explanation of monkey and ape intelligence. Only chimpanzees, baboons, and capuchin monkeys regularly kill mammals and birds in the wild. Of these, the captures by baboons and capuchins are normally opportunistic grabs by animals that find themselves in convenient circumstances; the organization, co-operation, and sharing components of hunting that might be supposed to require greater intelligence are lacking. The hunting hypothesis is therefore aimed squarely at the chimpanzee (and the subtext is the 'man the hunter' scenario portrayed in many accounts of human evolution).

Does chimpanzee behaviour deserve comparison with hunting by modern human hunter-gatherers? Chimpanzee hunting has been studied extensively in the secondary forests of Gombe and Mahale in Tanzania, where very long-term data are now available. Chimpanzees there catch and eat a wide range of mammals, usually juveniles (monkeys of several species, especially *Colobus badius*, bushpig, duiker, giant rat, etc). Both these sites have been provisioned in the past (researchers set out bananas or sugar cane to lure animals into view and reduce their natural initial fear of humans), and it has been claimed that hunting mammals is an unnatural consequence of the resulting dietary inbalances. However, mammal bones in faeces of unprovisioned chimpanzees at many other sites show that

Figure 12.4 Male chimpanzees eating of red colobus monkey at Mahale. The alpha-male, Ntologi (right), retains control of the carcass, but allows his closest ally, Lubulungu (left), to feed from it. The very old male behind them is also allowed to feed.

killing mammals is normal behaviour, not a result of provisioning. Hunting is seasonal in Tanzania, the season corresponding to the time when young prey animals are available. Techniques of hunting are hard to observe in tangled forest, but the end results are obvious. Males are found monopolizing carcasses, and overall they obtain much more meat than females (Fig. 12.4). Meat is shared by these males, to the extent that they will tolerate some theft and respond positively to some begging. The sharing is more generous to animals who are old, are close relatives of the possessor, or are females in oestrus (Fig. 12.5). Not all chimpanzees gain any meat, and females and young animals are especially likely to eat none for long periods. Although meat is thus not an essential part of chimpanzee diet, their hunting has major effect on prey populations (at Gombe, this has been calculated to be as great as the effect of lions on antelope in the Serengeti National Park).

When we come to look at details of the hunting, the picture seems different at the two sites, though they are separated by only 130 km along the shore of Lake Tanzania. At Gombe, hunting has been described as involving active co-operation among males and deliberate sharing out of the carcass among the participants immediately afterward (Teleki 1973). At

Figure 12.5 A female chimpanzee begs with outstretched hand, a request to a male in possession of a small piece of colobus monkey meat.

Mahale, the behaviours are described differently. All animals are seen to capture prey, and captures by females are noted frequently, but subsequent robbing of weaker animals by males in the party results in male monopolization of carcasses (Nishida *et al.* 1979); the division of a large carcass is seen as unpreventable by the alpha-male, so other large males gain big hunks (Nishida *et al.* 1979). The two accounts sound totally different, but it is possible the behaviour is the same in both cases. One has to remember that chimpanzees often travel in a large party centred about the top-rank male and his male friends. The spread of a chimpanzee party may be quite large on the ground, and may entirely encompass a colobus monkey troop's small home range: the monkeys have nowhere to go, since there are chimpanzees all around them. Suppose individual chimpanzees hunt opportunistically, intending no co-operation. Once one chimpanzee finds a colobus sufficiently vulnerable to attack and pursue, then the monkey on the run is especially vulnerable to attack by others as well. A group of chimpanzees each after the same monkey and each taking only their own best line of attack, would end up blocking each escape route the monkey had available—just as if they were intentionally co-operating. From the colobus monkey point of view, this may indeed feel like chimpanzee co-operation! But whether the co-operation is planned beforehand, as with human hunter-gatherers, is very hard to be sure. Similarly, there is a fine line between grudging acceptance that one's share is too big to monopolize, and intentional division of spoils. Perhaps chimpanzee hunting in Tanzanian sites merely 'simulates' the co-operative enterprise of human hunters.

However, at Taï Forest, Ivory Coast, chimpanzees' hunts are interestingly different (Boesch and Boesch 1989). Almost the whole community is involved in any given hunt, and observers can predict when a group is 'going hunting'. Hunting occurs year-round, and adult animals are regularly taken. With opportunistic hunting, it is occasionally likely that several prey are killed at the same time; this never happens at Taï, although it is quite frequent at Mahale and Gombe. Researchers who have watched these hunts describe male chimpanzees apparently taking pre-assigned roles in an organized, 'team play'—scout, decoy, catcher. This sounds much closer to human hunter-gatherer behaviour, but the varied and disputed interpretations of Gombe chimpanzees' hunting caution against hailing even Taï chimpanzees' behaviour as co-operative in a human way.

Striking differences remain between chimpanzee and human hunting, even if the co-operation observed at Taï were to be accepted as similar. In all known cases, chimpanzee hunting involves only 'small game', one-fifth the body size of the captors, whereas from upper palaeolithic times to the present day humans have slaughtered wild animals larger than themselves. Nor is any transport of the meat seen, the normal sequel to human hunting, although this, of course, reflects the chimpanzees' lack of a single home base. Most crucially, modern hunter-gatherers always employ weapons, and plan tactics in advance. Hunting by hominids before the Upper Palaeolithic was less sophisticated: there is no good evidence before that time for killing of large game or use of weapons for hunting. This argument has been used to dismiss the claims of elaborate and co-operative societies in hominids before anatomically modern humans. However, it remains of interest to understand how early hominids hunted, and the current best bet is that they may very well have hunted in a closely similar manner to chimpanzees.

Tool use

As we have seen already, a number of birds and mammals use objects as tools. These animals may select objects carefully for the purpose, but they do not *modify* them into tools, whereas common chimpanzees do. Further, only common chimpanzees use tools for many purposes in the wild, and have been seen to fashion a set of different tools for separate tasks in the attainment of a single goal. Individuals of other species only ever show a single technique.

Chimpanzees also readily invent *new* tool uses: for instance, a banana leaf as an umbrella, after researchers introduced the plants; a long stem to test a fire without getting burnt (Fig. 12.6). To use the jargon of psychological work on problem-solving, common chimpanzees seem to have a *set* to the use of tools—they tend to solve novel problems by using objects. (Other

Figure 12.6 Chimpanzees readily invent new uses for tools. A fire has been lit in the grass, and this rehabilitant chimpanzee is fearful but interested (note the facial expression); it uses a long probe to investigate the flames.

great apes in captivity readily invent novel tool uses, so it may be that all apes have a similar set, but only chimpanzee feeding ecology requires tool use in practice.)

Just as with the hunting hypothesis, tool use is largely relevant only to chimpanzee and human comparison; it has nothing to say about the intellectual fortes of monkeys, and little about other great apes. (Occasional cases of tool use in the wild by orang-utans, such as using a large leaf as a 'glove', and by pygmy chimpanzees, such as using branch dragging as a signal, seem unlikely to reflect a major pressure towards intelligence in these species.) An obvious test of the hypothesis' relevance, then, is comparison of chimpanzee tools with human tools.

Some modern hunter-gatherers use highly elaborate tools, like the intricate spears and arrows of !Kung San hunters, which leave the tip embedded in the prey. Others, like the sadly persecuted Tasmanian Aborigines, reduced to a single pure-bred individual by the 1880s, had very simple toolkits. Bill McGrew (1987) has directly compared the tools used to get food by Tasmanian Aborigines and Tanzanian chimpanzees, concluding that the level of sophistication is quite similar. (This result should not be misunderstood. Tasmanian Aborigines, unlike chimpanzees, used tools for many other purposes, and made clothes, jewellery and living shelters.)

Turning to the tools of extinct hominids, there is increasing evidence that the sophistication of hominid tools has been overestimated. The crude flake tools of the Oldowan culture of around 2 My, attributed to *Homo habilis*, lack any symmetry or clear sign of construction to an intended design; the intellectual abilities required are not much greater than those needed to fashion a chimpanzee fishing stick, and well within the ape range of competence (Wynn and McGrew 1989). Nicholas Toth (1985) has shown, by making replica tools experimentally, that much of the variety in types of tool that can be discerned in Oldowan assemblages is likely due to no more than accidents of flaking and the original variability of rocks. Right up to the Mousterian stone culture of the Neanderthals, most stone tools lack any sign that the makers had a preconceived design in mind. Mousterian tools consist mainly of small flake 'points' and bifacial cores. Evidence that Mousterian points were attached to wooden shafts has been questioned, and many of the bifacial core tools resemble those found in the earliest levels at Olduvai (Gowlett 1986). Great variation in Mousterian tools occurs, resulting from differences in the availability of raw materials (e.g. where these are abundant, little retouching is seen, but where stone is scarce, tools are retained and retouched: Rolland 1981), and from technique of construction. But in an important way, their lack of design, tools of hominids before anatomically modern humans suggest little intellectual advance over the Oldowan. The famous 'handaxe' of the Acheulean industry, associated with *Homo erectus* and still found in Neanderthal sites, appears to be an exception to this rule: the stone is bilaterally symmetrical viewed from above or the sides, and in some of the more recent examples (the Acheulean spanned 400 000 years) the edge follows a straight line projected through three-dimensional space (Wynn 1988). Now, even the cognitive significance of Acheulean handaxes has been questioned. Davidson and Noble (1993) note that the flakes detached from handaxes were themselves used as tools. Perhaps, they suggest, the Acheulean shape would often tend to emerge from flaking off small pieces of sharp stone that could be used as tools, and perhaps the 'handaxe' is simply a core, useful mainly for the production of small flake tools? Certainly this would explain the retention of the Oldowan style of tool throughout the Acheulean period, if all that had changed was the use of a handy-sized core for producing the same old flake tools. Similarly, they suggest that the Levallois technique, of a prepared 'tortoiseshell' core from which a single large flake can finally be struck, may be instead a discarded, failed attempt to rejuvenate a core: taking off the large flake would produce an edge with more obtuse angle so that more small, useful flakes could be removed. This would better account for the frequent finds of core and final flake together, hard to interpret if the final flake is the tool to be used.

These ideas are controversial, but there is no doubt that at the Upper Palaeolithic, a completely different level of sophistication suddenly emerges: many blades are split from prepared cores; tools become standardized, they show imposed form, and many unequivocal types are found; bone, antler, and ivory are used for the first time; and regional variation is found at each site, no mere reflection of raw material (Mellars 1991). This advance is associated with personal adornment by beads and pendants, the first signs of specialized, systematic hunting of large game, the colonization of Australia despite a minimum of 90 km ocean crossing, and, in Europe, beautiful representational art. Modern humans had arrived.

Before these anatomically modern humans of the Upper Palaeolithic, stone tools could all have been produced by animals with little more cognitive sophistication in tool-making than chimpanzees. This modern re-evaluation increases the relevance of chimpanzee studies to interpretation of early hominid behaviour, but it also weakens the case that tool use was a major selective pressure for human intelligence. Neanderthals had larger brains than ourselves, even *Homo erectus* had huge brains by chimpanzee standards, yet these creatures used tools only a little more sophisticated than those chimpanzees make. Tool-making remains a possible candidate for selecting intellectual advance in the common ancestors of humans and apes, but seems unlikely to have been the source of the subsequent massive brain-size changes in the hominid lineage.

Extractive foraging

Many foods are obvious to the eye, once found. But some edible matter is embedded in a matrix or hidden in some other way so that it cannot be seen, and first needs extraction. If food processing that requires extraction is cognitively demanding, then this could relate feeding to intelligence over a wide range of primates. However, many other mammals forage extractively (for instance, opening nuts and making caches to dig up later, probing for nectar, digging for water) and there is no sign of any systematic relationship with their general intelligence. Susan Parker and Katherine Gibson (1979) suggested that the crucial distinction is ecological. Specialist extractive foraging on one class of food available year-round (abalones for sea otters, cockles for herring gulls, nuts for squirrels) tends to promote tool use of an 'unintelligent', context-specific nature, they argue. It is only omnivores, confronted with foods seasonally available only by extractive foraging, that develop 'intelligent' tool use. In support of this they point out that the gorilla, which in captivity shows intelligence in manipulation of objects, nevertheless does not use tools in the wild (where most food plants are available year-round), despite having regularly to extract plant food from a concealing matrix. The chimpanzee, whose wider diet range includes seasonal foods (nuts, ants, termites) that require extraction, uses tools for the purpose. Parker and Gibson also labelled the capuchin monkey as an intelligent tool user but, in the light of the modern exposé of capuchins' failure to understand tool properties (Chapter 7), this is unwarranted; nor does this change weaken their hypothesis, since capuchins do not use tools in the wild. Parker and Gibson's theory, then, emerges as a variant of the tool-use hypothesis, in which they give theoretical justification for discounting tool using by non-chimpanzees. (Whether the criterion of seasonality will prove of any importance is perhaps dubious, since Mahale chimpanzees forage on *Campanotus* ants with tools year-round.) Their theory differs in seeing tool use as a *result* rather than a cause of intelligence, and specifies the circumstances (omnivory + extraction + seasonal availability) in which the intelligence is shown up by tool-making. They do not propose extractive foraging as itself the origin of the intelligence. However, the underlying implication—that there might be something special about extracting foods from a hidden place or a concealing matrix, making intelligence useful for success—would also be worthy of empirical investigation.

Complex food processing

There are other ways in which feeding technique can be complex besides needing a tool to do it. We have met an example of this already: when introducing the possibility of program-level imitation, I described the logical complexity of the technique that a mountain gorilla uses to process a stalk of a wild celery. In fact, gorillas use several different techniques as complex as that, for dealing with all their major food plants (Byrne and Byrne 1991, 1993); only rarer foods are simply picked and eaten. The reason is that the common foods, although nutritious and chemically innocuous, are defended by various physical problems—stings, prickles, hard casing, or surfaces covered with tiny hooks. Before they can be eaten, the gorilla has to neutralize the defences in some way. Eating the wild nettle, *Laportea alatipes*, shows this clearly (Fig. 12.7). First the soft leaves at a stem top are gently held to bring the stem into reach, then one hand is half-cupped at the stem base and stripped upwards (sometimes the other hand is needed to give firm support to the stem base, against the force of stripping). This detaches the leaves in a bunch, with the least-stinging undersurfaces in contact with the gorilla's hand, and the viciously stinging leaf-stalks downward. Next the bunch is gripped firmly with both hands (a firm grip makes the stings least liable to hurt), and the two hands rocked or twisted against each other to detach the leaf-stalks, which are discarded. Finally, the tight bundle of leaf-blades is carefully folded over and held folded for insertion into the mouth, which results in only the undersides possibly contacting the tender lips. The method is effective, adults eating nettles with apparent relish whereas youngsters who lack the technique eat only the tender tips and avoid holding the stem or touch it gingerly. It is also quite different to that used for wild celery, as comparison with Fig. 6.2 will show; this is true also of the techniques for eating the bedstraw, *Galium ruwenzoriense* (Fig. 12.8), and thistle, *Carduus nyassanus*. Some of these involve extractive foraging (e.g. getting the pith from celery

(a)

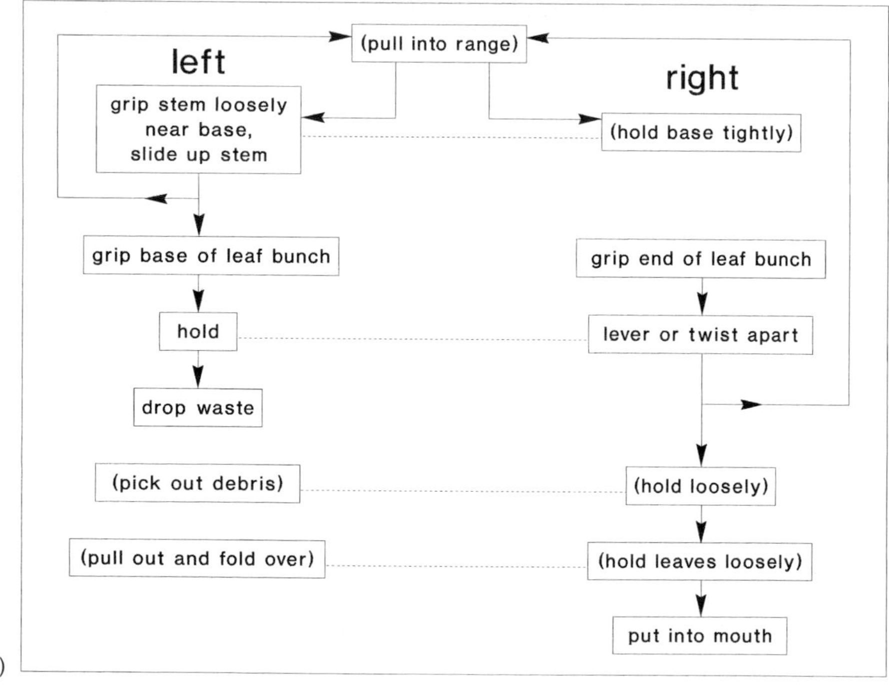

(b)

Figure 12.7 Problem and solution to eating the leaves of nettle *Laportea alatipes*. (a) Close-up photograph of a nettle stem, showing the plant's painful stings. (b) Flow chart to show how juvenile and adult mountain gorillas deal with the problem (key as in Fig. 6.2).

(a)

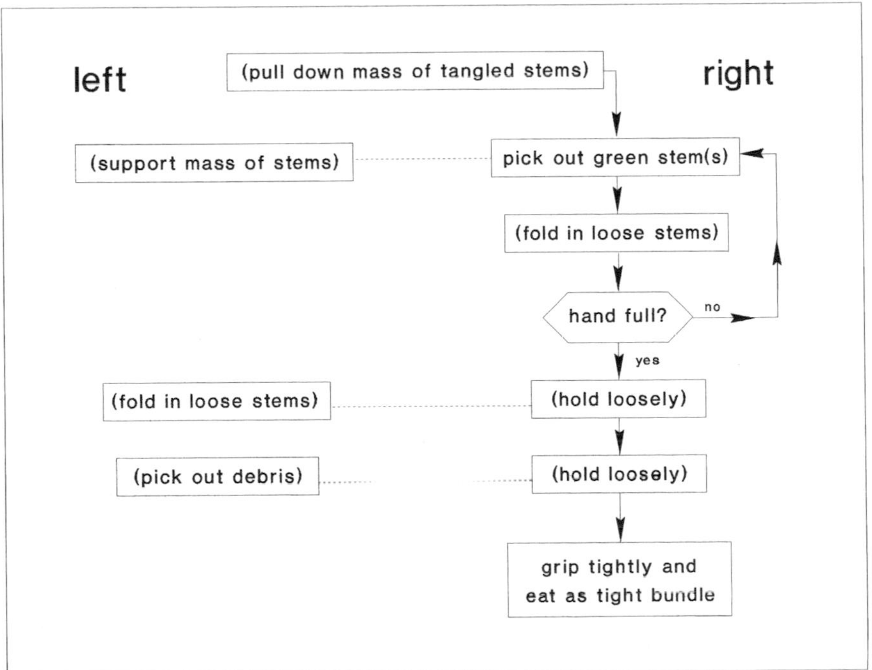

(b)

Figure 12.8 Other food plants of mountain gorillas require different techniques. (a) A silverback eats *Galium ruwenzoriense*, using the technique shown in (b).

or thistle stems), but none involve tools. Yet they are clearly of a similar order of logical organization to chimpanzee termite-fishing, and require similar dexterity. If learning the skills requires the ability to understand and copy the organization of another's behaviour, then intelligence may be just as necessary as it is for tool manufacture and use.

Gorillas have unspecialized guts, so cannot eat the mature leaves that a colobine's stomach allows it to digest; but the herbs of the mountain gorilla's habitat are fast-growing and free of most toxins, rather like a salad. Most gorilla populations live in lowland forest, lacking much herb-layer vegetation, so they must eat ripe fruit like chimpanzees, supplementing this nutrient-poor source with a wide range of other foods to obtain a balanced diet. Their ability to develop deft and complex food-processing skills has allowed them access to the 'salad bowl' of the high mountain meadows; an interesting example of habitat enlargement mediated by intellect. Nothing similar to these skills has been reported in monkeys, which is consistent with the overall picture of a monkey–ape difference in type of intelligence. It would be intriguing if orang-utans were to prove to share with gorillas and chimpanzees a real complexity of techniques in feeding, since this would then present a possible origin of the special intelligence 'package' of apes.

There is thus a range of hypotheses, lumped together under the banner 'food for thought', on the environmental selective pressures that might have selected for intelligence in simian primates. However, in recent years a very different form of 'challenge' has been proposed as a possible alternative to any of these: social complexity within a primate's group of acquaintances. Before we come to attempt a test between hypotheses, we must first examine this alternative—in the next chapter.

Further reading

Milton's theory of environmental pressures towards intelligence is described in Byrne and Whiten (1988*b*), but for modern discussion of the interaction of tool-making and intelligence, see Gibson and Ingold (1993). For the other topics, the journal papers will need to be consulted.

13
Machiavellian intelligence

In recent years, there has been growing interest in the radical idea that the *social* world has been the principal challenge shaping primate intelligence. This hypothesis is not unitary and precise, because it derives from several different theorists at different times, and has also undergone modification over time. All versions share the assertion that interactions with conspecific social companions present an intellectual challenge to an individual simian primate and that primate 'intelligence' has adapted in response to this challenge; Andrew Whiten and I have labelled the general idea as the 'machiavellian intelligence' hypothesis (Byrne and Whiten 1988*b*). Versions differ in which aspects of the social world are seen as most challenging; in whether environmental problems are also considered to have played some part in the evolution of primate intelligence; and in whether or not a specifically social type of intelligence been the result. These distinctions will emerge gradually in this chapter, as I explain the background and evidence for the Machiavellian intelligence hypothesis.

The 'environment' for a social animal includes not only other species of animal and plant (setting problems if they are predators, competitors, parasites, or foods) and the physical world (setting problems of temperature control, light and dark, and so on), but also its own companions. An individual's social companions are serious potential competitors for mates and food. Their behaviour can change rapidly, often as an interactive consequence of its own, and, having the same intelligence as itself, they are likely to present peculiarly challenging problems. Nevertheless, for many reasons, animals of some species benefit from long-lasting associations.

Nicholas Humphrey (1976), making these points, argued that the resulting need for compromise would select for those individuals with greatest intelligence: to maximize individual gains yet retain the benefits of group living. Humphrey argued that this would be a particularly *social* type of intelligence, poorly measured by the laboratory tasks of psychologists. That could explain why primates often do not emerge as qualitatively better than other animals on laboratory tests, because these do not tap social intelligence. Similarly, he suggested, that is why the natural lives of primates seem so unchallenging when we only look at environmental problems, and primate intelligence seems 'surplus to requirements'—the really tough problems are social ones. (Supporters of environmental challenge theories would dispute both these impressions, of course, pointing to the challenges inherent in primate feeding and to those laboratory tasks on which primates do emerge as superior.) Humphrey's theory leads to a either a *modular* view of intelligence, in which intelligence in one sphere can develop independently of that in another, or one in which all intelligence as we know it is *inherently* social.

Allison Jolly (1966) had a similar insight that social living might be important in the evolution of intelligence. She noted that the group-living ring-tailed lemur lacked the social complexity of any monkey. Therefore, she argued, while social living could not result from high intelligence, perhaps increased intelligence might be a consequence of social living. Unlike Humphrey, she did not suggest modularity of intelligence; she noted that the ring-tailed lemur is rather poor at laboratory tasks, suggesting that what these measure is indeed *not* unrelated to social skills. Therefore, while social living might promote intelligence by favouring individuals that best solve social problems, the intelligence thus evolved would be useful for other purposes.

Although there are small differences between Humphrey and Jolly's proposals, the essence of the machiavellian intelligence hypothesis is that intelligence evolved in social circumstances. Individuals would be favoured who were able to use and exploit others in their social group, without causing the disruption and potential group fission liable to result from naked aggression. Their manipulations might as easily involve co-operation as conflict, sharing as hoarding—but in each case the end is exploitative and selfish. (I use 'selfish' in the sense of Dawkins (1976), meaning acts that ultimately increase the probability of the individual or its kin passing their genes on to future generations, relative to the gene survival of unrelated or less closely related individuals.) Consistent with the machiavellian intelligence hypothesis, social species of primate display both complexity of social manipulation and considerable knowledge of social information. This social complexity needs to be fully appreciated, to understand the strength of the case for machiavellian intelligence, and I will go through the evidence in full, although some of it we have met already.

Social complexity: it's who you know...

In the long-lasting social groups of monkeys and apes, power is more often a matter of having the right allies than having physical strengh. Monkeys and apes in a social group can usually be ranked in order of their dominance. Knowing an animal's relative dominance rank allows observers to predict when it will take precedence at a feeding site, when it will succeed in gaining a mate, and in general when it will win in a competitive situation. In baboons, rank has even been shown to predict accurately how heavy a load of internal parasites an animal carries, and how long it will typically feed uninterrupted. Very often the ranks are 'linear': if A beats B, and B beats C, then the transitive inference follows—A beats C. (Despite this prevalent linearity, the order is usually called a 'hierarchy', as if a more complex structure of control were involved.) The original term for dominance rank, 'pecking order', points to the origin of the concept, in chickens, and indeed dominance is not unique to primates. Most social animals can be ranked for dominance, and their ranks are often linear.

What is special, however, is that ranks in monkeys and apes often do not correlate with physical power. In most mammals, researchers can make a pretty good guess at relative ranks simply by weighing the individuals. In species with dangerous horns or antlers, they might also take account of size of these weapons. This approach would often not work in monkeys and apes. For instance, in the many species of cercopithecine monkey that have been studied, female rank runs in families (Sade 1967; Harcourt 1988). Daughters 'inherit' a rank one below that of their mother; where there are several daughters, the daughters' ranks are the inverse of their ages. The reason for this is that mothers come to the aid of their daughters in any contests: thus, only individuals who outrank the mother can win against the daughter. The same applies to sons, but in Old World monkeys males transfer troops at adolescence; once in new troop, their mother's support is missing, and they are on their own. But not quite: often these young males already know individuals in the troop which they are entering—including elder brothers who transferred before them—and, if so, they too may get help (Meikle and Vessey 1981).

The advantage of having a relative to help is perhaps most dramatic in chimpanzees. Bill McGrew (1992) has analysed the rise to alpha status (top rank) of seven males at Gombe, and found that in every case it was a male with an elder brother, if any of the eligible males had one, who gained the top rank. Attaining alpha status has major consequences for chimpanzees, and not every male will reach this rank. Caroline Tutin (1979) showed that alpha-males will almost invariably father the baby of a female who comes into oestrus and remains with the core subgroup of males. At Gombe, this means that about 50 per cent of births are fathered by the alpha-male, and at Mahale it is probably even higher (Hasegawa and Hiraiwa-Hasegawa 1986). And a male can remain at this rank for a long time: the record is Ntologi at Mahale who was the alpha-male for at least 12 years. Without alpha status, a male chimpanzee will only have a good chance of becoming a father if he goes 'on safari' with a female at the time of her oestrus, well away from male competitors. This, however, is entirely at the female's choice and discretion (Tutin 1979); only if the female keeps silent and chooses to accompany a male, will the alpha-male and others remain in ignorance. Thus, once again, the personal relationship is what counts: 'it's not what you are, it's who you know'.

Youngsters' choice of playmates may be tuned to potential benefits of support in later life. Dorothy Cheney (1978) studied the play partners of juvenile baboons, and found that young males play with their same-sex peers—that is, just the animals who will need to transfer troops at the same stage as themselves—whereas young females play with babies. In particular, they play with the baby daughters of high-rank females. These babies will grow up to remain in the troop and 'inherit' their mothers' high ranks, and their alliance would therefore be highly beneficial to the young female when she is an adult. Support can come from friends as well as relatives.

Figure 13.1 Coalitions are important among primates. (a) Two male baboons make a temporary alliance in order to displace a higher-rank male from his coalition with a female (photo by R. Barton). (b) Two male mountain gorillas, half-brothers, jointly repel a lone male that threatens the group; often the dominant Ziz (left) will go forward to attack an intruder, while the younger, subordinate Pablo (right) herds females away from the conflict.

This is shown dramatically in the mating behaviour of savannah baboons (*Papio cynocephalus* and *P. anubis*). The top-rank male is only able to monopolize about 50 per cent of matings with potentially fertile females (Hausfater 1975). For the other 50 per cent, he is outwitted by pairs of other males, acting in coalition (Fig. 13.1). One male will solicit another's help by characteristic head and face movements; one of the pair then threatens the consorting top-rank male; when he retaliates in defence, the other male is often able to obtain a mating with the fertile female. The decoying action seems altruistic, but this is *reciprocal altruism*—because on a future occasion, the other helps him in turn (Packer 1977). Craig Packer's study was on *anubis* baboons at Gombe; elsewhere the rules of the coalition game may be different. Ronald Noë (1990) studied *cynocephalus* baboons at Amboseli in Kenya, and found that there the coalitions were not fair and reciprocal: the higher-rank winner took all, almost every time. Obviously, lower-ranking baboons were reluctant to form coalitions when they could expect no reward, and in fact only the two lowest rank males regularly allied in this way. Noë explained this as a *veto game*: each male baboon would do better to ally with a lower-rank animal, and only the lowest rank baboon has no choice! Presumably, even he would occasionally stand to attain some chance of mating as a result of an alliance, but would have none otherwise.

Sharing food, making friends, keeping allies

A mating cannot be shared, but food sharing can result in reciprocal sharing in the future or in rewards of other kinds. Few primates share food regularly. Several callitrichids, such as the golden lion tamarin *Leontopithecus rosalia*, share food extensively with younger relatives in their extended monogamous families, and chimpanzee mothers share with their offspring. But only the two chimpanzee species share food with unrelated adults, and announce their finding of shareable food sources with loud calls. When chimpanzees encounter small amounts of a rare and preferred food, they do not make these calls (Hauser and Wrangham 1987), suggesting a voluntary system in which information can be given or withheld at will. Frans de Waal (1989*a*) experimentally induced sharing by providing captive chimpanzees with tight bundles of a not-too-attractive food source: foliage. When food was presented, there was an outbreak of kissing and embracing—appeasement behaviours—and extensive bluff displays and submissive greeting—behaviours known to establish and confirm dominance rankings. Consistent with this, levels of aggression were increased during the ensuing feeding; however, subordinates acted with confidence towards dominants during feeding and food was shared with subordinates as much as with dominants: priorities of rank were suspended. Instead, food transfers were reciprocal: transfers from A to B correlated with those from B to A, and animals who shared little were 'sanctioned' by meeting refusal when they requested sharing themselves. In the wild, however, the rewards of sharing may not be in the same currency. Adult male chimpanzees regularly share the meat of the larger animals that they kill, and it has long been known that rank does not predict success in begging food: instead, meat goes more to old animals and to females in oestrus. Ten years of observation by Toshisada Nishida and his colleagues, of Ntologi, the alpha-male of Mahale, shows that the pattern of sharing can be complex (Nishida *et al.* 1992). Ntologi did not share with young males rising in the dominance hierarchy, nor with the beta-male; in other words, he avoided sharing with any animal who presented a threat to his high status. It was not a matter of personalities or grudges: when one beta-male dropped in rank, then Ntologi began to share meat with him. Ntologi regularly shared with middle-rank males who did not threaten his position, and with certain old but influential males—animals whose small size or emaciated condition meant that they posed no threat were allowed to share meat, and often also became close companions of Ntologi (Fig. 12.4). But even of the very old males, only some were allowed to share; Nishida speculated that those males retained influence from days when they themselves were alpha-males. Reciprocation in food cannot explain Ntologi's rules, but the males allowed to share were those who sometimes supported Ntologi in power contests: meat-sharing appears to be a strategy for building-up coalitions. In both de Waal's and Nishida's studies, a possessor was also more likely to share with those who had previously groomed them.

Old World monkeys and apes spend an inordinate amount of time grooming each other, as any visitor to a zoo knows (Fig. 13.2). Contrary to what many adults tell their children at the zoo, the animals are not continually finding fleas, eating salt, or picking off scabs—although when they do occasionally find fleas or salt grains they eat them with relish, and they certainly pick off scabs when they are there (without antibiotic dusting powder, this is a good strategy to prevent sepsis in the hot and often humid climates in which primates mostly live). For catarrhines, these primary, utilitarian functions of grooming are only a small part of the explanation. (Whereas, for strepsirhines and platyrrhine monkeys, the utilitarian function is the major one.) Most of the grooming time we observe is not necessary for the animals to maintain healthy skin condition: Old World monkeys and apes groom far too much for this to be the whole story, and in fact the amount of grooming received is not normally correlated with external signs of health. Grooming denotes a willingness to invest time and effort in the welfare of another: what we would normally call friendship. Animals that groom together, look after each other.

As would be expected, female Old World monkeys who are relatives groom each other frequently, and they come to each others' aid when they are in need. More interestingly, unrelated monkeys also groom: does this

Figure 13.2 Male and female simian primates interact far more through mutual grooming than through violent display or overt sexual behaviour. (a) A male chimpanzee grooms a female with a young infant. (b) A female baboon grooms the leading adult male of her group.

also lead to helpful alliances? To find out, Seyfarth and Cheney (1984) examined the sequels to grooming interactions in vervet monkeys. They played distress calls from hidden loudspeakers, on two occasions for each individual whose call was used. Once was within a few minutes of its grooming another animal, and once was not. How did this other animal react? If it was a relative, as we would expect, it reacted strongly whether or not it had recently received grooming. However, if it was unrelated, its reaction was stronger if it had recently been groomed.

Long-term relationships are also found between unrelated individuals. In a baboon troop, for instance, Smuts (1985) showed that each female has a particular male friend whom she grooms very frequently; the two are often found together; as there are usually more females than males in a baboon troop, one male may have several female friends. Friendship has benefits for both parties: as well as the grooming itself, the male has more chance of mating with his female friends than other females when they are in oestrus. Females gain protection for themselves and their infants from a male friend—the help of an animal twice their size. Also, males often contribute quite a bit of general infant care, of a less dramatic nature, to their friends.

Grooming, then, can be used as a sort of 'trade currency', it can be exchanged for benefits of other kinds at later dates. Grooming an animal is an investment for the future. The investment, however, is not without costs: grooming takes time. Robin Dunbar has shown that Old World monkeys and apes groom for proportionately more of their lives if they live in bigger groups (Dunbar 1991). Indeed, if groups contained many more than the few dozen adult animals that is the maximum seen in non-human primates, the time needed for servicing relationships by grooming would become a major drain on the animals' time and energy. The link between group size and the percentage of the overall time-budget spent grooming is a close one, but this is not because time grooming is distributed evenly over all animals. Instead, close friends are groomed more intensively as the overall group size increases, although in addition the actual number of an animal's 'close friends' also increases with the size of the group (Dunbar 1991). It seems that the larger the group, the more important these close alliances are in buffering individuals against social conflict—and the larger the group, the more stress and harassment an individual faces. For an investment that has real costs, it would make sense if the animals were selective in who they choose to groom—and they are. In fact, Harcourt (1992) has shown that, while other sorts of animal also use alliances, only catarrhine primates cultivate alliances on the basis of the individual's ability or readiness to give useful help.

Inevitably, relationships will sometimes become strained and fights take place with individuals which, in the long run, are important as allies. Old World monkeys and apes can deal with this problem too: by reconciliation. After a fight, the losing party will often seek out the winner for especially friendly contact, and when this happens a subsequent fight is less likely than when it does not. Frans de Waal (1989*b*) has studied this phenomenon in several species, and found reconciliation to be effective in maintaining peaceable relations within a group—avoiding 'rocking the boat', to the benefit of all parties that depend on group living.

Learning to manipulate and deceive

In Old World monkeys and apes, therefore, much of an individual's success depends on its network of relatives and friends. The latter are built up over years, sometimes from its childhood, and especially by using the currency of social grooming. Beyond nepotism and the old boy network, an individual can use behavioural tactics to manipulate those who are not allies or relatives into unwitting help. We have seen one form of manipulation already, in primate tactical deception. Although the insight necessary to *plan* or *understand* deception seems to be restricted to great apes, monkeys *use* deception often, apparently learning the tactics from lucky coincidences by the trial and error of conditioning. The survey that Whiten and I carried out in fact showed that all groups of monkeys (including New World species) and apes use deception, whereas no strepsirhine primates have been shown conclusively to do so (Fig. 9.4). The tricks are many and various. Most concern the manipulation of attention (Whiten and Byrne 1988), where an animal's focus of attention is shifted towards or away from just what will most profit the agent of the deceit. The example I gave of the baboon which behaved as if a predator had been sighted is one of these: the 'look behind you' ruse of cowboy movies. Others involve leading animals towards or away from places; making them think that the agent has been hurt (as used by the young baboon who screamed but had not been attacked) or has gained reward; deflecting aggression on to innocent third parties; concealing the excited glances that would reveal a hidden food, or concealing the food itself in the hand or under the body; and so on (Fig. 13.3). The hardest category to analyse that we encountered was eventually called 'creating an image', because the deception seemed to function by changing the way other animals viewed the agent. The case of the juvenile gorilla who made six day-nests *en route* to her real goal of contacting a baby, was put in this category, since it apparently functioned by creating the neutral image of 'only nest-building' to outside observers. The prevalence of deception among simian primates shows their learning ability in social circumstances—dramatically rapid compared with most non-primates, resulting in far more complex behaviour patterns.

Complex social manipulation need not involve deception. Hans Kummer has described a frequent tactic used by female hamadryas baboons (Kummer 1967). These baboons are unusual in living in small, one-male harems. Females sometimes succeed in threatening a rival yet avoiding the return of aggression, by sitting directly in front of the powerful harem-leader male. Any threat aimed at her, will seem to be aimed at him. Once again, chimpanzees offer the manipulations of most flambuoyant complexity. Frans de Waal (1982) has delightfully described the power shifts of three powerful males in a captive colony of chimpanzees. He noted that an alpha-male that required the support of a powerful male ally was weak in

Figure 13.3 Illustrations of various primate tactics of deception; codes as in Fig 9.1. The 'thinks bubbles' suggest planned, intentional deception, whereas in fact in none of these cases was there strong evidence for an intentional interpretation (Byrne and Whiten 1990). (a) Grooming a dominant animal in possession of prized food, used to allow snatching the food (baboon). (b) Playful attack on inappropriate adult, used to gain maternal comfort and milk (gelada *Theropichecus gelada*). (c) Neutral expression, used to allow close approach for attack (chimpanzee). (d) Leading away by manner of departure, used to allow return to prized food patch (chimpanzee). (Drawings by D. Bygott.)

his control, compared with a previous leader who had the support of the females. These manipulations led de Waal to draw a parallel with the advice of Niccolo Machiavelli, 'he who attains the principality with the aid of the nobility maintains it with more difficulty than he who becomes prince with the assistance of the common people, for he finds himself a prince amidst many who feel themselves to be his equals, and because of this he can neither govern nor manage them as he might wish' (Machiavelli 1532). Female chimpanzees are lower in rank and power than any male, but several together make worthwhile allies; with the bonus that none can ever become a competitor! For a similar reason, de Waal argued, the top-rank male in many primate groups acts like a 'policeman', defending the weak against the strong in conflicts: the motivation is not altruisitc social conscience, but sensible undermining of potential rivals. De Waal's group of chimpanzees lived in a large enclosure, where no animal could get fully away from others; and they were fed, thus having plenty of spare time for trying out machiavellian strategies. But such behaviours are not unique to captivity. Toshisada Nishida has observed a comparable pattern in the wild, and examined its reproductive consequences (Nishida 1983). The period was one in which the power of the alpha-male, Kasonta, was declining, and the younger male, Sobongo, was gradually able to assume alpha status. However, for a month, Kasonta was outranked by Sobongo and yet was able to keep his alpha rank because of a close alliance with the low-ranking Kamemanfu. During this time, Kamemanfu several times switched allegiance between the two top males, apparently playing off one against the other. What is more, during this time of instability Kamemanfu's copulatory share was significantly higher than before or since.

Monkeys and apes of many species, therefore, use a wide range of behavioural tactics in social manipulations. Social manipulation must be based on social knowledge. Unless information is represented in the brain, it cannot become a discriminating stimulus for tactics; this is true whether the tactics are acquired by reinforcement or by comprehension. The next section looks specifically at the social knowledge that must underlie social manipulation.

Knowing about others' social lives

That monkeys and apes have extensive social knowledge has been confirmed independently in several ways, but especially in the playback experiments by Dorothy Cheney and Robert Seyfarth. They have used the recorded calls of vervet monkeys to pose a number of interesting questions to the monkeys in the field. The work has shown a range of sophisticated knowledge in this monkey, including knowledge of the dominance ranks, patterns of close association, and group membership of individuals (Cheney and Seyfarth 1990).

Playback of calls given specifically to subordinates, or to dominants, shows that monkeys take into account the rank of the caller in interpreting the calls' meaning. For instance, if X is heard to give a 'grunt to dominant', and X is below the hearer in rank, there is no reaction (and in fact, the call might plausibly have been given on seeing the hearer); but if X is higher in rank than the hearer, there is a significant reaction from the hearer (the call implies the nearby presence of an animal dominant also to the hearer). Getting this difference in reaction means that vervet monkeys have some understanding of the relative ranks of third parties, not just their own position relative to others as researchers had always assumed.

In another experiment, an infant 'lost call' was broadcast to several mothers, none of whose infants were in view. Usually the mother whose infant's call was used was the first to react, and showed most agitation, confirming that mothers can identify their offspring by call alone. However, occasionally she was slow to react, and in these cases Cheney and Seyfarth noticed that the other females looked at the biological mother, as if to say 'It's yours, no?'. This impression was quickly checked by detailed examination of the films the researchers made of each experiment, and confirmed that vervets are aware of whose mother an infant call belongs to, even when it is not their own. A specific test of whether monkeys understand relationships like 'mother of' and 'sibling of' was made by Verena Dasser (1988). She taught long-tailed macaques to pick out the pair of photographs that matched the sample given. The sample showed a mother and daughter, two maternal siblings, or two unrelated animals (which could, however, belong to a single matriline, and so be associates of each other). Monkeys rapidly learnt the rule underlying each task and could use the relationships to obtain the rewards of correct performance—they did not have to learn the rewarded pairings one by one. This means that monkeys not only know the identity of their own infants, siblings, or mothers, they seem to know more generally who is whose infant, mother, or sibling. Probably this would strictly be an overstatement: remember that mothers, infants, and siblings are the closest associates and allies, and monkeys may not think of the relationships as any more than that.

Knowledge of group membership was shown by playback of a female vervet's call from a neighbouring group range (Cheney and Seyfarth 1988). In each case the female was from one of the neighbour groups (and female vervets do not change groups, so no female in another group would have 'met her socially', as it were), but in some cases her call was played from the wrong neighbour range. In the normal run of things, this is of course impossible. Vervets' reactions showed that they thought it very strange, too: attention was much greater to the calls from the wrong place, and this applied to females as well as males. So even females, who never experience living in other groups, are nevertheless aware of which group other females belong to.

Until this work, no one had been sure that any animal categorized its social companions in the sort of ways that we scientists do routinely. However, this knowledge had been strongly suspected in macaques (Judge 1982) and baboons (Smuts 1985), when it was found that 'redirected aggression' after losing a fight—long regarded as a functionless outpouring of annoyance—was not random. Losers in fact target their aggression specifically at relatives of the monkey who beat them. What is more, Seyfarth and Cheney later showed that vervets prefer to threaten the relatives of monkeys who have recently attacked *their* relatives. This monkey 'vendetta' suggests that they know very well who everyone else's allies are, and remember grievances. Nothing similar has been shown in non-primates or even strepsirhine primates.

Vervets are small monkeys with many predators in their savannah-edge habitat, and they are very sensitive to vocal warnings of their presence. In fact they have specific alarm calls to several different types of predator: leopards, eagles, pythons, small cats, baboons, humans (Struhsaker 1967). Seyfarth *et al.* (1980) checked whether the calls really referenced predators, rather than perhaps indicating different levels of fear, by experimental playback. The researchers used the distinctively different anti-predator tactics to three of these calls to find out. Artificially changing the volume, length of call, or identity of caller had no effect on the type of reaction observed (the strength of reaction, of course, was greater in response to a loud, repeated alarm by an old male, than to a single call by an infant). The reaction was always specific to the alarm call: looking up at the sky and jumping out of trees after hearing an eagle-alarm, scanning the horizon and running for a tree to climb after hearing a leopard-alarm, and so on. Nor was the association slavishly rigid. When there was a real leopard, callers who had seen the leopard often did not scan the horizon, or move at all if they were already in a favourable position; those who heard alarm calls often did not themselves call. That the calls really have *specific referents* is confirmed by vervets' reaction to misleading calls. Cheney and Seyfarth (1988) played one individual's leopard-alarm call repeatedly when there was no leopard, then looked at whether other monkeys still treated his calls seriously. The monkeys habituated to his leopard call, and largely ignored it, whereas they still reacted fully to other individuals' leopard calls. Interestingly, when the 'misleading' animal's eagle-alarm was played, they gave a full reaction. It's as if, knowing from long experience that Charley always gives you rotten financial advice, you still take his word about which is the best restaurant to go to. Eagles and leopards are categorically different to vervets, not members of a single 'dangerous' group which inspires different levels of fear.

Study of what things inspire young vervets to give alarm calls shows that each referential category is shaped by experience (Seyfarth and Cheney 1986). At first, infant vervets give eagle-alarms to almost anything flying, even a big leaf. Gradually this narrows to only large, broad-winged birds; then finally to only the two large hawk-eagles which are serious predators of monkeys. The local starlings also distinguish among some of these predators, and playback of their calls to the monkeys showed that vervets use the starlings' alarm calls too (Cheney and Seyfarth 1988).

Given vervet monkeys' sensitivity to social warnings of predators, and to subtle social distinctions among themselves, some of their failures to react to apparently interesting environmental events are striking (Cheney and Seyfarth 1988). When the distinctive deep chuckle of a hippopotamus is played from an open patch of desert sand, vervets apparently do not notice. A hippopotamus is no threat to vervets, but even when the researchers hung a stuffed antelope up a tree as if a leopard had cached it, vervets did not react. Every tourist to East Africa knows what a carcass up a tree means: how much more should vervet monkeys, whose lives might depend on it? When the researchers faked a python track (with an old rubber ball, apparently giving a fine imitation of a python trail), the monkeys did not seem to notice. Once, a group of vervets was watched walking unconcerned past a real python track ... until they met the python and panic ensued! Once again, why hadn't the vervets expected it, when the humans had? Interpreting 'failures' is always difficult. For instance, finding the track of a python does not indicate which way it went or when, and a reaction of alarm may be inappropriate. As one critic put it, cars are the major killers of Western humans below the age of 50—yet we don't react with alarm to finding oil on the ground in a car park!

Nevertheless, vervets are so good at using *social* signals to warn of danger, and seem so very inept when it comes to interpreting environmental signs of predators, that the possibility of domain-specific intelligence must be considered. Could it be that vervet intelligence is specifically of a social kind—a module of social intelligence, unavailable for other purposes—as Humphrey initially suggested for all primates? Even in humans there is an echo of this pattern of enhanced intelligence in the social sphere. Childrens' acquisition of the concept of rank and of the principle of transitive inference (for instance, if A is stronger than B, and B stronger than C, then A must be stronger than C) are both shown first in social judgements, only later in artificial contexts (Smith 1988). The trouble is, it is rather subjective of us to say that vervets or children are 'better' in one domain or other. Since we are not all-knowing beings able to measure each aspect of intelligence on an absolute scale, we can only confidently say how monkeys or children deviate from our own, adult human norm. There is no measuring scale on which to compare intelligences. Also, the fact that in human intelligence all the supposedly independent 'factors' correlate with each other (Heim 1970) should make us cautious of claiming independent modules without very strong evidence.

Returning to the big question, was primate intelligence an evolutionary adaptation towards environmental or towards social problem-solving? As we have seen, there is plenty of evidence in favour of both theories. In each case, this supportive evidence has been the complexity of tasks that simian primates do solve—their memory, their manual aptitudes, their social manoeuvres, the depth of social knowledge they take into account, and so on.

These different kinds of complexity cannot be fairly compared against each other on a single measuring scale. Moreover, finding a wealth of data consistent with a theory does not prove it correct.

Nor is it clear that one theory is right, the other wrong; there are two other possibilities. It could be that *both* theories are correct in suggesting a single selective pressure as the key, but at different *times* in our evolutionary history. Or perhaps the answer is not 'either/or' at all. Social and technical skills are not independent in practice. The greatest sophistication in social manoeuvre and understanding of any animal is undoubtedly by the chimpanzee; yet this is just the primate species that uses tools the most to forage extractively, hunts most regularly, inhabits the largest home ranges (350 km^2 at Mt. Assirik; Tutin *et al.* 1983), and eats the largest variety of plant and animal foods known (328 plant items, 12 mammals, 5 birds, 15 genera insects, at Mahale; Nishida and Uehara 1980). The two pressures may be inextricably linked in the lives of primates.

What we need is a discriminatory test. To test between theories properly we need measures that can be used to assess a wide range of species, comparing the assessment with the predictions of each theory. The next chapter attempts to do this, in a way that does not use any of the data we have seen so far.

Further reading

Many of the key papers on 'machiavellian intelligence' are in Byrne and Whiten (1988*b*); these include Humphrey and Jolly's original statements of ideas, chapters on tripartite interactions and political manoeuvring, deception, and social manipulation, and Cheney and Seyfarth's work. R. I. M. Dunbar's (1988) *Primate social systems* (Croom Helm, London) gives the best modern treatment of social relationships and grooming in primates.

14
Testing the theories

In Chapters 12 and 13, we met the two broadly competing types of 'challenge' theories (Fig. 14.1) for the origin of enhanced primate intelligence. In order to evaluate them, we need to find out which challenge best predicts intelligence, across a range of species. We therefore have to find out two things about any species that we are going to use:

(1) evidence of the complexity it is able to deal with in the social and environmental arenas; and

(2) evidence of its intelligence.

Both are problematic, but in this exercise we will have to accept less-than-ideal sources of evidence; the area is unfortunately one in which perfect data will simply never be on offer.

Estimating complexity

The first requirement, estimating the complexity an individual can handle in social and environmental problems, can certainly be met for many species, albeit in a very rough-and-ready way. Social complexity must

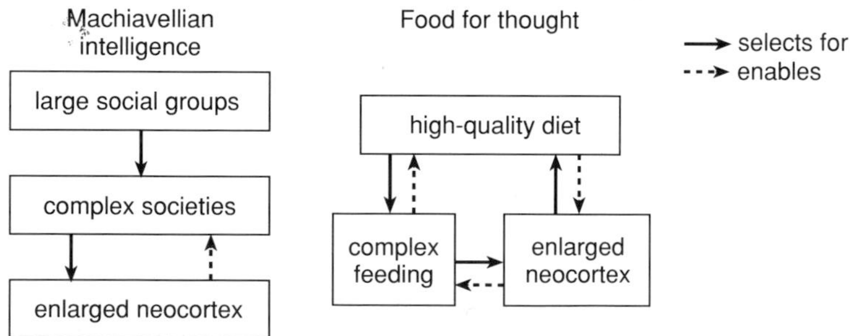

Figure 14.1 Comparison of the alternative models for the increase in brain size and intelligence in simian primate ancestry. Note that the machiavellian intelligence hypothesis identifies an external cause—a need for larger social groups—to trigger the feedback cycle, whereas the food-for-thought approach could cycle in either direction, selecting either for larger-brained complex-feeding species, or smaller brained simple-feeding ones.

surely increase with the number of separate individuals that an animal has to take into account. Primate social groups have stable social structure, and some individuals are permanent members. (This is not the case for groups in many other species, for instance the large herds of wildebeest or other antelope.) As a result, primate group members know one another individually and establish enduring relationships: an individual needs to keep track of more information the larger the group. An approximate index of the social complexity that each species can handle is, therefore, given by the species-typical (or maximum) group size. At first sight, the maximum would seem to be the most appropriate index. However, primate groups, unlike the temporary aggregations of many species of animal, do not vary in size continuously, with individuals joining and leaving; they tend to grow up to an unstable point, and then split up (see Dunbar 1988). Because of this, maximum observed size is likely to reflect an unstable group, and the average size will represent a better estimate of the social complexity the individuals can handle comfortably.

Environmental complexity, as a selection pressure for intelligence, is, for all but a few species, a matter of memory in foraging. If knowledge is used to aid foraging, as is believed to be the case for many primates (see Chapter 12), then memory load will increase with the size of the range area needing to be searched to obtain an adequate diet. The species-typical home range area will therefore give a rough idea of the foraging memory problem to be met. Again, the maximum home range might seem a more appropriate measure, but remember that groups may sometimes have ranges larger (temporarily) than strictly necessary for subsistence, or a group may (temporarily) be of an unusually large size. As with average group size, the average range area is probably a safer estimate of environmental complexity.

These measures are, of course, simplifications. In reality, social complexity presumably also varies with the quality and depth of the relationships between individuals. Complexity may be a non-linear function of social network size, since we know that primates can take the relationships between third parties into account. Foraging, in reality, presumably varies in difficulty depending on the type of food: with spatial and temporal unpredictability, and whether some processing techniques require technical skill. Are these flaws fatal, for our hopes of discovering the causes of primate intelligence? The possibility of non-linear increase in complexity with group size is certainly not, since this is an empirical question best answered by comparing group size with intelligence and discovering the shape of any relationship obtained. Similarly, variation in diet type may not be such a problem, as spatial and temporal unpredictability is reflected in range size anyway. More unpredictable diets, like frugivory, require larger year-round ranges, whereas more predictable ones can be met from smaller catchment areas. And the special technical challenges of locomotion, food catching, or food processing apply only to a few species, chiefly the great apes. In general, I think the various problems are best held in mind for later, when they may help to explain deviations from whatever pattern we find; in themselves they suggest no better way of proceeding at this stage. The great advantage of group size and range size is that they are known quite accurately for a wide range of primate species, whereas if we insist on more subtle indices they may never be available.

Estimating intelligence

More problems emerge when we move to the second requirement, a measure of intelligence. For a few primate species, good evidence exists of sophistication in dealing with social or environmental challenges, as we saw in Chapter 13. But now we need a more systematic measure; what would be ideal is an 'intelligence test' that could be applied even-handedly to each species. This goal has often been sought, and if it had ever been reached we would not need to take the more indirect approach of this chapter.

The trouble with finding an intelligence test for animals is analogous to the difficulty of designing a 'culture-fair' IQ test for people (a problem first touched on in Chapter 3). Tests devised for one human population, and calibrated on it, usually give deflated scores when applied to other populations: the questions are less appropriate and less well-understood, and so the test instrument gives a faulty reading. Similarly, human tests will not be as appropriate for other animals. Only a few animals are motivated by similar rewards to ourselves, see the world in rather human ways, and interact with the world in a similar way to humans. If we rely on human estimation of difficulty in some 'behavioural IQ test for primates', we are liable to equate similarity to ourselves with cleverness. This is not just a theoretical cavil. For instance, for years it was thought that fish couldn't manage simple discrimination learning, until someone realized that their eyes largely focus downwards. With the stimuli placed on the pool floor, they do just as well as rats. It is much easier to assess a monkey's ability (with its prehensile hands, primary reliance on eyes similar to our own, and a known fondness for peanuts) than a sloth's or a marine turtle's, but even within the relatively homogeneous group of the primates, there are no guarantees of species-fairness. Chimpanzees are more similar to humans than monkeys in many ways, but especially in their non-verbal communication which is almost identical. Consequently, we can describe and interpret their actions and guess their intentions much more accurately than we could interpret those of a monkey—let alone a nocturnal, scent-marking strepsirhine. As a result, there is no generally agreed measuring scale of intelligence on which to compare species, even for primates (see reviews by Warren 1973; Passingham 1982).

Brain enlargement reflects intelligence

Instead, we will have to use an indirect measure of intelligence, brain enlargement. The advantage of a large brain is always taken to be because of the benefits of intelligence,* and there are real reasons for believing that brain enlargement *must* confer evolutionary advantage. The extreme example of our own brain size will serve to illustrate this (occasionally disputed) point.

The human brain is uniquely large among primates, but this does not come without severe costs. The costs argue that such an evolutionary increase in brain size must have been driven by strong selective advantages. First, the brain is energetically expensive (for references see Milton 1988) In a quiet, resting state the body still requires a continual supply of energy. The rate at which energy is used in this resting state is called the 'basal metabolic rate' (BMR); when we take active exercise, our metabolic rate increases. In adulthood, the brain consumes about 20 per cent of BMR. During childhood, this percentage rises to 50 per cent. Moreover, this demand for energy is remorseless: unlike other organs, the supply to the brain has to be constant. Indeed, no more energy is used when thinking hard than when resting or sleeping. If the supply of energy is interrupted, such as by heart failure, brain tissue will be irreparably damaged after about 4 min. A large brain is thus an energy-expensive piece of equipment to have to rely on; this cost must have been worth paying for, in some way. Having a relatively large brain has incurred other disadvantages for us, as well as this remorseless energetic drain. At birth, the human child's head is a very tight fit in the birth canal compared with the easy passage of other great-ape babies (Leutenegger 1982); birth is a prolonged, often painful, and sometimes dangerous process for mothers. (Even in Third World countries, 2 hours' labour is still commonplace.) By contrast, birth for other great apes takes only a few minutes, an obvious consequence of looser fit in the birth canal. True, human bipedalism has imposed a pressure towards narrower hips, but mainly the difference is a matter of humans' much larger brains at birth. Finally, human brains grow for an unusual amount of time, considering their size at birth. Primates show a general 'trade-off' between species whose brain is near-adult size at birth, and in which little postnatal brain growth occurs (such as cebines); and those whose brain is still rather undeveloped at birth, and much postnatal growth is seen (such as lorisines). Again, humans are exceptional, an outlier from the neat straight-line

*Occasionally other possibilities have been suggested, such as William Calvin's intriguing suggestion that the rapid increase in brain volume seen in hominid evolution was because it permitted accurate aiming of throws (Calvin 1982). However, this suggestion cannot apply to non-human primates, and some sort of intellectual advantage would seem the only general explanation of specific increases in brain size.

relationship between brain size at birth and postnatal growth (Harvey *et al.* 1986). Despite their relatively large size at birth, human brains continue to grow for years afterward, and the adult size is as much a consequence of postnatal growth as in lorisines. During this phase of postnatal brain growth, human babies are relatively immature and helpless, so require years of time-consuming care from the mother or family. Large brains *must* be good for something, or they could never have evolved against all these costs! The only plausible explanation is intelligence.

Although humans are an extreme case for the primates, the logic applies more generally. To test between theories, therefore, we should be able to use brain size as an indication of species' intelligence—if we can first specify exactly what is meant by 'size'.

Allometry: getting the right scale of measurement

Larger animals, in general, have larger brains; this is not particularly surprising, since for most mammals, much of the brain is taken up with sensory and motor processes which might be expected to need brain tissue in proportion to their size. But as the absolute size of living things changes, so the relative proportions of their parts are generally found to change. In this case, absolutely larger animals have relatively smaller brains than one would expect from linearly scaling-up smaller animals (imagine how large a head a mouse would have if it were cow-sized). Simply weighing brains and comparing the weights, directly or in proportion to body weights, ignores these regular trends.

A technique that takes account of the way bodily form changes with size is called allometric scaling. In allometric scaling, a double logarithmic plot of something, in this case brain size, is made against body size for a given group of animals. Provided the two things are related by some sort of power relationship, this forces the species points onto a straight line. For brain size, plotting against body size on logarithmic coordinates gives a reasonably straight line for primates, as for other groups of animals. Then one can see whether any particular animal in the group lies *above* the line (has a relatively larger brain than one might expect); *on* the line (has average brain size); or *below* the line (has a relatively small brain). This technique has many limitations (including doubt as to whether a straight line is the best fit to the log–log transformed data; see Deacon 1990), but it is the one now used most often to compare animals' brain sizes. With this approach, one finds that humans have brains three times as large as we would expect from a monkey or ape of human size (Passingham 1982), which of course tends to give us smug confidence in the relationship between relative brain volume and intelligence.

An underlying assumption of this method of comparing relative brain sizes is that the extra volume (over that expected) is best viewed as a proportion of the total volume. five per cent extra brain is assumed to be equally useful for intelligence in a 5 kg animal or a 50 kg animal, even though the extra brain tissue is far larger in the second case, and contains far more neurones. This is a very odd assumption for anyone used to computational (Turing) machines, since these are ultimately limited in power by the number of their elements.

The oddity comes from mixing metaphors of what the brain is doing. If the brain is a sort of '*on-board computer*' (Dawkins 1976) that governs intelligent function, then the *absolute* number of neurones would be relevant, not the number relative to body size. (It always has to be assumed, and it is quite a reasonable assumption, that the efficiency of programming will not vary. The logic here is that evolution will have optimized neural programming in each species, and neural transmission speed is the same in all mammalian brains.) But the more traditional idea that animal brains function by making responses to stimuli in a more-or-less reflex or S-R manner, results in a model that is closer to a telephone switchboard. 'Lines from/to subscribers' in a telephone system would correspond, in bodies, to sensory and motor neurones. Thus, if the brain resembles a glorified automatic *telephone exchange*, the input/output connections will determine how big the system to handle them needs minimally to be; larger bodies need more connections. On this model, brain tissue *relative* to body size will show the extent to which processing can be more flexible and subtle than the minimum, justifying traditional allometry. The on-board computer and telephone exchange metaphors cannot both be right. Or rather, they probably *are* both right, but with regard to different systems within the brain.

Suppose the brain is a device in which different parts subserve very different functions (not an implausible claim). Those parts used for non-computational body-function should increase in size in some regular way with body size, whereas those parts used for computation should not; only the size of the latter will tell us the potential intelligence the brain can show. The underlying assumption, unlike that of traditional allometry, is that the brain is *additively* made up of the volume (or the number of neurones) free for intelligent functions, plus the volume needed for mundane other things. The *absolute volume of brain tissue free for computation* is what matters, not any volume relative to body size. Deciding how large this is, where the partition lies, is the tricky part. Before looking at how it might be done, let us see what can be learnt from more straightforward allometry, but not forget the alternative, messier, but rather more valid methods.

Primate brain sizes

When traditional allometric scaling is done for brain sizes of mammals, the primate order as a whole is found to be larger brained than most other groups (Jerison 1973); and this result emerges even with the alternative, 'two-part' methods. But when the strepsirhine primates (the more primitive lemurs, lorises, and galagos) are partitioned from the rest, the strepsirhines turn out to have typical brain sizes for mammals (Passingham and Ettlinger 1974): they have brains about the size one would expect from their body sizes. The monkeys and apes, however, have brains twice as large as average mammals of their size.

Primates with home ranges that are large in area tend to have relatively large brains (Clutton-Brock and Harvey 1980), and this has been used to argue that the origin of primate intellect lies in dealing with environmental complexity. Unfortunately, the effect may instead be an artefact of selection for bigger *bodies* in more folivorous species. True folivory relies on a complex (and thus large) stomach, for example the fore-gut fermentation chamber of colobine monkeys. But even in other primates, animals with simple stomachs, eating mature leaves requires a large gut for efficient hind-gut fermentation, and hence a large body to support it. Mature leaves are relatively abundant in most primate habitats, so primates with more *folivorous* diets can find sufficient food for their nutrition in *smaller* home ranges. By contrast, frugivory requires a larger range area—for year-round access to a variety of fruit species, and to other sources of nutrients to balance the energy-rich fruit—but the high sugar content allows digestion by a shorter gut. Other things being equal, primates that eat more fruit will have smaller bodies, and yet larger home ranges, than those that eat more leaves. Variations in 'brain size *relative* to body size' may therefore be caused solely by differences in body size due to diet type: a larger gut makes the abdomen heavier but requires little or no brain expansion, so it is misleading to compare species adapted to different diets. Scaling against body length instead of weight helps a bit, but the length of primate bodies is still heavily influenced by gut size. This effect, rather than selection for big brains in species needing good cognitive maps, may have artefactually caused a correlation between frugivory and relative brain size.

Gut tissue is as metabolically costly as brain tissue (although the demand for energy is not so remorseless); so primates with small guts are likely to be better able to 'afford' large brains, on the whole. Combined with the additional factor that diets requiring only small guts (frugivory, meat-eating) often provide a surplus of energy by the time a nutritional balance is obtained, a real correlation between high-energy diets and relative brain enlargement would seem likely. However, this would not in itself explain why evolution would favour the 'risky' strategy of relatively large brain, high-energy diet in certain species. Evolution would not be expected to invest in an energetically costly organ just because it is possible—only when it confers advantage. We are left with the question of *why* in haplorhine evolution it paid to adapt to a more fruit-based diet, losing the security of the relatively small brain, more folivorous strategy of most strepsirhines.

Apes as a group do not differ strikingly from monkeys in their relative brain to body size, as assessed by traditional allometry, but vary greatly among themselves. Similar problems with guts apply to such interspecies differences: although all great apes have a broadly similar type of gut, they do vary in their adaptedness to coarse food, i.e. in the size of their large intestines. In fact, the gut sizes rank gorilla > orang-utan and chimpanzees >> human, and this order is the inverse of their relative brain sizes. This hints that selection on body size rather than brain size has been responsible for much of the variation, and there are independent reasons to believe that body size is more labile than brain size over evolutionary time-scales (Shea 1983; Deacon 1990). The chimpanzees and the gorilla, whose brains are nearly identical in absolute size, illustrate the principle. Gorillas are able to live in smaller home ranges than chimpanzees because they can eat coarser food, having considerably longer large intestines. This contrast probably arose by recent selection favouring different diets, and consequently different gut lengths and range sizes; their brains have been 'conservative', changing less in evolution than their bodies. Relative brain to body size is unlikely to be a good way of comparing intelligence among apes.

Given these theoretical and practical problems, one of the estimates of 'free computing space' will be a much better way of testing theories—but which? Several methods have been tried, and usually depend on one of two assumptions. Either they identify animals of little intelligence and then assume the computational share of their brains is zero; or they assume the two components (computational and maintenance) are served by different physical locations in the brain, and point to which part is for computation. Estimating the amount of brain tissue required for visceral function (e.g. Jerison 1973) requires assuming that some animals have no computing capability, all their brains being devoted to body regulation. This assumption is somewhat naïve, as it is based largely on *ad hoc* judgements of the stupidity of insectivores like tenrecs, or edentates such as sloths. Given the difficulties of evaluating animal intelligence fairly, it is not surprising that this method has fallen into disrepute. Attempting to estimate the computational/non-computational ratio without such naïve assumptions, Passingham (1982) used medulla volume as a measure of input/output connections to the brain, assuming this to be proportional to the amount of brain tissue devoted to maintenance. This is hard to justify without a good theory of how the brain operates computationally; but worse, medulla volumes are known for few primates. Spinal cord cross-sectional areas would be a better measure, making only the reasonable assumption that interneurones relay information, but again these data are largely unavailable.

The idea of localized computational function would be much more tractable, and just *might* be right, if we are lucky. The increase in brain size in the primates, over that of other mammal groups, is chiefly due to neocortical enlargement; and among primates, it is the the neocortex that varies most strikingly between species, whereas the rest of the brain shows much less evolutionary change (see Passingham 1982). This implies a strong selection pressure for neocortical enlargement in primates, and an intellectual function is the only serious candidate for this selection pressure. So if we want to make the assumption of localization, the neocortex is the best-bet location for computation—for the 'thinking part of the brain'.

Testing the theories

Neocortical enlargement, then, measures the extent to which primate brains are specialized for intelligence: but does it help discern the cause? Sawaguchi and Kudo (1990) found that the neocortex was larger in species living in bigger social groups, both in strepsirhines and in frugivorous platyrrhines. Also, in frugivorous haplorhines, polygynous species (one male living with more than one female) had larger neocortices than monogamous species.

These findings hint at a social origin of intelligence, but Robin Dunbar (1992) has gone further, using neocortex size to test directly between the two candidate theories, asking whether neocortical volumes match measures of social or environmental complexity. He examined both raw neocortical volume and several more complex functions; all gave similar trends, but *neocortex ratio* (ratio of neocortex size to that of the rest of the brain) gave the clearest effects. Measures of environmental complexity—range area, day journey length, and the amount of fruit in the diet—were found to be unrelated to neocortex ratio when body-size effects are removed (Fig. 14.2b). In complete contrast, group size did correlate with all measures of neocortical enlargement (Fig. 14.2a), strongly supporting a social origin of primate intelligence. Dunbar proposes specifically that neocortical size limits the social complexity that an individual can cope with: social complexity increases with group size, so groups begin to fragment when their size increases past a complexity limit set by neocortical size.

Nevertheless, neocortical enlargement is still an indirect way of estimating intelligence. It would be nice if there were a direct way of validating the assumption that a larger neocortex allows greater machiavellian intelligence. Perhaps there is. Although collected in an unsystematic way, the data on primate tactical deception (described in Chapter 9) are extensive, ranging over all groups of primates. Deception of a conspecific within the social group is surely a classic case of machiavellian intelligence. In order to correct in a rough-and-ready way for variations in how much different species have been studied, Andrew Whiten and I tested whether the number of cases reliably reported matched the number of observational studies undertaken (Byrne and Whiten 1992). They did not: some types of primate do more deception than expected, some less. Calculating a decep-

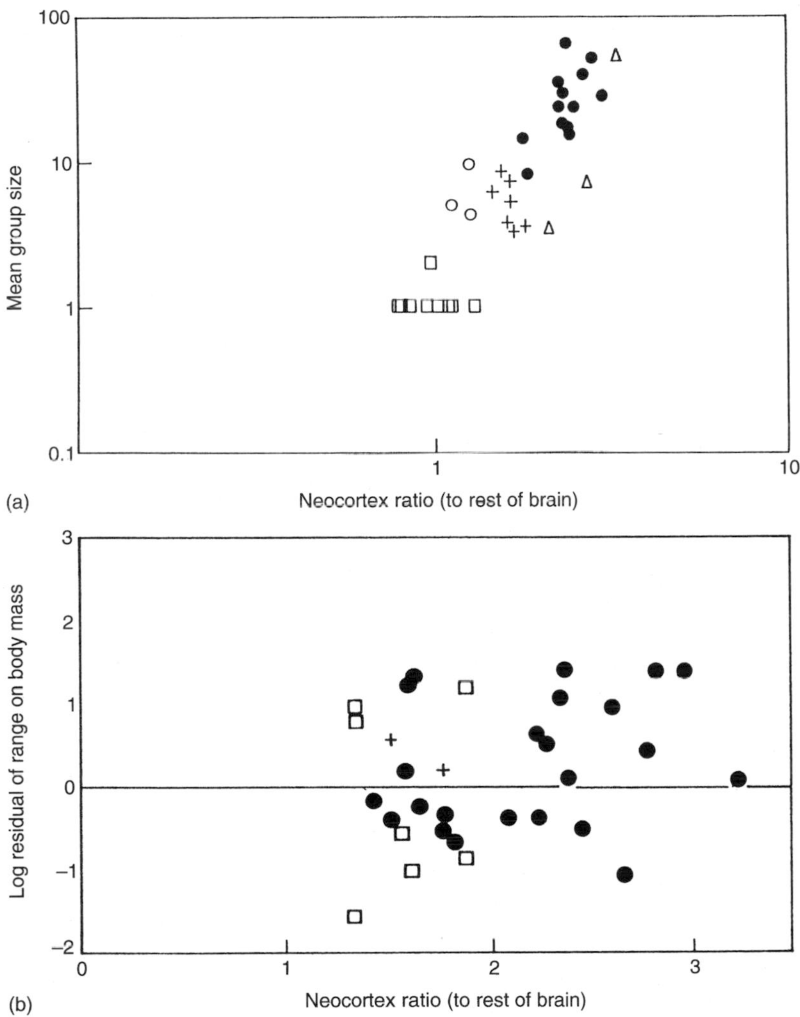

Figure 14.2 Dunbar's comparison of social group size and foraging range areas, as potential predictors of primate neocortex enlargement. (a) Group size and neocortex ratio for great apes (triangles), polygamous anthropoids (solid circles), monogamous anthropoids (plus signs), diurnal prosimians (open circles), and nocturnal prosimians (squares). (b) The components of range area not explained by body mass, against neocortex ratio for arboreal anthropoids (solid circles), prosimians (squares), solitary species (plus signs). (Copyright Academic Press, reprinted with permission from Dunbar 1992).

tion index—how much tactical deception has been seen in a species in excess of what one would expect from how much it has been studied—gives a direct, albeit rough, measure of social intelligence. When I tried plotting the index against Dunbar's neocortex ratio for different primate groups

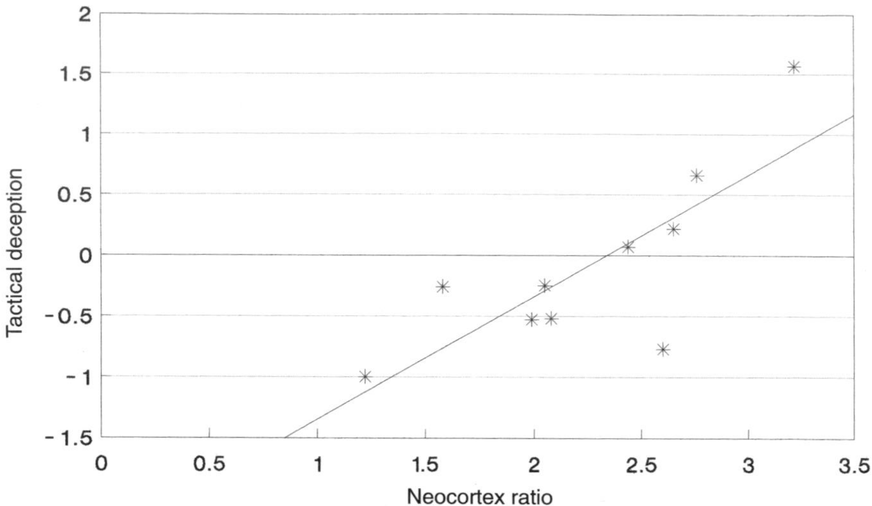

Figure 14.3 The relationship between the neocortical ratio and the prevalence of tactical deception (measured by the excess fraction reported over that expected on the simple assumption that the more study, the more reported), for various primates.

(Fig. 14.3), they matched; in fact the correlation of 0.77 is highly significant (Byrne 1993). Despite the approximations involved, the close relationship of this measure of machiavellian intelligence to enlargement of the neocortex suggests that the complex social manipulations shown by all haplorhine primates depend on neocortical enlargement.

The *insight* special to great apes—into mechanical function, into the structure of behaviour, and into intentions of other individuals—is not obviously related to brain volume. On Dunbar's neocortex ratio, for instance, *Papio* baboons are as large brained as gorillas, yet they show only rapid learning, no insight. The only brain measure that sets all the great apes completely apart from the monkeys is raw weight of neocortex (or brain), and this differs widely among apes in ways unrelated to any behavioural index (for instance, a gorilla's neocortex is much larger than a chimpanzee's). Possibly the sharp intellectual differences subsumed under the label 'insight' require a *critical* cortical size before they are possible, whereas above this size their expression does not depend on cortex size. Alternatively, the great-ape specialities may result from a change in type of information processing or neural organization within the brain, the result of a 'gene for insight'.

We are now in a position to give a (tentative) answer to the question, what selected for intelligence among primates? It seems more than a coincidence that the neocortical enlargement of primates correlates neatly with differences in social complexity and machiavellian intelligence. The evidence from deception shows that the social manipulations of monkeys and apes rely on having a large neocortex; at the least, neocortical enlargement must give an enhanced ability to learn quickly, especially in social contexts. Dunbar's comparison between measures of environmental and social complexity implies that the selection pressure for this neocortical enlargement was most likely a social one.

Social complexity does not explain the intellectual difference between monkeys and apes, however. Great apes live in groups of a size and complexity comparable to those of monkeys. (Anomalously, the orang-utan is actually solitary, although its more social nature in captivity and its large neocortex have led many to propose that solitary living is a recent adaptation.) And the insight of apes is not restricted to social problems. (Nor is it very obviously dependent on further neocortical enlargement above that of monkeys; the anatomical basis that results in ape insight remains a matter of speculation.)

Instead of social pressures, for an explanation of the insight shown in ape intelligence perhaps we should look again at environmental challenges. In dealing with several apparently complex environmental problems, great apes show remarkable abilities. Extensive tool use and manufacture, aided by imitation and sometimes teaching, is seen in common chimpanzees; but the readiness of all great apes to make and use tools in captivity hints that the origin of tool-making abilities may lie earlier than the common ancestor of chimpanzees and humans. We have also seen use of logically complex programmes of manual action, in gorillas (and orang-utans may be similar); complex diets and large ranges, exploited with economical route choices in foraging, in chimpanzees and orang-utans; and fluid but planned arboreal movements involving all four limbs, in the orang-utan alone. Any or all of these complex skills might have selected for insightful intelligence in the ancestor of modern great apes.

Further reading

There is no straightforward text on brain size and evolution that can be recommended at present; the papers referenced in this chapter are the best starting point.

15
Taking stock

It must be apparent by now that the field of primate cognition is a fast-moving one at present. This means that any generalizations are liable to be qualified by new results, and we must expect refinements and corrections to the provisional account that we can now give of the origins of human cognition. Nevertheless, even this provisional account is an exciting one, especially as it is based on solid, behavioural evidence. Speculations will still be necessary in places, but these can be differentiated clearly from the more sturdy, testable framework. I will first give a succinct review of the findings of Chapters 4–11 on animal learning and intelligence (with a digression on the intellect of cognitively advanced non-primates), and then map these results on to the evolutionary sequence of ancestor species that emerged from modern taxonomic analysis in Chapter 2.

The pattern of intelligence among animals

We have seen that what might be called 'intelligence' actually has a number of facets. Many dramatic achievements of animals, important ones for their survival, should perhaps not even be treated as a matter of their intelligence at all. These learning performances are tightly channelled by constraints on what the individual attends to; learning is highly efficient but narrow in scope. The results—imprinting, bird song-learning, food-aversion learning, star-compass learning, and so on—are striking, but the tight channelling means that the behaviour lacks flexiblity. The term 'intelligence' is more usefully reserved for more flexible, general-purpose cognitive functions.

Other animal learning is indeed much less constrained, such as learning by the mechanisms of classical and instrumental conditioning. These enable efficient learning of event correlations in the environment, and record the results of the individual's trial-and-error exploration. This sort of learning is found in all animals, but there are important species differences. The differences lie not in how the conditioning processes operate to produce useful knowledge, but in what the animal becomes aware of in the first place. Social circumstances, in particular, serve to 'prime' brain records of certain objects in the environment, possible actions, and desired goals, resulting in more efficient learning. This makes social species tend to show more cognitive skills than solitary ones, regardless of any real differences in basic aptitudes.

The way in which objects and events are represented in the brain—what is noticed, and whether it is coded in specific or abstract ways—affects the level at which knowledge can be generalized from one circumstance to another. In this case, species differences in what information is noticed and to what extent it can be generalized are *not* just a consequence of different environmental needs. Animals that can represent a wider range of categories of event, and generalize at a more abstract level, can solve problems that in humans we would treat as more intellectually demanding. Remember, though, this does not mean that such species are 'better adapted' than those with more inflexible and constrained learning; rather, they are adapted in a different way. Perhaps most likely, adaptations allowing more intelligent learning are needed by generalist species rather than specialist ones, and are of more benefit to social species rather than solitary ones. Social-living and generalist species often genuinely acquire more powerful and flexible behaviour than specialized and solitary ones.

Mainly, these species differences in intelligence have singled out simian primates from other animals. In most other species, differences seem largely to be due to specific learning mechanisms, rather than general intelligence. There is much evidence that converges on the fact that monkey and ape learning is more flexible, quicker, and less tightly bound to immediate circumstances than that of most other animals. Also, much of this evidence comes from the social arena, as if monkey and ape intelligence was somehow better developed on this 'topic' than any other. Monkeys and apes are quick at learning and tend to acquire much knowledge in the social domain. They are able to remember kinships and friendships, not only their own but those of third parties, and use this information in their social manipulations. Living in long-lasting groups, they are nevertheless able to benefit as individuals by manipulation of their fellow group members, for instance by deception in various ways. Social knowledge also allows them to build up complex social alliances, serviced by social grooming in catarrhine species. This might be summed up by saying that monkeys and apes are *better than most other animals at representing socially relevant information, and using it to gain rewards in their everyday lives*. (Whether their social aptitudes are usefully described as showing 'domain-specific social intelligence' is a matter of dispute. Alternatively, they can be viewed as a product of the beneficial 'channelling' imposed by social living, on individuals that are capable of learning rapidly in any domain.)

Because they have an extended social database, monkeys and apes develop tactics in the social arena which are impressively intelligent, but there is usually no evidence to suggest that the tactics are acquired by a qualitatively different mechanism than those of other animals. Instead, monkeys and apes are quicker at learning, especially socially, and this seems to be related to a greater relative size of the neocortex. Not only do haplorhine primates have relatively large brains for their body sizes, but this disproportion is largely due to neocortical expansion. In monkey and ape species, the size of the neocortex is related directly to how much tactical deception the species has been seen to commit, as well as the size of the social group in which it typically lives. The larger the neocortex, the more it seems the species relies on intelligence in its social living.

However, in addition to this continuous variation among haplorhine primates in neocortex size and the accompanying machiavellian intelligence, there is also a sharp discontinuity between one type of primate and another: a 'Rubicon' of cognitive capacity. This intellectual watershed lies between monkeys and apes. The great apes, especially chimpanzees, give abundant evidence of a greater depth of intelligence than possessed by any monkey: the quality that we call 'insight' in humans. Some of the special abilities that demonstrate this are social ones. Depth of social understanding shows up in varied ways, although there is often a common underlying theme: the ability to represent the intentions and knowledge of other individuals. Intentions and knowledge of others can, of course, only be inferred, not observed, but making the inferences seems beyond the minds of monkeys. Monkeys are apparently unable to imagine the mental states of other individuals.

Greater social understanding in great apes has implications for their social manipulation and comprehension of each other. Manipulations are potentially made more complex; but they may not be more conspicuous or common, since representation of intentions also confers the ability to anticipate and counter the manipulations of others. The ape/monkey difference in social comprehension shows up particularly in the abilities demonstrated by the common chimpanzee. Chimpanzees are sometimes able to: take account of others' ignorance; take over the role of a co-operator without explicit learning; anticipate solutions to problems experienced by others; and, in a few instances, teach their young in ways that show real understanding of gaps in knowledge. Although most evidence comes from chimpanzees, we know that this underlying depth of social understanding is not restricted to them because all the great-ape species show behaviour that relies on understanding mental states. Pygmy chimpanzees, orangutans, and gorillas can deceive intentionally and anticipate and counter the deception of others, can comprehend the self–other distinction in images reflected in mirrors, and can imitate others' actions at various levels of behavioural organization.

It might seem, then, that most of the special ape abilities are associated with the social arena—as with the more general learning excellence of simian primates. This is not so, and making the comparison is in any case problematic. Currently we know of no unbiased way of comparing social skill with mechanical or practical skill, they do not appear to be on a single scale of measurement. Also, the two domains are often hard to separate, and in practice they often intertwine. For instance, whether watching the skilled actions of others will be useful in learning new actions, depends both on having understanding of other individuals' behaviour and goals, and on being able to comprehend the logical structure of hierarchical processes.

Even in technical domains where social influences are minimal, such as in understanding the cause-and-effect relationship of tool and task, great apes still emerge as having insights that monkeys lack. Understanding the mechanical properties of objects used as tools is most clearly shown by the common chimpanzee, the only ape to make a range of tools in the wild. However, the other apes are perhaps mentally no different, since in captivity all learn to make and use tools similarly, in fact both orang-utans and pygmy chimpanzees have learnt to flake stone tools. In the wild the gorilla shows technical skill, using logically complex, hierarchical actions in feeding on plants defended by stings and other deterrents, although no tools are used: other apes may in time be shown to share their aptitudes.

One possible way of looking at the insight of great apes is to say that apes seem to have the ability to *think*, *plan*, or *compute* (in the sense of a Turing machine)—although admittedly, only in a limited way. Thinking could, in principle, allow computation of other 'possible worlds' than the current reality. A number of great-ape achievements can all be viewed as flowing from the ability to plan: deceiving intentionally, and forestalling the deceptive intentions of others; selecting or making an appropriate tool for the job, in advance of attempting the task; organizing several familiar processes into a new programme for a new goal; anticipation of future outcomes of current actions; and taking account of knowledge gaps in infants (teaching) and of the problems and plans of other individuals.

Rudimentary planning, as suggested by great-ape behaviour, is perhaps as far as an animal might be expected to get without a formal language in which to remember and express speculation and plans. When given the formal mechanisms artificially (in 'ape language' experiments) several individual great apes have shown that they can go well beyond the skills their wild counterparts ever show. This supports the idea that great-ape understanding of knowledge and ideas of other individuals has been a necessary springboard for the evolution of language. It also suggests that, while certainly supported by hard-wired brain systems, human language is much more a matter of learnt 'software' than often realized. Neocortical size variation does not clearly separate monkeys from apes, nor correlate with cognitive differences among the apes. The crucial advance in insight that the apes possess does not seem to be a simple function of brain size, but is perhaps instead a reflection of brain reorganization or reprogramming.

Postscript: are we (and other great apes) alone?

I have concentrated on primates, since this book's aim is to understand human intellectual origins. Building up a case for a 'pinnacle' of primate intellectual capacity, however, does not mean that *other* pinnacles might not exist. Other groups of animals might also have become specialized for intelligence, perhaps in quite different ways, and in response to different selective pressures, than primates. We have already met evidence of various sorts of intelligent behaviour in non-primates: might the evidence reflect a systematic pattern? On the basis of what we have seen for primates, we can predict where we should find evolutionary convergence with aspects of human intelligence: in species with complex social systems, perhaps in species that meet complex problems in foraging, and in species with large brains.

If social complexity acted generally as a selective pressure, facilitating the brain enlargement that allows rapid learning in social contexts, the carnivores and the pinnipeds are obvious mammal groups in which to seek signs of intelligence. Many carnivore species live in groups, some more structured than any primate's. Dwarf mongooses (*Helogale hirtula*) take turns to 'baby-sit' youngsters while the rest of the group is off hunting (Rood 1978). Males of several species form coalitions, either with kin or non-kin, in order to gain and hold more than one female (lion: Packer *et al.* 1991; cheetah: Caro and Durant 1991; slender mongoose (*Herpestes sanguineus*): Waser *et al.* 1994). Both carnivores and pinnipeds are large-brained, and some species meet the potentially demanding foraging problem set by hunting prey that are larger than themselves (wolves (*Canis lupus*) eating moose; lions eating buffalo), or occur in tight groups of many individuals (seals eating fish), or both (wild dogs (*Lycaon pictus*) eating wildebeest). Some species hunt socially, and co-ordination potentially gives an additional problem. Although Stander's work shows genuinely co-operative hunting by lionesses (Stander 1992), in general the evidence on the nature of co-operation in carnivores and pinnipeds is slim compared with that for primates, usually amounting only to hunters' tales. One reason for this is the nocturnality of many social carnivores. This would not prevent good evidence for cognitive skills being obtained in captivity, but little has been found. There is no convincing evidence in any of these species for imitation, intentional deception, or intentional teaching, no suggestion of any ability to understand others' roles or knowledge, nor of understanding self-reflection in a mirror. Schusterman has shown that sealions are able to learn the syntax of an artificial language, but this work gives no evidence of mental-state attribution (Schusterman *et al.* 1986). Perhaps social carnivores and pinnipeds can match monkeys' quantitatively enhanced learning, but they certainly do not show any sign of ape-like insight and understanding.

If we judge by brain size, toothed whales (e.g. dolphins, *Tursiops* spp., orca, *Orcinus orca*, and sperm whale, *Physeter catodon*) should show intelligence: their brains are unique among animals in being as large as humans in proportion to body size, and are far larger in absolute terms. Some of the smaller cetaceans are also now known to live in long-lasting groups; and for thousands of years they have forced their cognitive and social tendencies to human attention. Despite a lack of hands and despite inhabiting a wholly different world to ourselves (the two factors that comparative psychologists have most often found useful in explaining failures of animals) dolphins and other toothed whales are first-class at laboratory tasks—if they are in the mood, for they are temperamental animals. When not given tasks, dolphins will in fact often invent their own. The minor difficulties of studying nocturnal carnivores pale into insignificance when compared with the problems of studying dolphins in the field, although dolphins' legendary exploits in saving drowning sailors tantalizingly hint at some kind of empathy. Understandably, dolphin fieldwork is in its infancy but already there is evidence that suggests teaching (Sayich *et al.* 1993). In captivity, much more progress has been made. Herman's work shows that dolphins can learn a communication system with grammar and interpret novel commands (Herman 1986), and Taylor and Saayman (1973) showed that dolphins can imitate actions and sounds. Recently, dolphins have also been found to comprehend their image in a mirror, using the Gallup mark test; their contorted swimming pattern indicated that they were deliberately looking at the hidden marks on their bodies (Marten and Psarakos 1994). It seems that some of the package of intellectual abilities which are specialized in apes have evolved independently in cetaceans.

Perhaps just the same has happened at least once in far more remote relatives of ourselves: parrots. In the African grey parrot, Pepperberg's work on linguistic and number comprehension (Pepperberg 1990), combined with Moore's on the impersonation of actions (Moore 1993), begins to make a case for this. African greys, like other large parrots (macaws, cockatoos) are large-brained among birds, but what mentally challenging tasks (if any) they meet in the wild is not known. It is intriguing that these large parrots are also highly manipulative, using one foot as a vice with almost 360° manoeuvrability, and the tongue and upper mandible as tools. So far, there is no convincing evidence of intentional deception, teaching, or other signs of intentionality in these birds, but it would be unwise to assume that it will not emerge in time.

How humans became intelligent: reconstruction of evolutionary history

Returning to the theme of this book, the evolutionary origins of *human* intelligence, we can now begin to reconstruct the sequence of changes that took place before the first bipedal hominid emerged. For this exercise, we must map the pattern of primate cognition on to the secure history of human ancestors that is derived from extant species.

This process has several stages. First, the *ancestors* of modern groups are deduced with cladistic taxonomy, as we saw in Chapter 2. In general, these creatures will lack scientific names, because it is rare when a specific known fossil can be identified as the precise ancestor of modern forms. To create fossils, very special conditions are needed, especially for terrestrial animals; few individuals of few species will actually leave any. Far more often, the fossils that *have* been found will be on 'side-branches' of the known evolutionary tree. To name the deduced ancestral species, I shall use the device of 'the X/Y ancestor', where X and Y are the most divergent species among the modern descendants of the ancestor. Since we are especially interested in the evolution of human attributes, 'human' will usually be species Y. The lemur/human ancestor is thus the earliest primate about which we can get any evidence by the comparative method, whereas the chimpanzee/human ancestor is the most recent, our last common ancestor with a living great ape. Lemurs and lorises are *equally* closely related to humans, as are common chimpanzees and pygmy chimpanzees; either name could be used for the X species and would specify exactly the same common ancestor.

Then, from behavioural evidence about modern species, we estimate the behaviour and aptitudes of these ancestral species by 'reversing' cladistic analysis. Each clade (valid evolutionary taxon) defines an ancestor. Behaviours *shared* by descendant species in a clade (whether these traits are derived or primitive) are taken to be traits of the deduced ancestor. Confidence in this deduction depends on the number of modern species about which we have evidence, and the variance within each clade. If all modern descendants share a similar skill, and there are many descendents, then we can be sure about their common ancestor's ability. Where there are only two branches deriving from the ancestor (there must be at least two, since ancestors are only deduced where branches meet), and these show quite opposite cognitive traits, we gain no evidence about the ancestor. In such a problematic case, we would do best to take the approach that requires the least stretching of the imagination. That is, we should assume that the ancestor possessed the 'primitive' level of ability: that of all *other* species outside the clade. The basis for this assumption is reasonable: a character is more likely to evolve once, than evolve in one lineage and then later disappear in some species within it. (But the latter *can* occasionally happen, characters may be lost with evolution after previous selection for them, so we must be wary.) The other problem is the matter of counting traits. In general, traits of only a few clade members are unlikely to reflect the clade's ancestral state; for instance, if one species in a clade has a unique trait, it is most likely to be a new (derived) characteristic of this species alone. Therefore, rather than the 'most advanced' level of any species within a clade, we must infer average capabilities to an ancestor. The correct way to determine this average is by counting branches in the cladogram, regardless of the number of species on each branch. For instance, if we were using this method to deduce the ancestral social system of apes, the fact that the nine or so modern species of gibbon are monogamous would not lead to a deduction of monogamy as the gibbon/chimpanzee ancestor's likely mating system. The closely related gibbons are on one branch in the phylogeny (gibbon ancestor: 'monogamous'), the great apes another (great ape ancestor: 'indeterminate', since each modern species has a different mating system); given this conflict, the safest, 'default' conclusion would then have to be the primitive state. With these rules, what account of the evolution of human intelligence do we derive? (In what follows, data to reconstruct ancestral social organizations come from Smuts *et al.* 1986.)

The lemur/human ancestor, the earliest primate species for which we have modern descendants available to study, lived around 65 My ago (Fig. 15.1); but cladistically the lemur/human does not give us much to go on. It is ancestral to two modern branches, strepsirhines and haplorhines; the average strepsirhine is small-brained, socially unsophisticated, poor at laboratory puzzles, nocturnal and solitary; the average haplorhine is the exact reverse! Because most other mammals are like strepsirhine rather than haplorhine primates, we know that this was the primitive condition for mammals in general. Following the rules described above, we therefore infer that the lemur/human was no more intelligent or socially sophisticated than other mammals; it was small-brained, socially unsophisticated (and would have been poor at laboratory puzzles, had it been tested), nocturnal, and solitary. In other words, it was very like a modern lemur, because in fact strepsirhines show many primitive primate traits. As it happens, these

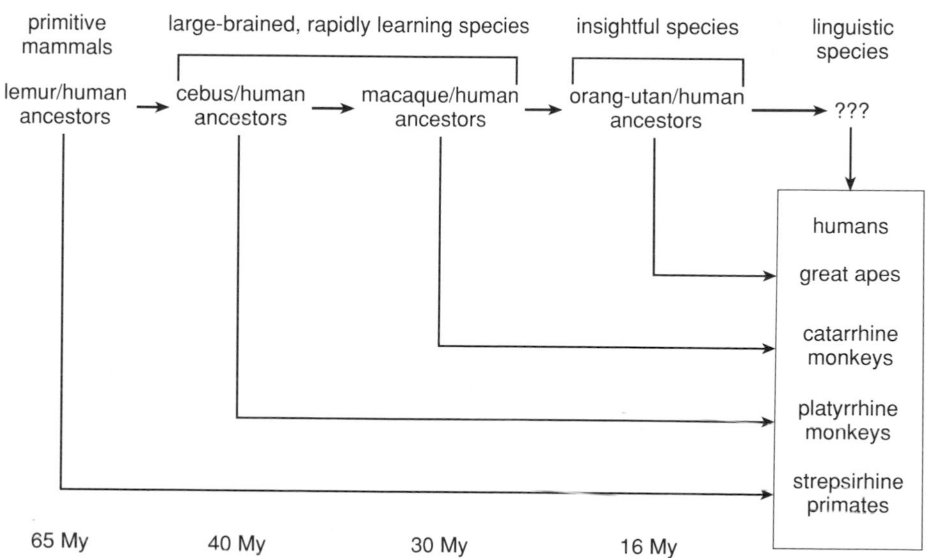

Figure 15.1 Diagrammatic representation of the reconstruction of human ancestry, with the dated chain of inferred ancestors and their cognitive attributes (top), all based on evidence from living species (box, right).

deductions are supported by the fossil record: the earliest primate fossils *are* the sort that we would call strepsirhines if they were alive today. It is therefore not unrealistic to view modern lorises and most lemurs as similar to the earliest primates: as 'living fossils'. (And this has, in fact, routinely been done in texts on primate evolution.) Although of course no living species is an ancestor of any other, the commonsense idea of a 'living fossil' can be very useful in understanding evolutionary history; it helps most people to view nocturnal lemurs as living fossils of the earliest primates. Of course, these are not species on the 'scrap heap' of evolution—their very survival proves their evolutionary success—and the similarities to the ancestral common ancestor will not be exact. With these provisos, modern survivals similar to early ancestors are invaluable in fleshing out the dry history.

Some modern lemurs do not correspond to this pattern: they are diurnal and live in large, long-lasting social groups. Living on Madagascar, free from competition with monkeys, these social lemurs have converged with monkeys on several traits. Even so, they are relatively small-brained, poor at laboratory tasks, and retain the specialized vision of a nocturnal animal, with a reflective tapetum behind the retina, like a cat's. And, as Jolly (1966) emphasized, their large groups are not socially complex like those of monkeys. These few species of group-living lemur are best viewed as recent divergences from the characteristic pattern retained in most modern strepsirhines, thus are of little relevance to the process of reconstructing origins of human cognition. Similarly uninformative, but for a different reason, is the tarsier. On most currently accepted cladistic taxonomies, the tarsier/human is deduced as an ancestor. However, the modern tarsiers are little-known and apparently differ little from strepsirhines on most parameters, so little can be concluded from this intermediary.

From the lemur/humans, unspecialized for intelligence, the simian primates (monkeys and apes) represent an important *quantitative* shift in cognitive ability. The earliest simian ancestor, the cebus/human, diverged from the strepsirhine (or tarsier) line before 40 My ago. The cebus/human was very different to strepsirhines: diurnal, group-living, and with a larger neocortex of the brain—almost certainly an adaptive response to the increased social complexity of living in semi-permanent groups. (We deduce these facts because almost all its modern descendants live diurnally in semi-permanent social groups; and among these modern simians group size predicts neocortex ratio, whereas in modern strepsirhines it does not.) Relatively larger brains allow more efficient learning. This made cebus/humans good at representing socially relevant information (giving them an extended social database) and using it to gain rewards in group living (giving more sophisticated behaviour in social contexts). However, there is no reason to suppose that their brain mechanisms of learning differed qualitatively from those of other mammals. Because of the potential for *priming* (by stimulus enhancement and response facilitiation in their social groups) to enhance associative learning, and because an extended range of social knowledge would allow discrimination of subtle differences of circumstance, their social manipulations might sometimes have looked clever and insightful. In a sense, just like many modern monkeys, cebus/humans may have been good mimics of insightful, thoughtful animals—but only mimics.

Unfortunately, it is not easy to decide which living species, if one exists, is similar to an ancestral cebus/human. Cladistic tree analysis gives no clear pointer to whether the primitive simian social organization was multimale/multifemale groups, one-male groups, or even extended monogamous families; nor whether males or females would have transferred between groups. The tiny callitrichids *seem* primitive, having claws on their fingers (not the big toe), but modern evidence reinterprets them as a recent, derived form, adapted to a squirrel-like niche in rainforest. If so, their apparently primitive characters result from secondary re-selection in this process, and one of the cebine or pithecine monkeys would be a better bet for a modern model of a cebus/human; we shall never know for sure.

Around 30 My ago, macaque/human ancestors diverged from cebus/human stock, and their descendants include all Old World monkeys and apes. Like cebus/humans, these animals were socially sophisticated, but their social skills extended beyond deception and dyadic manipulation, using social grooming as a currency to build up more complex alliances, and reconciliation to repair alliances after conflict. However, macaque/human ancestors would not have reached the heights of monkey 'insightless intelligence' shown today in modern open-country monkeys (especially baboons, but also some macaques, and vervet and patas monkeys). The enlarged neocortex of these species is linked to their large body size: colonization of niches that select for body size was critical. In the main, this means open savannah environments: larger body size allows longer cruising range between resource patches, and less risk of predation for animals away from the safety of trees. Monkeys adapted to these open habitats are restricted to the Old World, but savannahs are relatively new habitats on Earth, generally post-Miocene. Thus, the most socially smart Old World monkeys of today probably reflect an increase of intelligence *since* divergence with the human line of evolution: like the social lemurs, these species have no direct relevance to human ancestry. Several groups of social carnivores and pinnipeds (all post-Miocene genera) show similar insightless intelligence to monkeys; this convergent evolution was presumably in response to parallel needs for enlarged social groups.

The quantitative shift to an enlarged neocortex, allowing enhanced learning in social contexts, may have been an essential prerequisite for a more fundamental, *qualitative* development: the evolution of insight, giving a 'quantum leap' in intelligent behaviour. Only one descendant of the macaque/human evolved the insight needed to understand, and perhaps consequently plan, its actions: the orang-utan/human ancestor. This species lived about 16 My ago and is ancestral also to modern gorillas and chimpanzees; from cladistic evidence, its locomotion involved brachiation, and was most likely similar to that of a modern orang-utan. Fortuitously, as noted in Chapter 2, a *Sivapithecus* skull exists from 12 My; this closely resembles a modern orang-utan in cranial form; it is therefore reasonable to treat the modern orang-utan as a living fossil of the orang-utan/human ancestor.

The intellectual abilities of orang-utan/humans—and hence all modern great apes—are not especially associated with enlarged brain or neocortex, and some more subtle, organizational brain change seems to have occurred. What caused the quantum leap in orang-utan/human intelligence is not certain, but social challenges do not fit the bill: even assuming orang-utan/humans were socially more chimpanzee-like or gorilla-like than the solitary orang-utan, does not suggest groups larger than those of modern monkeys. The orang-utan/human ancestor would, no doubt, have shown insight in social contexts, but it had no greater *need* of such social insights than monkeys.

Environmental challenges are more plausible as selection pressures that led to ape insight, since several apply specifically to one or more great apes. Likely candidate challenges include a need to use and learn complex programmes of manual action, in which imitation and teaching would help; locomotor problems, in which advance calculations about the self would help; hunting large mammals, in which anticipation of future actions of prey and companions would help; tool use and tool-making, especially for extractive foraging, in which symbolic representation of object properties and the ability to imagine unseen objects would help. However, the evidence that suggests possible insight (by convergent evolution) in dolphins cautions against too ready speculation, since none of these ape challenges seem to apply to dolphins on our current, admittedly fragmentary, knowledge. If dolphins do share ape-like insight, this would be more consistent with a 'critical brain mass' hypothesis, since a dolphin has a large neocortex by any measure. Perhaps sheer, absolute size of neocortex, rather than any organizational change in the brain, can allow complex, symbolic representation to develop as an emergent property?

Whatever led to the cognitive advance in the orang-utan/human ancestor, the implications of the change were profound. For the first time, an animal could mentally represent and conjure with other 'possible worlds': what other animals might be thinking, and what other animals might think of it; what a novel object might be used for, and what sort of object would be needed to solve a current problem; how other animals' behaviour could be manipulated by changing their beliefs, with deception or teaching; which particular aspects of another individual's actions and intentions are crucial to copying a skill.

For the first time, animals could be said to be capable of 'thought' in the sense of anticipatory planning or Turing machine computation. No doubt the extent of this thinking was—and still is, in non-humans—highly limited. But if a clear cognitive boundary were to be sought between 'man and beast' other than language, this would have to be it, and great apes come down on the human side. The implications of this statement for ethics of animal usage by humans are obvious and profound.

There is no evidence of further cognitive advance, compared with the orang-utan/human, in the gorilla/human ancestor. This diverged about 7.5 My ago, and since all its descendants—the gorilla, two chimpanzee species, and apparently also humans—are African then presumably it was an African species. We cannot get any clear evidence of its locomotion from comparative study: the descendant branches have different modes of locomotion, bipedalism and knuckle-walking. Fossil great apes are known from 4 My ago, but these are of hominids, animals already capable of bipedal walking: the australopithecines. They still show a number of orang-utan-like features suggesting arboreality, and no anatomical signs of knuckle-walking, so it seems probable that the gorilla/human ancestor retained the orang-utan style of locomotion (but the possibility that gorilla/human ancestors were bipedal walkers has also been suggested: Kortlandt and Kooij 1963).

The chimpanzee/human ancestor of 6 My ago may well have shown cognitive advance, however. Certainly, one of the two chimpanzee species always seems to be represented in the most impressive demonstrations of cognitive skill: intentional teaching, intentional deception, grammatical comprehension, distinguishing between malice and accident, and so on. In particular, the more extensive evidence of tool-making and mechanical comprehension in the chimpanzee line cannot be ignored. Nevertheless, the chimpanzee/human's behavioural expression of insight would most likely not have been very conspicuous, any more than it is in modern chimpanzees. Why these animals, which give evidence of the insight that we humans consider so crucial to behavioural intelligence, show so few signs of its use in everyday life, remains a mystery.

The other great qualitative change in cognition during human evolution was that of *language*. When the first use of language occurred will remain a mystery, since no direct signs of language are preserved in the fossil record. However, it is no coincidence that only in the great-ape clade did one animal develop this further capability. The ability to imagine other mental viewpoints is a necessary precursor to language, and it certainly evolved first. Over the years, linguists have always hotly debated the origins of language, and whether there are precursors of language in other species' communication. In the main, their answer has been 'no', but they may have asked the wrong question. Asking instead whether there are precursors of language in other species' *cognition* gives a different answer: there are several precursors of language evident in the behaviour of all great apes. These include attribution of intentions and beliefs to others; understanding individuals' differences of mental perspective, belief, and role; comprehension of cause and effect, and hierarchical structure in behaviour; and rudimentary anticipatory planning. In the limiting case, a species unable to take account of another's current intentions and needs would not be capable of benefiting from linguistic communication at all. Already, the experimental provision of sign-language to apes has, among other things, shown chimpanzees capable of undertanding true (Gricean) communication. The relationships of hierarchical structuring and anticipatory planning to language are less clearly defined, but on many theoretical viewpoints these would also be linked.

It is tempting at this point to speculate among the possible scenarios that might bridge from the chimpanzee/human at 6 My to anatomically modern humans at 0.2 My. But this is where we came in, in Chapter 1! Any such bridge can never be more than plausible hypothesis, so it is safer to leave that story to a different sort of book. What this book has shown is that, from the chimpanzee/human's array of cognitive capacities, the gulf to 'the thinking primate' is a bridgeable one: human cognition has a long history, extending back in time to well before the inscrutable era of the hominids.

References

Adams, E. S. and Caldwell, R. L. (1990). Communication in asymmetric fights of the stomatopod crustacean. *Animal Behaviour*, **39**, 706–16.

Anderson, J. R. (1984). Monkeys with mirrors: some questions for primate psychology. *International Journal of Primatology*, **5**, 81–98.

Bailey, W. J., Hayasaka, K., Skinner, C. G., Kehoe, S., Sieu, L. C., Slightom, J. L., and Goodman, M. (1992). Re-examination of the African hominoid trichotomy with additional sequences from the primate ß-globin gene cluster. *Molecular Phylogenetics and Evolution*, **1**, 97–135.

Baron-Cohen, S. (1991). Precursors to a theory of mind: understanding attention in others. In *Natural theories of mind evolution, development and simulation of everyday mindreading* (ed. A. Whiten), pp. 233–51. Basil Blackwell, Oxford.

Baron-Cohen, S., Leslie, A. M., and Frith, U. (1985). Does the autistic child have a 'theory of mind'? *Cognition*, **21**, 37–46.

Baron-Cohen, S , Leslie, A. M., and Frith, U. (1986). Mechanical, behavioural and intentional understanding of picture stories in autistic children. *British Journal of Developmental Psychology*, **4**, 113–25.

Bateson, P. P. G. (1973). Internal influences on early learning in birds. In *Constraints on learning* (ed. R. A. Hinde and J. Stevenson-Hinde), pp. 101–16. Academic Press, London.

Bauer, P. and Mandler, J. (1989). One thing follows another: effects of temporal structure on 1- and 2-year-olds' recall of events. *Developmental Psychology*, **25**, 197–206.

Beck, B. B. (1980). *Animal tool behavior*. Garland Press, New York.

Binet, A. and Simon, T. H. (1915). *Method of measuring the development of the intelligence of young children*. Chicago Medical Book Company, Chicago.

Binford, L. R. (1981). *Bones: ancient men and modern myths*. Academic Press, New York.

Birch, H. G. (1945). The relation of previous experience to insightful problem-solving. *Journal of Comparative Physiological Psychology*, **38**, 367–83.

Boesch, C. (1991*a*). Teaching in wild chimpanzees. *Animal Behaviour*, **41**, 530–2.

Boesch, C. (1991*b*). Symbolic communication in wild chimpanzees. *Human Evolution*, **6**, 81–90.

Boesch, C. and Boesch, H. (1984). Mental map in wild chimpanzees: an analysis of hammer transports for nut cracking. *Primates*, **25**, 160–70.

Boesch, C. and Boesch, H. (1989). Hunting behaviour of wild chimpanzees in the Taï National Park. *American Journal of Physical Anthropology*, **78**, 547–73.

Brown, D. H. and Norris, K. S. (1956). Observations of captive and wild cetaceans. *Journal of Mammology*, **37**, 311–26.

Byrne, R. W. (1975). Memory in complex tasks. Ph.D. thesis, University of Cambridge.

Byrne, R. W. (1977). Planning meals: problem-solving on a real data-base. *Cognition*, **5**, 287–332.

Byrne, R. W. (1993). Do larger brains mean greater intelligence? *Behavioral and Brain Sciences*, **16**, 696–7.

Byrne, R. W. (1994). The evolution of intelligence. In *Behaviour and evolution* (ed. P. J. B. Slater and T. R. Halliday) pp. 223–65 Cambridge University Press, Cambridge.

Byrne, R. W. and Byrne, J. M. (1988). Leopard killers of Mahale. *Natural History*, **97**, 22–6.

Byrne, R. W. and Byrne, J. M. E. (1991). Hand preferences in the skilled gathering tasks of mountain gorillas (*Gorilla g. beringei*). *Cortex*, **27**, 521–46.

Byrne, R. W. and Byrne, J. M. E. (1993). Complex leaf-gathering skills of mountain gorillas (*Gorilla g. beringei*) variability and standardization. *American Journal of Primatology*, **31**, 241–61.

Byrne, R. W. and Whiten, A. (1985). Tactical deception of familiar individuals in baboons (*Papio ursinus*). *Animal Behaviour*, **33**, 669–73.

Byrne, R. W. and Whiten, A. (1988*a*). Towards the next generation in data quality: a new survey of primate tactical deception. *Behavioral and Brain Sciences*, **11**, 267–73.

Byrne, R. W. and Whiten, A. (1988*b*). *Machiavellian intelligence: social expertise and the evolution of intellect in monkeys, apes and humans*. Clarendon Press, Oxford.

Byrne, R. W. and Whiten, A. (1990). Tactical deception in primates: the 1990 database. *Primate Report*, **27**, 1–101.

Byrne, R. W. and Whiten, A. (1991). Computation and mindreading in primate tactical deception. In *Natural Theories of Mind* (ed. A .Whiten), pp. 127–41. Basil Blackwell, Oxford.

Byrne, R. W. and Whiten, A. (1992). Cognitive evolution in primates: evidence from tactical deception. *Man*, **27**, 609–27.

Byrne, R. W., Whiten, A., Henzi, S. P., and McCulloch, F. M. (1993). Nutritional constraints on mountain baboons (*Papio ursinus*): implications for baboon socioecology. *Behavioural Ecology and Socioecology*, **33**, 233–46.

Calvin, W. H. (1982). Did throwing stones shape hominid brain evolution? *Ethology and Sociobiology*, **3**, 115–24.

Caro, T. M. (1980). Predatory behaviour in domestic cat mothers. *Behaviour*, **74**, 128–47.

Caro, T. M. and Durant, T. M. (1991). Use of quantitative analyses of pelage characteristics to reveal family relationships in genetically monomorphic cheetahs. *Journal of Heredity*, **82**, 8–14.

Caro, T. M. and Hauser, M. D. (1992). Is there teaching in non-human animals? *Quarterly Review of Biology*, **67**, 151–74.

Chagnon, N. A. (1974). *Studying the Yanomamö*. Holt, Rinehart and Winston, New York.

Cheney, D. L. (1978). The play partners of immature baboons. *Animal Behaviour*, **26**, 1038–50.

Cheney, D. L. and Seyfarth, R. M. (1988). Social and non-social knowledge in vervet monkeys. In *Machiavellian intelligence: social expertise and the evolution of intellect in monkeys, apes and humans* (ed. R. W. Byrne and A. Whiten), pp. 255–70. Clarendon Press, Oxford.

Cheney, D. L. and Seyfarth, R. M. (1990). *How monkeys see the world: inside the mind of another species*. University of Chicago Press, Chicago.

Chomsky, N. (1957). *Syntactic structures*. Mouton, The Hague.

Chomsky, N. (1959). Review of Skinner (1957). *Language*, **35**, 26–58.

Clutton-Brock, T. H. and Harvey, P. H. (1980). Primates, brains and ecology. *Journal of Zoology, London*, **190**, 309–23.

Craik, K. J. W. (1943). *The nature of explanation*. Cambridge University Press, Cambridge.

Dasser, V. (1988). Mapping social concepts in monkeys. In *Machiavellian intelligence: social expertise and the evolution of intellect in monkeys, apes and humans* (ed. R. W. Byrne and A. Whiten), pp. 85–93. Clarendon Press, Oxford.

Davidson, I. and Noble, W. (1993). Tools and language in human evolution. In *Tools, language and cognition in human evolution* (ed. K. R. Gibson and T. Ingold), pp. 363–88. Cambridge University Press, Cambridge.

Dawkins, R. (1976). *The selfish gene*. Oxford University Press, Oxford.

Deacon, T. W. (1990). Fallacies of progression in theories of brain-size evolution. *International Journal of Primatology*, **11**, 193–236.

Dennett, D. C. (1983). Intentional systems in cognitive ethology: the 'Panglossian paradigm' defended. *Behavioural and Brain Sciences*, **6**, 343–90.

Dibble, H. L. (1989). The implications of stone tool types for the presence of language during the Lower and Middle Paleolithic. In *The human revolution* (ed. P. Mellars and C. Stringer), pp. 415–32. Princeton University Press, Princeton.

Dickinson, A. (1980). *Contemporary animal learning theory*. Cambridge University Press, Cambridge.

Dowsett-Lemaire, F. (1979). The imitative range of the song of the marsh warbler, *Acrocephalus palustris*, with special reference to imitations of African birds. *Ibis*, **121**, 453–68.

Dunbar, R. I. M. (1988). *Primate social systems*. Croom Helm, London.

Dunbar, R. I. M. (1991). Functional significance of social grooming in primates. *Folia Primatologia*, **57**, 121–31.

Dunbar, R. I. M. (1992). Neocortex size as a constraint on group size in primates. *Journal of Human Evolution*, **20,** 469–93.

Eldredge, N. and Tattersall, I. (1982). *The myths of human evolution*. Columbia University Press, New York.

Emlen, S. T. (1970). Celestial rotation: its importance in the development of migratory orientation. *Science*, **170**, 1198–201.

Fisher, J. and Hinde, R. A. (1949). The opening of milk bottles by birds. *British Birds*, **42**, 347–57.

Fouts, R. S., Fouts, D. H. and Van Cantfort, T. E. (1989). The infant Loulis learns signs from cross fostered chimpanzees. In *Teaching sign language to chimpanzees* (ed. R. A. Gardner, B. T. Gardner, and T. E. Van Cantfort), pp. 280–92. State University of New York Press, New York.

Galef, B. G. (1988). Imitation in animals: history, definition and interpretation of data from psychological laboratory. In *Comparative social learning* (ed. T. Zentall and B. G. Galef Jr), pp. 3–28. Erlbaum, Hillsdale, NJ.

Gallup, G. G., Jr (1970). Chimpanzees: self-recognition. *Science*, **167**, 86–7.

Gallup, G. G., Jr (1975). Towards an operational definition of self-awareness. In *Socioecology and psychology of primates* (ed. R. H. Tuttle), pp. 309–41. Mouton, Paris.

Garber, P. A. (1989). Role of spatial memory in primate foraging patterns: *Saguinus mystax* and *Saguinus fuscicollis*. *American Journal of Primatology*, **19**, 203–16.

Garcia, J. and Koelling, R. A. (1966). Relation of cue to consequence in avoidance learning. *Psychonomic Science*, **4**, 123–4.

Garcia, J., Ervin, F. R., and Koelling, R. A. (1966). Learning with prolonged delay of reinforcement. *Psychonomic Science*, **5**, 121–2.

Gardner, R. A., Gardner, B. T., and van Cantfort, T. E. (1989). *Teaching sign language to chimpanzees*. State University of New York Press, New York.

Gargett, R. H. (1989). Grave shortcomings: the evidence for Neanderthal burial. *Current Anthropology*, **30**, 157–90.

Gibson, K. R. and Ingold, T. (1993). *Tools, language and cognition in human evolution*. Cambridge University Press, Cambridge.

Gisiner, R. and Schusterman, R. J. (1992). Sequence, syntax and semantics: responses of a language-trained sea lion *Zalophus californianus* to novel sign combinations. *Journal of Comparative Psychology*, **106**, 78–91.

Glander, K. E. (1978). Howling monkey feeding behavior and plant secondary compounds. In *The ecology of arboreal folivores* (ed. G. C. Montgomery), pp. 561–74. Smithsonian Institution Press, Washington DC.

Gomez, J. C. (1991). Visual behaviour as a window for reading the mind of others in primates. In *Natural theories of mind: evolution, development and simulation of everyday mindreading* (ed. A. Whiten), pp. 195–207. Basil Blackwell, Oxford.

Goodall, A. G. (1977). Feeding and ranging behaviour of a mountain gorilla group (*Gorilla gorilla beringei*) in the Tshibinda-Kahuzi region (Zaire). In *Primate ecology* (ed. T. H. Clutton-Brock), pp. 450–79. Academic Press, New York.

Goodall, J. (1986). *The chimpanzees of Gombe: patterns of behavior*. Harvard University Press, Cambridge, MA.

Goodall, J., Bandora, A., Bergmann, E., Busse, C., Matama, H., Mpongo, E., Pierce, A., and Riss, D. (1979). Intercommunity interactions in the chimpanzee population of the Gombe National Park. In *The great apes* (ed. D. Hamburg and E. R. McCown), pp. 13–54. Benjamin Cummings, Menlo Park.

Gould, S. J. (1981). *The mismeasure of man*. Penguin Books, Harmondsworth, Middlesex.

Gowlett, J. A. J. (1986). Culture and conceptualisation: the Oldowan–Acheulian gradient. In *Stone Age prehistory* (ed. G. N. Bailey and P. Callow), pp. 243–60. Cambridge University Press, Cambridge.

Green, S. (1975). Dialects in Japanese monkeys: vocal learning and cultural transmission of locale-specific vocal behaviour? *Zeitschrift für Tierpschologie*, **38**, 304–14.

Groot, A. D. de (1966). Perception and memory versus thinking. In *Problem solving* (ed. B. Kleinmuntz). Wiley, New York.

Harcourt, A. (1988). Alliances in contests and social intelligence. In *Machiavellian intelligence: social expertise and the evolution of intellect in monkeys, apes and humans* (ed. R. W. Byrne and A. Whiten), pp. 132–52. Clarendon Press, Oxford.

Harcourt, A. (1992). Coalitions and alliances: are primates more complex than non-primates? In *Coalitions and alliances in humans and other animals* (ed. A. H. Harcourt and F. B. M. de Waal), pp. 445–71. Oxford University Press, Oxford.

Harlow, H. F. (1949). The formation of learning sets. *Psychological Review*, **56**, 51–65.

Harvey, P. H., Martin, R. D., and Clutton-Brock, T. H. (1986). Life histories in comparative perspective. In *Primate societies* (ed. B. B. Smuts, D. L. Cheney, R. M. Seyfarth, R. W. Wrangham, and T. T. Struhsaker), pp. 181–92. University of Chicago Press, Chicago.

Hasegawa, T. and Hiraiwa-Hasegawa, M. (1986). Sperm competition and mating behaviour. In *The chimpanzees of the Mahale Mountains* (ed. T. Nishida), pp. 115–32. University of Tokyo Press, Tokyo.

Hauser, M. D. and Wrangham, R. W. (1987). Manipulation of food calls in captive chimpanzees. *Folia Primatologia*, **48**, 207–10.

Hausfater, G. (1975). *Dominance and reproduction in baboons* (Papio cynocephalus). S. Karger, Basel.

Hayes, K. J. and Hayes, C. (1952). Imitation in a home-raised chimpanzee. *Journal of Comparative Physiological Psychology*, **45**, 450–9.

Heim, A. (1970). *Intelligence and personality*. Penguin Books, Harmondsworth, Middlesex.

Herman, L. M. (1986). Cognition and language competencies of bottlenosed dolphins. In *Dolphin cognition and behaviour: a comparative approach* (ed. R. J. Schusterman, J. A. Thomas, and F. G. Wood), pp. 221–52. Lawrence Erlbaum Associates, Hillsdale, NJ.

Heyes, C. M., Dawson, G. R., and Nokes, T. (1992). Imitation in rats: initial responding and transfer evidence from a bidirectional control procedure. *Quarterly Journal of Experimental Psychology. Section B: Comparative and Physiological Psychology*, **45B**, 229–40.

Hinde, R. A. (1970). *Animal behaviour*, (2nd edn). McGraw Hill, New York.

Hiraiwa-Hasegawa, M. (1986). A note on the ontogeny of feeding. In *The chimpanzees of the Mahale Mountains* (ed. T. Nishida), pp. 277–83. University of Tokyo Press, Tokyo.

Hiraiwa-Hasegawa, M., Byrne, R. W., Takasaki, H., and Byrne, J. M. (1986). Aggression towards large carnivores by wild chimpanzees of Mahale Mountains National Park, Tanzania. *Folia Primatologica*, **47**, 8–13.

Hladik, C. M. (1975). Ecology, diet and social patterning in Old and New World monkeys. In *Socioecology and psychology of primates* (ed. R. H. Tuttle), pp. 3–35. Mouton , Paris.

Horai, S., Satta, Y., Hayasaka, K., Kondo, R., Inoue, T., Ishida, T., Hayashi, S. and Takahata, N. (1992). Man's place in hominoidea revealed by mitochondrial DNA genealogy. *Journal of Molecular Evolution*, **35**, 32–43.

Humphrey, N. K. (1976). The social function of intellect. In *Growing points in ethology* (ed. P. P. G. Bateson and R. A. Hinde), pp. 303–17. Cambridge University Press, Cambridge.

Humphrey, N. K. (1983). *Consciousness regained*. Oxford University Press, Oxford.

Ingmanson, E. J. (1993). Waging peace. *International Wildlife*, **26** (6), 30–7.

Jerison, H. J. (1973). *Evolution of the brain and intelligence*. Academic Press, New York.

Jolly, A. (1966). Lemur social behavior and primate intelligence. *Science*, **153**, 501–6.

Judge, P. (1982). Redirection of aggression based on kinship in a captive gruop of pigtail macaques. (Abstract.) *International Journal of Primatology*, **3**, 301.

Köhler, W. (1925). *The mentality of apes*. Routledge and Kegan Paul, London.

Kortlandt, A. and Kooij, M. (1963). Protohominid behaviour in primates (preliminary communication). *Symposia of the Zoological Society of London*, **10**, 61–88.

Kummer, H. (1967). Tripartite relations in hamadryas baboons. In *Social communication among primates* (ed. S. A. Altmann), pp. 63–71. University of Chicago Press, Chicago.

Lashley, K. S. (1951). The problem of serial order in behavior. In *Cerebral mechanisms in behavior: the Hixon symposium* (ed. L. A. Jeffress), pp. 112–136. Wiley, New York.

Lawrence, T. E. (1926/35). *Seven pillars of wisdom; a triumph*. Jonathan Cape, London.

Leslie, A. M. (1987). Pretense and representation: the origins of 'theory of mind'. *Psychological Review*, **94**, 412–26.

Leutenegger, W. (1982). Encephalization and obstetrics in primates with particular reference to human evolution. In *Primate brain evolution* (ed. E. Armstrong and D. Falk), pp. 85–95. Plenum Press, New York.

McGrew, W. C. (1987). Tools to get food: the subsistants of the Tasmanian Aboriginies and Tanzanian chimpanzees compared. *Journal of Anthropological Research*, **43**, 247–58.

McGrew, W. C. (1989). Why is ape tool use so confusing? In *Comparative socioecology: the behavioural ecology of humans and other mammals* (ed. V. Standen and R. A. Foley), pp. 457–72. Blackwell Scientific Publications, Oxford.

McGrew, W. C. (1992). Proximate causes for becoming alpha: fraternalistic coalitions in striving for dominance by male chimpanzees at Gombe. *14th Congress of the International Primatological Society, 16–21 August, Strasbourg, France*.

Machiavelli, N. (1532/1979). *The Prince*. Penguin Books, Harmondsworth, Middlesex.

Mackinnon, J. (1978). *The ape within us*. Collins, London.

Marler, P. (1976). Sensory templates in species-specific behavior. In *Simpler networks and behavior* (ed. J. C. Fentress), pp. 314–29. Sinauer Associates, Sunderland, MA.

Marten, K. and Psarakos, S. (1994). Evidence of self-awareness in the bottlenose dolphin (*Tursiops truncatus*). In *Self-awareness in animals and humans: developmental perspectives* (ed. S. T. Parker, R. W. Mitchell, and M. L. Boccia), pp. 361–79. Cambridge University Press, Cambridge.

Matsuzawa, T. (1991). Nesting cups and metatools in chimpanzees. *The Behavioral and Brain Sciences*, **14**, 570–1

Meikle, D. B. and Vessy, S. H. (1981). Nepotism among rhesus monkey brothers. *Nature*, **294**, 160–1.

Meinertzhagen, R. (1954). The education of young ospreys. *Ibis*, **96**, 153–5.

Mellars, P. (1991). Cognitive changes and the emergence of modern humans in Europe. *Cambridge Archaeological Journal*, **1**, 63–76.

Menzel, E. W. (1974). A group of chimpanzees in a 1-acre field: leadership and communication. In *Behavior of nonhuman primates* (ed. A. M. Schrier and F. Stollnitz), pp. 83–153. Academic Press, New York.

Miller, G. A., Galanter, E., and Pribram, K. (1960). *Plans and the structure of behavior*. Holt, Rinehart and Winston, New York.

Milton, K. (1981). Distribution patterns of tropical plant foods as a stimulus to primate mental development. *American Anthropologist*, **83**, 534–48.

Milton, K. (1988). Foraging behaviour and the evolution of intellect in monkeys, apes and humans. In *Machiavellian intelligence: social expertise and the evolution of intellect in monkeys, apes and humans* (ed. R. W. Byrne and A. Whiten), pp. 285–305. Clarendon Press, Oxford.

Mineka, S., Davidson, M., Cook, M., and Keir, R. (1984). Observational conditioning of snake fear in rhesus monkeys. *Journal of Abnormal Psychology*, **93**, 355–72.

Mitchell, R. W. (1986). A framework for discussing deception. In *Deception: perspectives on human and nonhuman deceit* (ed. R. W. Mitchell and N. S. Thompson), pp. 3–40. SUNY Press, New York.

Mitchell, R. W. (1993). Mental models of mirror-self-recognition: two theories. *New Ideas in Psychology*, **11**, 295–325.

Mitchell, R. W. and Thompson, N. S. (1986). *Deception: perspectives on human and nonhuman deceit*. SUNY Press, Albany NY.

Moore, B. R. (1993). Avian movement imitation and a new form of mimicry: tracing the evolution of complex learning behaviour. *Behaviour*, **122**, 231–63.

Moss, C. J. and Poole, J. H. (1983). Relationships and social structure of African elephants. In *Primate social relationships: an integrated approach* (ed. R. A. Hinde), pp. 315–25. Blackwell Scientific Publications, Oxford.

Natale, F., Antinucci, F., Spinozzi, G., and Poti, P. (1986). Stage 6 object concept in non-human primate cognition: a comparison between gorilla (*Gorilla gorilla gorilla*) and Japanese macaque (*Macaca fuscata*). *Journal of Comparative Psychology*, **100**, 335–9.

Newell, A., Shaw, J. C., and Simon H. A., (1958). Elements of a theory of human problem solving. *Psychological Review*, **65**, 151–66.

Nishida, T. (1983). Alpha status and agonistic alliance in wild chimpanzees (*Pan troglodytes schweinfurthii*). *Primates*, **24**, 318–36.

Nishida, T. and Uehara, S. (1980). Natural diet of chimpanzees (*Pan troglodytes schweinfurthii*): long term record from the Mahale Mountains. *African Study Monographs*, **3**, 109–30.

Nishida, T., Uehara, S., and Nyundo, R. (1979). Predatory behaviour among wild chimpanzees of the Mahale Mountains. *Primates*, **20**, 1–20.

Nishida, T., Hasegawa, T., Hayaki, H., Takahata, Y., and Uehara, S. (1992). Meat-sharing as a coalition strategy by an alpha male chimpanzee? In *Topics in primatology*, Vol. 1 (ed. T. Nishida, W. C. McGrew, P. Marler, M. Pickford, and F. B. M. de Waal), pp. 159–74. University of Tokyo Press, Tokyo.

Noë, R. A. (1990). Veto game played by baboons: a challenge to the use of the Prisoner's Dilemma as a paradigm for reciprocity and cooperation. *Animal Behaviour*, **39**, 78–90.

Packer, C. (1977). Reciprocal altruism in *Papio anubis*. *Nature*, **265**, 441–3.

Packer, C., Gilbert, D. A., Pusey, A. E., and O'Brien, S. J. (1991). A molecular genetic analysis of kinship and cooperation in African lions. *Nature*, **351**, 562–5.

Palameta, B. (1989). The importance of socially transmitted information in the acquisition of novel foraging skills by pigeons and canaries. Ph.D. thesis, University of Cambridge.

Parker, S. T. and Gibson, K. R. (1979). A developmental model for the evolution of language and intelligence in early hominids. *The Behavioral and Brain Sciences*, **2**, 367–408.

Parker, S. T. and Gibson, K. R. (1990). *Language and intelligence in monkeys and apes*. Cambridge University Press, Cambridge.

Passingham, R. E. (1982). *The human primate*. W. H. Freeman, Oxford.

Passingham, R. E. and Ettlinger, G. (1974). A comparison of cortical function in man and other primates. *International Review of Neurobiology*, **16**, 233–99.

Patterson, F. G. P. and Cohn, R. H. (1994). Self-recognition and self-awareness in lowland gorillas. In *Self-awareness in animals and humans: development perspectives* (ed. S. T. Parker, R. W. Mitchell, and M. L. Boccia), pp. 273–91. Cambridge University Press, Cambridge.

Pepperberg, I. (1990). Conceptual abilities of some non-primate species, with an emphasis on an African grey parrot. In *Language and intelligence in monkeys and apes* (ed. S. T. Parker and K. R. Gibson), pp. 469–507. Cambridge University Press, Cambridge.

Perrett, D. I., Harries, M. H., Bevan, R., Thomas, S., Benson, P. J., Mistlin, A. J., Chitty, A. J., Hietanen, J. K., and Ortega, J. E. (1989). Frameworks of analysis for the neural representations of animate objects and actions. *Journal of Experimental Biology*, **146**, 87–113.

Pilbeam, D. and Smith, R. (1981). New skull remains of *Sivapithecus* from Pakistan. *Memoirs of the Geological Survey of Pakistan*, **11**, 1–13.

Povinelli, D. J. (1991). Social intelligence in monkeys and apes. Ph.D. thesis, Yale University, New Haven, Connecticut.

Povinelli, D. J. and Cant, J. G. H. (1992). Orangutan clambering and the evolutionary origins of self-conception. *14th Congress of the International Primatological Society, 16–21 August, Strasbourg, France.*

Povinelli, D. J., Nelson, K. E., and Boysen, S. T. (1990). Inferences about guessing and knowing by chimpanzees (*Pan troglodytes*). *Journal of Comparative Psychology*, **104**, 203–10.

Povinelli, D. J., Parks, K. A., and Novak, M. A. (1991). Do rhesus monkeys (*Macaca mulatta*) attribute knowledge and ignorance to others? *Journal of Comparative Psychology*, **105**, 318–25.

Povinelli, D. J., Nelson, K. E., and Boysen, S. T. (1992*a*). Comprehension of role reversal in chimpanzees: evidence of empathy? *Animal Behaviour*, **43**, 633–40.

Povinelli, D. J., Parks, K. A., and Novak, M. A. (1992*b*). Role reversal by rhesus monkeys but no evidence of empathy. *Animal Behaviour*, **44**, 269–81.

Povinelli, D. J., Rulf, A. B., Landau, K., and Bierschwale, D. (1993). Self-recognition in chimpanzees (*Pan troglodytes*): distribution, ontogeny, and patterns of emergence, *Journal of Comparative Psychology*, **107**, 347–72.

Povinelli, D.T., Rulf, A. B., and Bierschwale, D.T (1994). Absence of knowledge attribution and self-recognition in young chimpanzees (*Pan troglodytes*). *Journal of Comparative Psychology*, **108**, 74–90.

Premack, A. J. and Premack, D. (1972). Teaching language to an ape. *Scientific American*, **227**, 92–9.

Premack, D. (1988). 'Does the chimpanzee have a theory of mind?' revisited. In *Machiavellian intelligence: social expertise and the evolution of intellect in monkeys, apes and humans* (ed. R. W. Byrne and A. Whiten), pp. 94–110. Clarendon Press, Oxford.

Premack, D. and Woodruff, G. (1978). Does the chimpanzee have a theory of mind? *The Behavioral and Brain Sciences*, **4**, 515–26.

Rasmussen, J. and Jensen, A. (1974). Mental procedures in real-life tasks: a case study of electronic trouble shooting. *Ergonomics*, **17**, 293–307.

Richards, D. G. (1986). Dolphin vocal mimicry and vocal object labeling. In *Dolphin cognition and behaviour: a comparative approach* (ed. R. J. Schusterman, J. A. Thomas, and F. G. Wood), pp. 273–88. Lawrence Erlbaum Associates, Hillsdale, NJ.

Riedman, M. L. , Staedler, M. M., Estes, J. A., and Hrabich, B. (1989). The transmission of individually distinctive foraging strategies from mother to offspring in sea otters (*Enhydra lutris*). *Eigth Biennial Conference on the Biology of Marine Mammals, 7–11 December, Pacific Grove*, C. A.

Rolland, N. (1981). The interpretation of Middle Paleolithic variability. *Man*, **16,** 15–42.

Rood, J. P. (1978). Dwarf mongoose helpers at the den. *Zeitschrift für Tierpsychologie*, **48**, 277–87.

Roosmalen, M. G. M. van (1988). Diet, feeding behaviour and social organization of the Guianan black spider monkey (*Ateles paniscus paniscus*). *12th Congress of the International Primatological Society, 24–29 July, Brasilia, Brazil.*

Roper, T. J. (1983). Learning as a biological phenomenon. In *Animal behaviour*, Vol. 3, *Genes, development and learning* (ed. T. R. Halliday and P. J. B. Slater), pp. 178–212. Blackwell Scientific Publications, Oxford.

Rumbaugh, D. M., von Glasersfeld, E., Warner, H., Pisani, P., and Gill, T. V. (1974). Lana (chimpanzee) learning language: a progress report. *Brain and Language*, **1**, 205–12.

Russon, A. E. and Galdikas, B. M. F. (1993). Imitation in ex-captive orangutans. *Journal of Comparative Psychology*, **107**, 147–61.

Russon, A. E. and Galdikas, B. M. F. (1995). The nature of imitation in rehabilitant orangutans. In *Reaching into thought; The minds of the great apes* (ed. A. E. Russon, K. A. Bard, and S. T. Parker). Cambridge University Press, Cambridge, in press.

Sade, D. S. (1967). Determinants of dominance in a group of free-ranging rhesus monkeys. In *Social communication among primates* (ed. S. Altmann), pp. 99–114. Chicago University Press, Chicago.

Sarich, V. and Wilson, A. (1967). Immunological time scale for hominid evolution. *Science*, **158**, 1200–3.

Savage-Rumbaugh, E. S. (1986). *Ape language: from conditioned response to symbol*. Columbia University Press, New York.

Savage-Rumbaugh, E. S. and McDonald, K. (1988). Deception and social manipulation in symbol-using apes. In *Machiavellian intelligence: social expertise and the evolution of intellect in monkeys, apes and humans* (ed. R. W. Byrne and A. Whiten), pp. 224–37. Clarendon Press, Oxford.

Sawaguchi, T. and Kudo, H. (1990). Neocortical development and social structure in primates. *Primates*, **31**, 283–9.

Sayich, L. S., Tyack, P. L., and Wells, R. S. (1993). Signature whistle development in bottlenose dolphins is affected by early experience. *23rd International Ethological Conference, 1–9 September, Torremolinos, Spain*.

Schiller, P. H. (1952). Innate constituents of complex responses in primates. *Psychological Review*, **59**, 177–91.

Schlesinger, I. M. (1971). The grammar of sign language and the problems of language universals. In *Biological and social factors in psycholinguistics* (ed. J. Morton), pp. 98–121. Logos Press, London.

Schusterman, R. J., Thomas, J. A. and Wood, F. G. (1986) *Dolphin cognition and behaviour: a comparative approach*. Lawrence Erlabaum Associates, Hillsdale, NJ.

Seyfarth, R. and Cheney, D. (1984). Grooming alliances and reciprocal altruism in vervet monkeys. *Nature*, **308**, 541–2.

Seyfarth, R. M. and Cheney, D. L. (1986). Vocal development in vervet monkeeys. *Animal Behavior*, **34**, 1640–58.

Seyfarth, R. M., Cheney, D. L., and Marler, P. (1980). Vervet monkey alarm calls: semantic communication in a free-ranging primate. *Animal Behaviour*, **28**, 1070–94.

Shea, B. T. (1983). Phyletic size change and brain/body allometry: a consideration based on the African pongids and other primates. *International Journal of Primatology*, **4**, 33–61.

Sherry, D. F. and Galef, B. G., Jr (1984). Cultural transmission without imitation: milk bottle opening by birds. *Animal Behaviour*, **32**, 937.

Shettleworth, S. J. (1975). Reinforcement and the organisation of behavior in golden hamsters: hunger, environment and food reinforcement. *Journal of Experimental Psychology: Animal Behavior Processes*, **1**, 56–87.

Sigg, H. and Stolba, A. (1981). Home range and daily march in a hamadryas baboon troop. *Folia Primatologica*, **36**, 40–75.

Skinner, B. F. (1981). Selection by consequences. *Science*, **213**, 501–4.

Slater, P. J. B., Ince, S., A., and Colgan, P. W. (1980). Chaffinch song types: their frequencies in the population and distribution between the repertoires of different individuals. *Behaviour*, **75**, 207–18.

Smith, P. K. (1988). The cognitive demands of children's social interactions with peers. In *Machiavellian intelligence: social expertise and the evolution of intellect in monkeys, apes and humans*, (ed. R. W. Byrne and A. Whiten), pp. 94–110. Clarendon Press, Oxford.

Smuts, B. B. (1985). *Sex and friendship in baboons*. Aldine, Hawthorne, NY.

Smuts, B. B., Cheney, D. L., Seyfarth, R. M., Wrangham, R. W., and Struhsaker, T. T. (1986). *Primate societies*. University of Chicago Press, Chicago.

Spence, K. W. (1937). Experimental studies of learning and higher mental processes in infra-human primates. *Psychological Bulletin*, **34**, 806–50.

Stander, P. E. (1992). Foraging dynamics of lions in a semi-arid environment. *Canadian Journal of Zoology*, **70**, 8–21.

Sternberg, R. J. (1985). General intellectual ability. In *Human abilities. An information processing account* (ed. R. J. Sternberg). W. H. Freeman, New York.

Struhsaker, T. T. (1967). Behavior of vervet monkeys. *University of California Publications of Zoology*, **82**, 1–74.

Sugiyama, Y., Matsuzawa, T., Fushimi, T., and Sakura, O. (1992). Hand preference and hammer-using of wild chimpanzees at Bossou. *14th Congress of the International Primatological Society, 16–21 August, Strasbourg, France.*

Swartz, K. B. and Evans, S. (1991). Not all chimpanzees (*Pan troglodytes*) show self-recognition. *Primates*, **32**, 483–96.

Taylor, C. K. and Saayman, G. S. (1973). Imitative behaviour by Indian ocean bottlenose dolphins (*Tursiops aduncus*) in captivity. *Behaviour*, **44**, 286–98.

Teleki, G. (1973). *The predatory behavior of chimpanzees*. Bucknell University Press, Lewisburg, PA.

Terborgh, J. (1983). *Five New World primates*. Princeton University Press, Princeton.

Thorpe, W. H. (1963). *Learning and instinct in animals, (*2nd edn*)*. Methuen, London

Thorpe, W. H. (1967). Vocal imitation and antiphonal song and its implications. *Proceedings of the International Ornithological Congress*, **14**, 245–63.

Tomasello, M. (1990). Cultural transmission in the tool use and communicatory signaling of chimpanzees? In *Language and intelligence in monkeys and apes* (ed. S. T. Parker and K. R. Gibson), pp. 274–311. Cambridge University Press, Cambridge.

Toth, N. (1985). The Oldowan reassessed: a close look at early stone artifacts. *Journal of Archaeological Science*, **12**, 101–20.

Toth, N., Schick, K. D., Savage-Rumbaugh, E. S., Sevcik, R., and Rumbaugh, D. M. (1993). Pan the tool maker: investigations into the stone tool-making & tool-using capabilities of a bonobo (*Pan paniscus*). *Journal of Archaeological Science*, **20**, 81–91.

Turing, A. M. (1937). On computable numbers, with an application to the *Entscheidungsproblem*. *Proceedings of the London Mathematical Society*, **2**, 42.

Tutin, C. E. G. (1979). Mating patterns and reproductive strategies in a community of wild chimpanzees (*Pan troglodytes schweinfurthii*). *Behavioral Ecology and Sociobiology*, **6**, 29–38.

Tutin, C. E. G., McGrew, W. C., and Baldwin, P. J. (1983). Social organisation of savanna-dwelling chimpanzees, *Pan troglodytes verus*, at Mt. Assirik, Senegal. *Primates*, **24**, 154–73.

Visalberghi, E. and Fragaszy, D. M. (1990). Do monkeys ape? In *Language and intelligence in monkeys and apes* (ed. S. T. Parker and K. R. Gibson), pp. 247–73. Cambridge University Press, Cambridge.

Visalberghi, E. and Limongelli, L. (1994). Lack of comprehension of cause–effect relationships in tool-using capuchin monkeys (*Cebus apella*). *Journal of Comparative Psychology*, **108**, 15–22.

Visalberghi, E. and Mason, W. A. (1983). Determinants of problem-solving success in *Saimiri* and *Callicebus*. *Primates*, **24**, 385–96.

Visalberghi, E. and Trinca, L. (1987). Tool use in capuchin monkeys: distinguishing between performing and understanding. *Primates*, **30**, 511–21.

Waal, F. B. M. de (1982). *Chimpanzee politics*. Jonathan Cape, London.

Waal, F. B. M. de (1989*a*). Food sharing and reciprocal obligations among chimpanzees. *Human Evolution*, **18**, 433–59.

Waal, F. B. M. de (1989*b*). *Peacemaking among primates*. Harvard University Press, Cambridge, MA.

Waddell, P. J. and Penny, D. (1994). Evolutionary trees of apes and humans from DNA sequences. In *Handbook of symbolic evolution* (ed. A. J. Lock and C. R. Peters). Clarendon Press, Oxford, in press.

Warren, J. M. (1973). Learning in vertebrates. In *Comparative psychology: a modern survey* (ed. D. A. Dewsbury and D. A. Rethlingshafer), pp. 471–509. McGraw Hill, New York.

Waser, P. M., Keane, B., Creel, S. R., Elliott, L. F., and Minchella, D. J. (1994). Possible male coalitions in a solitary mongoose. *Animal Behaviour*, **47**, 289–94.

Wechsler, D. (1944). *The measurement of adult intelligence*. Williams and Wilkins, Baltimore.

Whitcombe, E. (1994). *The power of speech: an essay in anatomy*. Clarendon Press, Oxford, in press.

Whiten, A. and Byrne, R. W. (1988). Tactical deception in primates. *The Behavioral and Brain Sciences*, **11**, 233–44.

Wimmer, H. and Perner, J. (1983). Beliefs about beliefs: representation and constraining function of wrong beliefs in young children's understanding of deception. *Cognition*, **13**, 103–28.

Wood, D. (1989). Social interaction as tutoring. In *Interaction in human development* (ed. M. H. Bornstein and J. S. Bruner), pp. 59–80. Lawrence Erlbaum Associates, Hillsdale, NJ.

Wright, R. V. S. (1972). Imitative learning of a flaked-tool technology: The case of an orangutan. *Mankind*, **8**, 296–306.

Wynn, T. (1988). Tools and the evolution of human intelligence. In *Machiavellian intelligence: social expertise and the evolution of intellect in monkeys, apes and humans* (ed. R. W. Byrne and A. Whiten), pp. 271–84. Clarendon Press, Oxford.

Wynn, T. and McGrew, W. C. (1989). An ape's view of the Oldowan. *Man*, **24**, 383–98.

Zajonc, R. B. (1965). Social facilitation. *Science*, **149**, 269–74.

Author index

Page numbers in *italics* refer to figures; those annotated *n* refer to footnotes.

Subject index

Page numbers in *italics* refer to figures; those annotated *n* refer to footnotes.